MAXIMIZE YOUR QL

SUSAN CURRAN and RAY CURNOW

MACMILLAN

Series consultant: Ray Hammond

First published 1985 by
PAPERMAC
a division of Macmillan Publishers Limited
4 Little Essex Street London WC2R 3LF
and Basingstoke

Associated companies in Auckland, Delhi, Dublin, Gaborone, Hamburg, Harare, Hong Kong, Johannesburg, Kuala Lumpur, Lagos, Manzini, Melbourne, Mexico City, Nairobi, New York, Singapore and Tokyo

Typeset by Bookworm Typesetting
Printed in Great Britain by Richard Clay (The Chaucer Press) Ltd, Bungay, Suffolk

British Library Cataloguing in Publication Data

Curnow, Ray
    Advanced techniques for the Sinclair QL.
    1. Sinclair QL (Computer)
    I. Title II. Curran, Susan
    001.64/04 QA76.8.S625

    ISBN 0-333-38415-6

MAXIMIZE YOUR QL

Contents

Acknowledgements

The QL was a very new computer when we began to write this book, and one with an architecture and operating system quite different from any we were familiar with. In large part we've been travelling in uncharted territory, but as we've been writing, reviews and articles (and even a couple of books) on the machine have begun to appear. The facts and opinions we've encountered have helped to shape this book. Our thanks are due to everybody who has published such material.

At a time when few QL users were around, we were lucky enough to enlist the help of an expert. Special thanks are due to Mike Marriage, of Norwich City College and Norwich Computer Users' Group. Mike wrote the machine code programs included in Chapter 15, reviewed that chapter, and spent long hours discussing the QL with us. We also used his machine to help test out the QLAN network discussed in Chapter 16.

Thanks, too, to Nick Chapman of Papermac, and to Ray Hammond, who together helped us to obtain information and assistance from Sinclair Research Ltd. Nigel Searle of Sinclair Research provided us with a copy of the draft QDOS documentation, which was particularly helpful.

We developed the material and programs in this book on a QL with a 1.02 version of the operating system and FB SuperBasic. The programs have been tested as fully as possible, but there always remains the possibility of undiscovered bugs or typesetting errors. We hope they will work correctly on your machine: our sincere apologies if they do not. In the later stages of the writing, our QL was upgraded to a 1.03 operating system and JM Basic. Most, but not all, of the programs have been tested on this latter version.

Some program listings have been directly reproduced from printouts from the QL on to an Epson FX-80 dot matrix printer. Our FX-80 has a Centronics parallel interface, and we linked it to the QL using a Miracle Systems serial to parallel interface. The FX-80 was also used to produce the screen dumps from Easel in Chapters 6 and 8.

Though we have tried to use the QL as fully as possible in the preparation of this book, the lack of reliability of our early model and of its Psion programs, and the lack of peripheral devices, have caused us to resort to other computing equipment as well. Our other printer, a Tandy daisywheel, is not easily interfaceable with the QL, and printed illustrations that are not in dot matrix style are taken from this printer, run by a Torch computer. The manuscript was written using the Wordstar word processing package running on the Torch.

Finally, some illustrations in Chapters 12 and 16 were drawn up on a Commodore printer/plotter, run by a Commodore 64. Though this machine is broadly representative of the type of cheap plotter that we expect to see appearing for the QL, it does not work with the QL at present – indeed, we do not know of any plotters that do.

Susan Curran
Ray Curnow
September 1984

1

Introducing the QL

This book is a guide to the Sinclair QL, designed to help personal computer users get the most out of the machine. It is aimed primarily at those who already possess a QL. We don't simply repeat information provided in the QL User Guide: instead we try to supplement the User Guide, explaining points not fully covered there, exploring topics in more depth, and taking a more critical look at the QL's shortcomings. We expect you to have a User Guide to hand, and we frequently refer to it in detail. Although there should be much to interest you in this book if you don't already possess a QL and User Guide, you will find it much easier to follow if you do.

This is not an introductory book to computers, nor a preliminary course in QL SuperBasic. We assume that you already have a basic understanding of what a computer is and how it works, and that you are able to write short and simple Basic programs. Our aim is to show you how to go on from this point, to expand your computing expertise and to make the most of this unusual and powerful computer. We do not expect you to be a programming expert, or to possess a detailed understanding of electronics. A few sections of this book are aimed particularly at low-level programmers, but an understanding of assembly language and machine code is generally not necesssary.

This book was written from experience gained using an early production model of the QL computer. The QL's Basic dialect and operating system were both still under development when the first QLs were released for sale, and later models of the machine may not be identical to the one we describe in every respect. We point out techniques and 'bugs' apparent in the FB version of Basic with which we worked, which may not be evident in later versions. The same is true of the QDOS operating system. The programs have been tested on our QL, but some may need slight modification on later models of the computer. Some advertised features of the computer were not fully operational on our machine, and these have necessarily been described from documentation rather than from practical experience.

We start, in this chapter, by looking at the hardware of the QL, setting it in the context of rival personal computers. In the following chapters, we will study the machine's suite of applications software: and later in the book we will go on to look in detail at other software including the operating system, and at networking and expansion possibilities which will push still further the boundaries of the QL's applications.

Our emphasis throughout is on the use of the QL for professional and semi-professional applications. This is a field for which we feel that the machine is particularly well suited, as we explain below.

THE QL IN CONTEXT

In the first years of development of the personal computer market – from 1979, when the first commercial personal computers emerged, to 1983 – two distinct development patterns could be distinguished. There were 'business' personal computers and 'home' personal computers. The business machines can be typified by models such as the IBM PC and the ACT Sirius; the home computers, by the Commodore VIC-20 and the Sinclair Spectrum. Of course, these are only examples: dozens of home computers and hundreds of business machines, have competed for a market share over this period.

Business micros developed as cut-down versions of the microcomputers and dedicated word processors which had earlier permeated offices. Though some machines were sold to private individuals, the major sales were to companies, for 'personal' (often in a rather loose sense, as we explain below) use by professionals, executives or secretarial/clerical staff. The software developed for such machines reflected their business orientation, with the major emphasis being on spreadsheet, word processing and database packages. Small business accounting and business graphics have also been significant application areas. The hardware of such machines – and by this, we mean not so much the silicon chips, as the supporting hardware, including the computer casing, its keyboard, its storage devices and so on – is of high quality, and this has been reflected in a high price tag. Software, too, has been both good (by contemporary standards) and expensive. Another factor behind the historically high prices has been the high level of dealer support – in consultancy, training and general trouble-shooting – provided in this market.

In the early 1980s, a business microcomputer system, complete with the necessary peripherals and software to enable it to work adequately, could have cost from £2000 to £10,000.

Home computers emerged as a distinctive product field from two different antecedents. One predecessor was the electronic kit machine in the late 1970s. Early home computers like the Sinclair ZX80 and ZX81 were sold as kits to electronic enthusiasts whose interest was at least as much in assembling the machine, and testing its capabilities, as in end-user applications. The other predecessor was the electronic game machine. The craze for electronic arcade games first spawned a generation of non-programmable game playing computers. As interest in home computers grew, these dedicated machines have increasingly been superseded by more general purpose, programmable machines for which large ranges of game programs are available.

The prices of home computers reflect the budgets of their purchasers and have generally tended to keep below the £200 level, leaving a massive price/performance gap between these machines and their business rivals. Home computers have often offered less powerful microprocessors; less memory; poorer quality casings and keyboards; cheaper and lower-performance storage media. Dealer support to purchasers is much less extensive, with the thirst for advice being met largely by the growing number of computer magazines and self-help groups. Software, too, has been cheaper than that available for business machines.

Application development in the home computer market has been shaped by the game-orientation of many machines and limited by the very low level of the hardware. For many machines, only a token range of 'serious' software was originally available; indeed before 1982-3, typical home computers did not offer sufficient memory or processing power to run even comparatively simple versions of the 'serious' programs offered on business micros. In the last two years, however, two developments have changed this picture. First, the computing power and memory capability of home machines has increased markedly, to the extent that cheap computers like the Commodore 64 now have the potential to run programs as complex as those developed on business machines only a few years earlier. And second, an increasing awareness has developed of the market for 'serious' personal computers (i.e. computers capable of running non-game application programs) at a price that individuals, and not just companies, can afford.

In short, the gap between home and business machines, in both price and performance terms, has begun to narrow. And into the as yet unfocused market that lies midway between the two have come an increasing range of 'semi-professional' personal computers, aimed at bringing computing power to the hands of those for whom business micros are just too expensive.

THE RISE OF THE GENUINELY PERSONAL COMPUTER

Though microcomputers have been sold so extensively over the past five years, people are still asking what they are used for – and still getting a wide, and often conflicting, variety of answers. Our impression, from informal personal research, is that most business microcomputers have so far been purchased, not as general purpose aids to professionals and executives, but as special-purpose machines. The company justifies the purchase because the machine is to run the company's accounts, to act as a word processor, or to be available to one or more staff in some other very specific capacity. A small range of software (perhaps only one word processing or accounting program) is bought with the machine, and it is not generally made available for other purposes.

Of course, business microcomputers (and larger machines too) have a very valuable role to play in this capacity. But they have an equally valuable potential role as a permanently available, general-purpose tool for an individual professional or executive with varied and sometimes unpredictable requirements. In this different sphere, applications are not laid down in advance, but are developed on an *ad hoc* basis, as the need for computer power becomes apparent. Applications software is not tightly tailored to specific applications, but provides a range of general 'thinking tools'.

How might a typical executive – if there is any such thing – use a personal computer? With a suitable range of applications programs, the computer can act in a very wide variety of ways. It can be used as an 'intelligent notepad', for filing informal as well as more formal data: developing ideas, notes on enquiries from customers or business leads, miscellaneous information that might be needed some time in the future. It acts as a message sender and receiver. It can act as a calculator, a worksheet. A word processor enables even the most butter-fingered individual to turn out a mistake-free urgent note or confidential memo, when a suitable professional typist isn't immediately available. A graphics package makes facts and figures come alive in visual form, bringing trends home to the executive him- or herself and providing an effective way of putting them across to a wider audience.

Five years ago, the professional with an informed need for a computer as a working aid, and with the background knowledge and experience needed to use such a machine effectively, running application packages unaided and even writing the occasional small program, hardly existed. Today, there are more and more such people. And as new generations of computer-literate school and college leavers enter our businesses, there will be infinitely more.

A personal computer, in this very real sense, can be an enormous aid to almost every member of the office staff. Few companies as yet have the inclination or the resources, however, to provide business computers on a one-to-one basis. This kind of purchase can't be cost-justified on a 'proven savings' basis: the benefits of the computing resource are far more open ended and, many would argue, less certain.

For companies reluctant or simply unable to invest speculatively and at a high level in what are still new machines with newly developing applications, the much cheaper semi-professional computer – like the QL – can provide an attractive alternative. To more and more computer-literate professionals, a moderately powerful computer with good applications programs and only limited dealer support is becoming an invaluable tool. The lower-quality hardware of a cheaper machine is inevitably a drawback, but it is infinitely better than having limited or no access to a machine.

Often these young professionals already have home computer experience, and they may use the same type of machine (if not exactly the same machine) at home. Computers with serious capabilities can now realistically be used both for working from home and for more domestic tasks such as keeping control of family finances, writing formal letters and running clubs and societies. An increasing number of home computer users are beginning to see the limitations of the very cheap home computers, and to feel the need for a more powerful machine that is capable of performing this kind of serious application. Money is still a constraint, however. Only a small minority will ever be able to contemplate spending at the business computer level for a personal machine that will be used far less intensively.

One more factor is apparent in looking at the market for semi-professional computers. It is important to remember too that many companies have been reluctant or unable to invest in business computers for specific applications, even where the need is clearly apparent and the cost could easily be justified.

These companies often make use of semi-professional computers for intensive, fully professional purposes.

The growing sales of machines such as the Commodore 64, with severely limited hardware and only marginal suitability for business applications, to small (and not so small) businesses, emphasize the market available to a computer with a dramatically lower price tag than its business rivals, however marked its shortcomings when compared to them.

The self-employed – journalists, shopkeepers, those running craft or service businesses from home, to give just a few examples – are also becoming aware how useful computers could be to them. Many couldn't contemplate buying an expensive business machine, and often the computer wouldn't be used for the long periods that would justify buying one. This group has an evident need for affordable semi-professional computers.

For different reasons, much the same type of powerful but cheap computer appeals to the educational market. It's a type of machine that's particularly attractive to older students. Arts students can use word processor packages to prepare their essays; science and engineering students need the computer's number crunching power. Students in all disciplines can benefit from the computer's ability to help them organize and manipulate their ideas. Individual students find working with machines like this a help in their studies, and a good preparation for their subsequent working life. Schools and colleges with a limited computing budget find them an affordable alternative to the previous generation of 'educational' machines.

THE QL: A SEMI-PROFESSIONAL COMPUTER

We've tried to sketch out a profile of the semi-professional computer user: and from this we can go on to draw up a profile of the kind of machine he or she needs. Power is top of the list. Reliability is essential. Ease of use comes lower down the table: and intensive dealer support is an expensive luxury that most will opt to do without.

Against this background we can evaluate the unusual blend of capabilities and limitations that the Sinclair QL offers. It's a computer that is – as its software makes clear – specifically tailored to the 'semi-professional' market. Its price puts it above the level of the typical home game-player, and into the range of serious home users, business users with a strictly limited budget, and of users in the field of education.

We will not be considering the QL's features in great detail at this point. We will of course return to both the hardware and the software later.

The QL's great strength is in its memory and processing power. While most home, and many cheaper business, computers provide 64K or sometimes substantially less RAM (random access memory) the basic QL provides a hefty 128K. The memory of the machine is directly reflected in the size and complexity of the application programs it can run, and this complement gives the QL the capability to run full-scale business-type applications: though still more memory can be a great advantage, as we explain later.

To handle this quantity of memory without resort to complex paging methods, it's necessary to use a microprocessor with a substantial address capability, and the 68008 chip which forms the QL's main processor provides just this. It is a powerful chip with processing abilities that are reflected in the speed and complexity of the QL's application programs. The machine also contains a second processor, the Intel 8049, which controls the keyboard, acts as a serial communications receiver and generates the QL's not very impressive sounds. This device, by taking these routine tasks from the main processor, frees it to work still more rapidly. Indeed, the machine can be very fast, as you can see particularly well in the QL Easel program.

That the machine should provide such remarkable capabilities for under £400 is amazing enough: it's hardly surprising that it should have shortcomings in other directions. Those shortcomings will be apparent to anyone who already owns the machine: for the sake of those considering whether to buy one, we'll outline them briefly.

The machine's casing, though reasonably robust, falls short of the quality you'd expect from a business-type computer, and it will obviously not stand up to very extensive long-term use – over years, that is, rather than weeks. The computer is adequately made for moderate intensity use, but not really designed for heavy bashing, day in and day out! The keyboard is particularly vulnerable. It's designed with a membrane of connection points underlaying the keys, and though this arrangement is admirably resistant to dust and spills, it can make it difficult to register a key-press. Light touch typists may find it particularly difficult to work with, as a fairly firm press is needed, and there is no way of adjusting the keyboard's sensitivity. The larger keys (particularly 'Enter') can be especially difficult to handle, though we've found that with reasonable care, it is possible to touch-type successfully and accurately. Membrane keyboards do become more difficult to use, and vulnerable to breakdown, as they age. It may however become possible to obtain better-quality replacement keyboards for the machine, as has been the case for earlier Sinclair computers with more drastically limited keyboards.

Floppy disk drives, the standard storage medium on lower-cost business systems, can be extremely expensive. In the QL, Sinclair have opted instead to provide two continuous-tape microdrives. The microdrives are admirably compact, and each tape cartridge holds around 100K (i.e. 100×1024 bits) of data, a very acceptable quantity; but the drives are quite slow in operation, and this does prove a drawback. The cartridges are extremely vulnerable (as indeed are the older 5¼ in. and 8 in. floppy disks) and should be treated with great care. In practice, the provision of microdrives is a less severe drawback than it may seem. Their tiny size makes the computer very easily portable, and conventional floppy- or hard disk drives can quite easily be added if they are wanted. We look in depth at the variety of expansion possibilities that the machine presents in Chapter 17.

A useful feature of the QL is its ability to work with either a television or a monitor. A monitor (ideally a colour one, though black and white is adequate for many uses) provides a far better picture, and makes it possible to use the eighty-column screen that's important in serious applications. However, the option to connect a television instead makes it possible for a user to keep a monitor in his/her office, for instance, and carry the machine home for use with a TV set there. It is admirably easy to adapt the Psion suite of programs to work with either an eighty-column screen on a monitor or a forty-column (or sixty-four-column in Quill) screen on a television, using the same files with both types of display. As with so many features, this reflects the conscious home/business orientation of the computer.

Psion's suite of software programs are another major plus of the QL. They rival the best of contemporary microcomputer software, and provide an impressive and adaptable range of capabilities. Though at first sight they may seem business oriented, they are equally suited to serious domestic use, as we shall show. Programs of this calibre are expensive to buy, and their inclusion with the computer greatly adds to its appeal. As the Psion programs have so much to offer to the QL user, we look at their features and their potential applications in detail in this book.

The QL also includes an impressive high-level programming language in SuperBasic. Some of the features of SuperBasic are quite different from those found in other dialects of Basic (including those on other Sinclair machines) and even experienced Basic users will need to take some time learning how to handle them. The powerful structuring commands in particular make it comparatively easy to write useful programs in SuperBasic, as is shown in Chapter 9. The QL's operating system, QDOS, also compares favourably with much of its competition, and will be even more impressive when its multi-tasking features are fully operational.

Learning to Use the QL

Our emphasis in this book is on hands-on use of the QL, and we have tried to slant our coverage towards the gaps in the documentation provided with the computer. First we look in some detail at the choice of a printer for use with the computer and at ways of programming a printer. Then we go on to look at Psion's four applications programs, Easel, Quill, Archive and Abacus, exploring the ways in which they work and interact, and outlining some potential uses for them. There's a brief general introduction to all four programs, a review of each, with comments on use and on the less obvious aspects of command structure; and finally a short chapter covering the development of integrated applications using all four programs.

Even those who intend to stick primarily to these programs will need to understand something of SuperBasic and of the QDOS operating system. In the next chapter, we look in detail at some aspects of programming in SuperBasic and of the operating system – like the windowing features – that are accessible to a Basic programmer. We include a wide variety of short programs, and a few longer programs with a particular emphasis on graphics.

Chapter 12 takes a more detailed look at the QL's hardware, with particular emphasis on the 68008 main processor. This information will be particularly interesting to low-level programmers, but it is intended as an introduction, not a full-scale guide to machine code programming on the QL. We go on from here to look at operating system operations in more low-level detail, and to sketch out some aspects of the QL's operation that are accessible only on this low level. In this part of the book we also look in detail at the microdrives, at their storage pattern, and present some utility programs which will simplify use of the microdrives.

The QL is unusual in having built-in networking capabilities: on most rival machines a network is provided, if at all, as an optional extra. Chapter 16 looks at QLAN's operation, and suggests some uses for networking. And a final chapter looks forward to expansion possibilities for this very open-ended computer.

2

Using a Printer with the QL

Your QL computer system will not be complete until you have a printer to enable you to obtain hard copy output. You can print program listings; you can print data and reports from the four Psion programs; you can dump graphs and drawings if you have a graphics-oriented printer; you can even do simple illustrations on some printers.

Choosing and using a printer can be operations full of unexpected pitfalls, however. In this chapter we look briefly at some of the issues involved.

Sinclair do not market a printer for use with the QL, and so it is up to you to select a suitable model. If you already possess a printer, you will obviously be keen to make that one work with your new computer. If you do not possess one, then you will of course want to select one that will enable you to make the maximum use of your new machine.

Note that the ZX Printer, a small and very cheap device which Sinclair sold until recently for use with the Spectrum and ZX81 home computers, will *not* work correctly with the QL.

PARALLEL AND SERIAL PRINTERS

Separate printers designed to be controlled by personal computers are linked to them by a cable. At each end of the cable is a connector: one to plug into the printer and one for the computer.

Obviously, it is necessary to obtain a cable that has the right type of connectors on both ends. Though printer connectors are fairly standard in design, computer connectors are not. The sockets on the QL are particularly unusual. A cable designed for use with a different computer will almost certainly not fit the QL's sockets. You need a cable that's specifically designed for use with the QL. You could either buy one from Sinclair (if you didn't receive one with your computer), look in a good computer store, or have one made up to the right specification by an electrician.

It is equally necessary to ensure that the printer and computer are able to communicate successfully. It's always necessary for the computer to be able to send data to the printer, and for the printer to be able to decode it successfully. It's often necessary for the printer to be able to send return signals to the computer to confirm its successful receipt of the data transmitted. For this to be achieved, the two devices must agree on the type and timing of the signals that they will exchange. The wires of the cable must be correctly connected, so that the two devices both know which of the several signals being sent serves which purpose.

We describe the combination of hardware and software that enables a computer or printer to send and/or receive signals as a port. There are a number of different types of port, depending upon the basic ways in which signals can be sent. For our purposes two types are important: parallel or Centronics ports and serial RS-232-C ports. Within these broad categories there are more variations in the exact set-up and use of the ports.

Printers typically have either a parallel port or a serial port. Computers, on the other hand, often have both types of port, enabling them to work with a wide range of different printers.

The QL has a major limitation in its printer support. It does not have a parallel printer port. A parallel port forms one end of a communications channel down which a number of bits of data can flow simultaneously. Typically the port (and cable) will contain enough lines to enable it to handle a byte of data and send complex control signals at the same time (anywhere between twelve and thirty-six of them).

Many parallel ports conform more or less exactly to what is known as the Centronics standard (often they are described as Centronics ports). Centronics is the name of a printer firm whose printer port design has been very widely copied. Today printers from many other companies comply with the communications standard pioneered on Centronics printers.

Parallel printers work faster, and tend to cause less interfacing problems, than do serial printers. On the debit side, they must be placed close to the computer with which they are used – the thick ribbon cables are typically only a metre or so in length, and it is not practicable to use a very much longer cable without causing synchronization problems.

The alternative type of printer interfacing uses a serial communications channel. Data flows through a serial port only one bit at a time, so that a full byte of data is built out of a succession of bits sent down the channel. Serial communications channels generally consist of more than a single wire, however – five or six is a typical number. These wires carry the single bit of data at a time in one or both directions, also the control signals and voltages required.

Most serial communications on computers conform more or less with the RS-232-C standard. This standard was originally designed primarily for computer-to-computer communications, but the same definition has now been adapted to link printers to computers and for a wide range of other uses. The QL contains two serial ports that conform to the RS-232-C standard. The QL User Guide (under 'communications' in the 'Concepts' section) describes them and explains the difference between them.

The RS-232-C standard does not cover every possible aspect of data communication, and there can be a variety of difficulties involved in linking different devices in this way. (There are far more difficulties than are involved in linking parallel devices.) The User Guide explains some of them, and in particular outlines the 'handshaking' control signals required by the QL in order to make the serial link work correctly.

It is possible to connect a 'serial' printer with an RS-232-C port of its own directly to one of the QL's serial ports (which one will depend upon the printer port configuration). A number of popular printers are available with a serial port: often the Centronics port is provided by default, but you can order the printer with a serial port instead. If you have a parallel printer, then you can only connect it to the QL if you obtain a special interface, which will do the task of converting the serial signals from the computer into the parallel signals required by the printer.

We use an Epson FX-80 printer with our QL. This comes with a standard Centronics parallel port, though it can be obtained with a serial port. Ours is a parallel model, bought originally for use with another computer. We have connected it to the QL using a Miracle Systems interface – a cable plus a little box, slightly smaller than a cigarette packet, which contains the interfacing circuitry. The interface plugs directly into the Epson's parallel port at one end and into the QL's serial port at the other end.

The task of sending control signals via the interface to our printer has caused us a great many problems; many of the signals we have sent have clearly been corrupted *en route*. It is not clear to us yet whether the majority of problems are caused by the evident deficiencies in the serial port itself, or by failings in the interface. At the time of writing (August 1984) the Miracle interface is the only interface specifically designed for use with the QL that we know of, though it would be possible to do a similar job with some more expensive, general purpose programmable interfaces. As a result we would recommend it to readers with some reservations.

Interfacing a parallel printer to the computer via a serial communications link will cause it to work no faster, and probably rather slower, than would a serial printer linked directly to the serial port.

Though many interfaces will, like ours, use the QL's serial port as a connection to the computer, other designs may make use of other connection points: for example, to the QL's user port. Note that the Psion programs provided with the QL assume that data destined for a printer will be sent via the serial port and so, doubtless, will many other commercial programs. You may have great difficulty in making such a program work successfully with a printer that is not connected to a serial port but is connected in some other way. However, you can use such an arrangement without difficulty when programming in SuperBasic.

DOT MATRIX AND DAISYWHEEL PRINTERS

The actual printing technology used by your printer has nothing to do with its method of interfacing: you can get dot matrix, daisywheel, and other types of printer with both parallel and serial ports. However, the printing technology has a lot to do with the uses for which your printer is suitable.

Broadly speaking, dot matrix printers are 'draft' printers. They produce that 'dotty' looking typeface that is fine for internal documents but that many people feel is not suitable for professional letters. Better quality dot matrix printers will often produce a 'near letter quality' (NLQ) type by overstriking, and this is much more acceptable.

Dot matrix printers are fast and versatile. Many machines are programmable to produce alternative typestyles. Some will handle proportional spacing, others will produce user-defined characters (useful for special symbols, or even for graphics); most will handle 'screen dumps' or copies of the computer's display screen. This latter, however, demands quite a bit of programming.

Daisywheel printers tend to be slower and less versatile and are not suitable for graphics. By changing the daisywheel, you can vary the typestyle quickly and easily. Their print quality is often better, and they are ideal for word processing applications.

We cannot go in depth into the many other factors which you need to consider when choosing a printer. Of course, there is always a trade-off between price and quality, and you cannot expect the cheapest printer to produce the neat, even, well-formed type that is characteristic of the best machines, or to work as fast. You must check, too, on the forms of stationery that the printer will accept. Continuous tractor-fed paper is a popular choice, but you may find it limiting if you wish to print envelopes, sticky labels, or letters on your pre-printed letterhead.

In theory the QL will support any model of printer that can be interfaced successfully with it. In practice, the use that you can make of your printer will depend upon the 'printer driver' routines included in the programs you obtain. The Psion programs are reasonably adaptable, as we explain below, but they certainly do not support every conceivable printer in every conceivable way. You may find it frustrating if you buy a printer with advanced graphic capabilities and the capacity for microspace justification, only to find that you can't access any of these using the Psion programs.

PROGRAMMING YOUR PRINTER

In order to send data to your printer, you must set up a suitable data channel. If you use a commercial program like the Psion programs, this will almost certainly be done for you. If you are programming in Basic or some other language, then you must do it yourself. Here we look at the steps involved in doing so.

We will look in detail at SuperBasic programming and at the QDOS operating system later in the book, and in Chapter 9 we explain the conventions we use in the statements in this chapter and elsewhere. Refer to these sections if you have any difficulty in understanding the programming we describe here.

We will assume that you have a printer connected to serial port 1 of the QL. If your printer is connected to serial port 2, then you'll simply need to change 'ser1' to 'ser2'. If you use an interface with some other form of connection, you should follow these notes in conjunction with the programming advice provided with your interface.

Whenever you use a serial port, it is necessary to select a baud rate: that is, a speed at which data will be communicated. The documentation for your serial printer or interface should tell you the baud rate at which your configuration needs to work. The BAUD is used to set the baud rate, and this can be given either before or after you open your communications channel. There's only one baud rate settable for both ports, so the command is something like:

BAUD 9600

– no port number is needed. 9600, incidentally, is the default, so if your printer works at 9600 baud you can omit this command if you wish.

Next it is necessary to open a communications channel for the printer. The SuperBasic OPEN command is used for this purpose. Choose any channel number that you won't be using for other purposes. We'll use #3, but you may wish to change this if you regularly use number 3 as a screen or microdrive channel. Your 'open' command will be something like:

OPEN #3, ser1

Depending upon the form of communication that you require, you may need to add additional arguments to describe the parity, handshaking and communications protocol with which the port is to work. You'll find details of these arguments under 'devices' in the Concepts section of the QL User Guide. You will of course need to read the documentation for your printer and/or interface in order to discover which ones to use. Our own configuration, like many others, uses the default settings and needs no further argument. A longer command might look like:

OPEN #3,ser1eic

QDOS doesn't normally differentiate between input and output channels, so that the serial channel will automatically support two-way communications.

The channel, once open, will stay open either until you specifically close it with a 'CLOSE #3' command, or until you turn off the computer. It should survive not just the end of a program but even re-sets of the computer.

A channel can be opened once only: if you attempt to re-open an open channel you will get an error message. Close all channels specifically at the end of each program in order to avoid accidentally re-opening open channels.

Opening a channel to the serial port automatically calls up a 'device driver' in the QDOS operating system, which handles the transmission of data to and from the port, whenever the system receives appropriate commands in SuperBasic or another programming language. The driver will appropriate a block of memory to use as a 'buffer': working storage to enable it to hold data awaiting transmission via the port, and to receive data that comes in. Data is stored in the buffer in the form of a simple serial queue. There's no need for you, as an end user, to set the size of the buffer or to do anything else to ensure that this works correctly.

The error message 'channel in use', or 'at line x in use' which comes up if you try to re-open a channel that you haven't closed may also occur, apparently, if you try to close a channel or use it for some purpose when for some reason the buffer is not empty and the data has not been transmitted. Sometimes when we had difficulty with communications we found that we received 'channel in use' messages when the channel in question was clearly not functioning properly and sometimes when we knew it had not been opened. If you get such a message, you can try to retrieve the situation by closing the channel in question and then re-opening it. If this fails, your best course of action is to turn off both the computer (first removing any microdrive cartridges from the drives and saving any new programs) and the printer, wait a minute or so and then try again. Resetting the computer will not clear the buffer or necessarily help the situation.

Once the communications channel is open, any PRINT or similar statement that addresses data to the channel will cause data to be printed. For example:

LIST #3

PRINT #3, "Hard Copy"

There is unfortunately no command in QDOS that will enable you to re-direct all screen output to a printer automatically. There's also no TAB command in SuperBasic and it is not possible to use the AT window-oriented command to affect PRINT statements to a printer channel. You can use the print formatting ',' (and other print formatting symbols) to set up rudimentary tab settings on a printer, or you may be able to send printer control codes (see below for more details) if you wish to change the margins, set tabs or otherwise format your output.

Note too the WIDTH command, which can be used to set the width of your printed page, and hence your right printer margin. It is used with the channel number, like this:

WIDTH #3, 60

The 'intelligent space' print formatter and the other print formatters will work with the width command just as they do on screen. We found, however, that in FB Basic the WIDTH command did not work correctly with LIST.

LINE FEEDS AND CARRIAGE RETURNS

It is important to be aware of the difference between two printer control signals: the line feed, and the 'carriage return'. The 'carriage return' on a printer will return the print head to the start of the line. It does not automatically advance the paper like the carriage return on a conventional typewriter. 'Line feed' advances the paper and will automatically return the print head or otherwise prepare to produce the next line of print.

In order to return for the next line of print the printer needs to perform either 'line feed' or both 'line feed' and 'carriage return' operations. Some printers are set up so that a 'carriage return' will automatically generate a 'line feed'. This means that a single 'carriage return' character will suffice to feed the paper (normally described as 'auto-line feed'). Others expect either 'line feed' or both codes to be sent by the computer.

One or the other (or both of these codes) are sent to the printer automatically by any Basic interpreter when your statement includes any PRINT statement that triggers a new line and during program listings at the end of each line of the program. One or the other, or both codes will also be sent by word processor and other application programs at suitable intervals. You can also send the codes yourself, as we will explain below. If the printer doesn't receive a line feed or carriage return code, it automatically performs a line feed when it has printed a full line of text, up to the right margin position.

On many (but not all) printers, it is possible either to set or disable auto-line feed. A dip-switch inside the printer will often do this (see your printer manual). Sometimes, a sequence of control codes (see below for more details) is required.

Auto-line feed is useful if the computer program you use (or Basic interpreter) doesn't automatically send a line feed signal, but simply sends 'carriage return'. It's a nuisance if the computer does this, as it may result in all your output being double spaced. Auto-line feed also prevents you from using 'carriage return' as a form of back-space – for example, to underline text. Some word processors make use of this feature. Disabling auto-line feed when the computer sends 'carriage return', however, will only cause all your printout to appear on the same line of the paper.

Our QL seemed to be set up so that from SuperBasic, printings and listings appeared correctly single-spaced whether we enabled or disenabled auto-line feed. Presumably the computer automatically adds a 'line feed' control code, but not a 'carriage return' control code at the end of each line. The Psion programs, however, appear to send 'line feed' and 'carriage return'. With auto-line feed, they double space output. We discuss below how you can adapt the Psion printer driver routine to allow for your computer's line-feed.

If you are using an Epson FX-80 or similar printer, you should disable the auto-line feed inside the printer in order to make the Easel screen dump routine work correctly: there's no provision for stripping out carriage returns within the Easel program. You can do this on Epson printers by changing a dip-switch setting inside the machine: your manual will tell you which switch to flick, and how to get to it.

OTHER PRINTER CONTROL CODES

On most printers, a variety of the ASCII codes from 0 to 31 (32 with 'space' starts the normal printable characters) are used for control purposes. Code 10, for instance, is 'line feed', the code we described above; code 13 is 'carriage return'. Other codes may back-space, tab, sound the buzzer, or perform other similar functions. To send these codes to the printer while in SuperBasic, you simply use the CHR$ function. Code 7 sounds the bell on the FX-80, for example, so:

   PRINT#3, CHR$(7)

will do just that.

Some printers are more fully programmable, and in order to program them (for example, to access alternate typestyles or to set up graphics modes) it is necessary to send quite complex sequences of control codes. These can be sent in the same way, using a combination of CHR$ and normal printable characters. Your printer manual should give you the code sequences. Note particularly the 'Escape' code, CHR$(27). You will not get the correct result by pressing Escape mid-way through typing your program line!

For example, in order to set a new print mode on the FX-80, you need to send a sequence consisting of Escape, '!' and an ASCII type code specifying the typestyle. To set mode 55, for instance, you'd need this statement:

   PRINT#3, CHR$(27); "!"; CHR$(55);

If you find it easier, you can enter '!' in ASCII coded form: it's CHR$(33).

Note that although these simple measures work well from SuperBasic, they will not work in exactly the same fashion from within the Psion programs or from within other commercial software. In Archive, for example, you can send printer control codes but 'CHR$' is replaced by 'CHR' and you must precede codes below 32 with a code 0 in order to ensure that they are sent correctly. We found this procedure did not work well on our own system. If you are anxious to set up a regular alternative print style for use in Archive or some other program (e.g. condensed type to enable you to print wide spreadsheets in Abacus), then you may find it easiest to do this in SuperBasic before you load and run the program in question. Provided your 'printer initialization' routine does not over-ride it (see below), the print style won't be affected by your loading the program.

SETTING UP A PRINTER DRIVER FOR THE PSION PROGRAMS

The four Psion software programs that come with the QL are set up to work with a printer, via a 'printer driver' routine. Abacus, Archive and Quill will work with almost any printer that is driven via the QL's serial port. There is no easy way to make them work with printers connected to the QL by a different route. Easel will dump graphic screens only to printers that it specifically supports. The early version of its printer menu contains the Epson FX-80 only. This makes a good argument for buying that printer! A few other models of printer work in a very similar fashion, and you may find that the FX-80 screen dump routine will work with them too. Many printers from other manufacturers are entirely different in their control code structure, however, and Easel will not dump data to these.

Easel does not have general non-graphic support for printers, which is unfortunate. If you wish to obtain a non-graphic hard copy of Easel data on a different printer you can do it by exporting your Easel file to Abacus (see our notes on file export in Chapter 8).

The Abacus, Archive and Quill printer drivers can be adapted to reflect many of the characteristics of your own printer. You will find an explanation in the Appendix to the QL User Guide of how this is done. You must use three different files, 'install_bas', 'install_dat' and 'printer_dat'. The manual suggests that the three files should all be contained on each of the Abacus, Archive, and Quill microdrives, but they weren't on all of ours. However, there's no need to work through the installation routine three times. If you generate the correct 'printer dat' file using Quill, you can copy it on to the cartridges for the other two programs. The other two files are not necessary in normal program running once you've used them to install the printer, and need not be copied over.

Among the printer features that are set via the printer driver routine are:
   – the parity (see the User Guide section on communications) and baud rate for your printer.

— the number of lines per page, which will of course depend upon the stationery you use. It's not affected by the line spacing selected inside a document, though it will be affected if your printer has automatic line feed. You can over-ride this setting inside Quill, using the 'design' command, or, with careful programming, inside Archive. (Note: on the first versions of Quill this over-ride did not work correctly.)

— the number of characters per line. This can be over-ruled by the margin settings in Quill: it is much more important in Abacus and Archive. If you set your printer to condensed type when using Abacus, you will want to set a suitably large number here.

— whether your paper is continuous or single sheet.

— the end-of-line code. See our notes on line feed and carriage returns above.

— various control code settings. Among these are a 'preamble code' which could be used to initialize your printer or to select a special print style (e.g. condensed), and a 'postamble code', to return the printer to its default settings.

As you can see, many of these features relate to your own applications as much as to your model of printer, and you may find it necessary to amend the printer details even if Quill nominally includes a driver for your printer.

You can only have one active 'printer_dat' file on a cartridge, though you can save a variety of potential 'printer_dat' files in the install_dat file. If you want to vary one of these settings regularly (e.g. to use different typestyles with Quill), your best course is to copy the Quill program on to two different cartridges, and set up a different 'printer_dat' file on each. If you are not prepared to use up microdrive cartridges in this way, then you will need to re-run the install program before running Quill in order to change your choice.

Quill contains very simple facilities for selecting bold type, underlining, sub- and superscripts. (In fact, you can select and deselect any four print styles: they need not be these, as we explain in Chapter 7.) These facilities are not available in Abacus and Archive, and setting up a printer driver for use with the three programs will not alter this fact. In order to use alternative typestyles with Abacus or Archive, you need to incorporate printer control codes into your sheet or file for printing. In Archive, the command 'LPRINT CHR(x)' can be used for this purpose. In Abacus, you simply put a suitable string of CHR(x) functions into cells of the sheet. You might, for example, do this to set up a title in emphasised type or to underline a figure.

The advantage of the more complex approach taken on Abacus and Archive is that within these programs, you can with care access just about any feature of your printer that is programmable via control codes. In Quill, on the other hand, it is not possible to switch to any typestyle at will: you have about five choices at the most (see chapter on Quill).

A NOTE ON SINGLE SHEET STATIONERY

One final note on the use of single sheet stationery. Many printers (including the Epson FX-80) will allow you to use single sheets of paper as an alternative to continuous tractor-fed paper. This can be very handy if you want to print your document on pre-printed stationery or to print envelopes or labels.

These printers often include a 'paper out' sensor: a simple device which reacts if the paper stack is running out. The sensor doesn't react right at the very end of the paper, it bleeps and stops the print run about two thirds of the way down the last page. Disastrous if you use single sheets: you'd never be able to print a complete page.

You can normally disable the paper-out sensor, to enable you to use single sheets without difficulty, in either of two ways. You can switch it off inside the printer, by changing a dip-switch setting, or you can send a control code that disenables it. The first of these approaches removes the worry, but it also stops the sensor from performing its very useful function when you are using continuous stationery. Most dip-switches are pretty inaccessible and you won't want to change the setting regularly. A neat alternative is to include a 'turn the paper-out sensor off' code sequence in your printer 'preamble' set-up, when setting up your printer dirver as we have already described. On the Epson FX-80, for example, 'Escape-8' disenables the sensor, and you can simply add this to the end of the list of codes given as a 'preamble' in the install__dat file for this printer. Escape-9 turns the sensor back on, and you could include this in the driver's 'postamble' sequence.

3

Introducing the Psion Programs

Psion, a software (and more recently microcomputer) company with a long tradition of close co-operation with Sinclair, had reportedly begun work on its set of four business-oriented programs (Abacus, Archive, Easel and Quill) long before the QL's design was finalized. The four programs were not specifically designed to run on the QL, and their code was not developed on a QL or even on a 68000-based computer with a broadly similar main processor. In fact, the programs were originally written on a VAX minicomputer and were 'cross-compiled' on to the 68008 – a complex procedure which is notoriously heavy on memory requirements. It helps to explain both why the programs are so large (with around 50-60K of code in each, massive by the standards of single-task programs) and why they run so slowly.

As the programs are not specifically QL-oriented, there is no technical reason why they should not be adapted to other computers. Indeed it is currently expected that the set will be launched on other popular personal business-oriented computers. On the whole, we believe this would be to the advantage of QL users. It should improve the level of support for the program as a whole and will certainly help those who can use the same programs on a QL at home or an IBM PC at work.

Of course, the four programs have been fully adapted to the QL's hardware and they make full use of the microdrives and the QL's screen features. However, they do not interface directly with QL SuperBasic. Archive's programming language, as you will notice, is by no means identical to SuperBasic. Although it has similarities, it is not a subset or an expanded set of the language and its syntax in some places is markedly different, suggesting that the similarities are no more than coincidental. It is not possible from within the other programs to issue general commands using Superbasic or the high-level QDOS commands and it is important to remember this: if you want to set the system clock, for instance, then this must be done before loading the application program.

As the main programs are not written in Basic, it is not, of course, possible for the average user to amend the listings or to 'tailor' them in any way.

Early Psion/Sinclair publicity suggested that the four programs would act as an integrated suite and even that the QL's multitasking features would be employed to enable more than one of the programs to be resident in memory at the same time. This has not been achieved, at least in the early versions of the programs. It's easy to see why. Though the QL's 128K of user memory is extremely generous by the standards of competitive semi-professional computers, the operating system and Psion programs eat into it with alarming rapidity. The screen display takes 32K. Up to 60K, as we have said, goes to the program itself. (The bulk of each program is loaded into RAM, though the programs do call overlays from microdrive to handle some command sequences.) Other chunks of memory are reserved for input and output handling, stacks and other system uses (see our comments on the QL's memory map in Chapter 14). When running Abacus, the spreadsheet, only 15K of memory is available for data and calculation purposes, a quantity which is far from adequate. In Easel, only 5K of user memory is provided; and in Quill and Archive too, memory requirements can become extremely tight. There is clearly insufficient memory to support multitasking at this level.

Two future developments of the QL may alleviate this situation. We understand that there are plans to release the four programs in ROM form in the near future. ROM programs use a different segment of the 68008's generous addressable memory and do not overlay the available RAM, making much more RAM available as work-space. A ROM based program should certainly perform more rapidly and impressively and with two or more programs it may indeed become possible to support multitasking.

Second, the QL's half megabyte RAM expansion, not yet launched at the time of writing, is apparently planned for release by early 1985. With four times as much RAM available as in the basic machine, many of the difficulties which beset operation of the Psion programs at present should be removed.

We look at both of these projected developments and at other possibilites for expanding the QL in much more detail in Chapter 17.

Though the programs are not integrated in this real sense, it *is* possible to export and import files from one to another. This is generally true of programs that can create or read simple sequential ASCII files, as do Abacus, Archive and Easel. There's nothing to stop you from cross-handling data files not only between these three programs, but also from within SuperBasic and any other programs using a similar file structure. Export from Quill, which would be a more complex matter, is not supported. In the earliest versions of the programs, import of data to Quill from the other programs did not work either, a major disappointment. File import and export sounds slow and dreary, but in fact it works well between Abacus, Archive and Easel. We look in detail at the way in which integrated applications can be built up using this feature in Chapter 8.

There are of course other advantages to be gained in using a coherent suite of programs from the same source. Psion's programs use, as far as is feasible, a common screen layout. Their use of function keys and special keys such as 'Escape' is broadly consistent and so is their handling of commands and default choices. This makes it far easier to learn the four programs than it would be to learn four programs not related in this kind of way.

PSION VERSUS THE COMPETITION

At the time of writing there *is* no competition to the Psion programs – at least, not on the QL! No serious large scale software from other sources has been made available for the machine at all. Even if it were, the fact that the Psion programs come free with the machine means that they are going to be used by the great majority of QL users. Competitive programs from other sources will certainly be expensive, perhaps extremely so.

We can compare the Psion programs with other word processor, spreadsheet, database and business graphics programs which are available on business-oriented personal computers with broadly the same resources as the QL, however. 'Broadly the same' must be taken loosely: all comparable computers tend to use floppy or hard disks rather than Sinclair's unique microdrives, and as microdrives are markedly slower in operation than are disks we must accept that when the programs involve microdrive access they won't perform comparably.

Because the comparison isn't a straight one, it would be pointless to try to produce a 'benchmark' timings of competitive programs against the Psion suite. Our comments are general ones, intended to give those not familiar with a broad range of business software a general idea of how the Psion programs rate.

Our comments are based largely on our in-depth experience with the versions of the programs that were shipped out with the very first QL computers to be issued. These programs were sold as part of the QL package to members of the public: in that sense, they are certainly not provisional products. Both Sinclair and Psion have publicly admitted some of their

shortcomings, however. These shortcomings were all too apparent in use:
features that did not work as advertised, features that did not work at all,
command sequences that crashed the entire computer, were alarmingly
common. They made all four programs largely unsuitable for serious use:
Quill and Archive, both of which were prone to 'lose' entire files without
warning, were entirely so. We'd rate these early versions as little short of
disastrous: we certainly couldn't contemplate writing any of the manuscript of
this book on Quill, for instance.

Psion's programs are not the only appalling products to have been issued
in the software field – but we cannot recommend them on this basis.
However, it was reasonably clear from these versions what fully functional
versions of the programs would be like. In the hope that such versions will be
made available by the time this book is published, we've proceeded to
evaluate the programs as best we can without further reference to their almost
total lack of reliability.

The Psion programs certainly score very highly on their general screen
display and presentation. The displays are clear and comprehensive, and it is
very handy to be able to swap between a help-oriented split screen and a
more uncluttered display. The help facilities are generally excellent though
the use of microdrive-based help files inevitably slows them down. Many
programs from other sources contain minimal 'help' facilities. The use of
on-screen help is much simpler and more flexible than is reading a manual.

Ah . . . the manuals! Here we are unable to be so enthusiastic. The
manuals for all four programs are very brief in comparison with those of most
competitive products. Of course, the Psion programs do come effectively free
to QL users, not with the hundreds-of-pounds price tags that are characteristic
of the competition. But no more data is available from Psion or Sinclair to
those who would willingly pay for it. It's possible to make the best use of, say,
Easel with only the help that is provided; but the manual for Archive, the most
demanding of the four programs, is grossly inadequate. It doesn't even
contain data on how files are stored or how long they can be. With such
limited data available, it's hard to make the best of the program while all is
going well, and virtually impossible to recover fully from a program crash (and
in the early days, there have been plenty of those). Using Abacus, too, we
wanted more explanation of how memory is allocated to help us build bigger
sheets without running out of the very limited memory available. And the
manuals for all four programs contain inadequate or even misleading
descriptions of how various commands work.

It's largely because of the inadequacies of the manuals that we've opted to
devote so much space in this book to Archive in particular. We still could
cover only a fraction of the material that would be useful to potential users. As
more books on the QL appear, we hope that some of them will fill the glaring
gaps that the program manuals leave.

In use, the features of Quill, Abacus, Archive and Easel all compare fairly well with the competition. We have mentioned individual strengths and weaknesses of the four programs in the succeeding chapters that concentrate on them individually. Taking the suite as a whole, it can certainly cope with the majority of small business-oriented applications. An obvious lack is the omission of any form-letter or mass mailing facility: it would be difficult or impossible to bend Quill and Archive jointly to this task at present.

The four programs have very little overlap of function and at times we found this a drawback. You can't print a textual record of your data in Easel, for instance: it's necessary to export a file to Abacus in order to do so. There's no number formatting and very little print formatting in Archive, though you can produce more effectively formatted reports by exporting Archive data to Abacus or Quill. Though the Abacus manual makes a brave attempt to outline a bar chart program, Abacus is basically completely lacking in graphic capabilities and only the very determined would bother to use it to produce a bar chart. This determined lack of overlap means that most users will need to make quite extensive use of the import/export feature and it really is not an ideal tool for this purpose.

A last serious drawback of the programs is their slowness of response when microdrive accesses are not involved. The version of Quill with which we worked suffered particularly badly in this respect: it was not difficult to find yourself typing (or worse, deleting) text more than a line ahead of the result appearing on screen. Abacus screen scrolling was slow; its overall calculation speed was generally adequate, but so it should be for the very small spreadsheets that it handles. Archive too seemed to respond slowly on screen. Easel, on the whole, was a welcome exception and charts were drawn and redrawn with admirable speed. Psion have suggested that later revisions of the programs will work markedly more rapidly.

USING THE PROGRAMS

Before proceeding to use the Psion programs you should, of course, take a security copy of each one. It would be a wise precaution to take two copies: one 'master' used only for recopying, and one 'working' program that you normally use. Put the original programs away in a quite different place, where natural disasters like floods, spills of coffee and children cannot reach them. Use them again only if your master as well as your working copy is corrupted.

You can safeguard the data on a microdrive cartridge by snapping off the 'write protect' tab, making the cartridge read-only. The Psion programs do not (as some do) require any write operations on the program cartridge, and you may feel that this is a wise precaution. However, it is a one-way operation, and if the program subsequently fails to load you won't have the option of reformatting and re-using the cartridge.

Abacus, Archive and Easel all operate with a simple 'default' printer definition. Before using the programs for the first time you should 'install' the programs so that the print features are set up as you wish. You may wish to set up several different cartridges, each with a slightly different printer definition, as we described in Chapter 2.

The neatest way to load the programs is by using the auto-boot feature described in the User Guide: any program called 'boot' in microdrive 1 is automatically searched for and run when the 'TV or monitor' prompt is answered. 'Boot' on the Psion cartridge is, incidentally, a short SuperBasic program. You can list it and, if you wish, copy its format as an outline for your own 'boot' programs, and, perhaps more to the point, add to it. If you want to set the system clock, print yourself a reminder on the 'loading' screen to switch on your printer, or include any other operation in your 'start-up' sequence, this is the place for it. Before amending the file, save the original version under a different name, and delete 'boot' from the cartridge. You can then save the revised file as 'boot', so that it will be the one that runs automatically.

Finally, do remember to take a back-up copy – on a different cartridge to the original – of every file you create and wish to keep. Microdrive cartridge failures are quite common and you may otherwise find that hours of work spent in composing a document or laying out a spreadsheet have been lost forever.

BACKUPS AND REVISED VERSIONS

The very inadequate Psion programs with which we worked while preparing this book were due to be replaced by upgraded versions when our QL went in for its internal ROM refitting. Purchasers of later models of the QL will not, of course, need to obtain an upgrade in this way.

The four programs should certainly be still further improved in future, and Psion have outlined a number of planned improvements such as three-dimensional graphics on Easel, as well as the ROM version we mentioned earlier. These enhanced versions of the program will *not* automatically be provided to QL owners. This is in line with general industry practice, where you get the version that is current when you buy, and pay extra if you want to upgrade to a later improved version.

It has been stated that members of the QLUB, the Psion/Sinclair QL user group, will be entitled to a free upgrade of the programs. This may well justify the hefty joining fee. After sending off our QLUB membership fee over a month ago, we've received absolutely nothing back (except for a curt receipt to show that Sinclair have taken our money) so we cannot as yet justify QLUB membership on any other grounds. It is likely that any upgraded programs will also be put on sale to the general public, but as yet we have no indication of the potential price level.

When programs provided on a fragile medium such as a floppy disc or microdrive cartridge are protected against copying, it is usual for the supplier to undertake to replace any damaged copy – perhaps at a fairly nominal fee. This is not generally true of copyable programs like the Psion suite and we do not understand it to be true in this case. If you wreck your only copy of one of the Psion programs, you have only yourself to blame. Take those security copies we mentioned earlier and it won't happen. If it does, you can of course beg for mercy from Psion: but you may find it preferable to hunt out another local QL user who can help you out of your fix. This is not intended as an incentive to piracy: it seems to us a reasonable recourse in a tight spot, but generally if you want a program or version of a program, that you haven't obtained legitimately in the first place, then you should pay for it.

As well as obtaining hardware backup from Psion, you may well need to ask for 'soft' help from Psion, if the programs don't work as you anticipate, or if you need help in developing applications. Sinclair and Psion have taken the unusual step of launching the QLUB as a general forum for help with the Psion programs. If you are a QLUB member you should eventually receive a membership number and 'help line' address that will enable you to request help with any problems that may come up.

Our own feeling is that, admirable as the QLUB may yet prove to be, this system should be additional to, and not a substitute for, Psion's normal responsibility to their customers. The company are under no obligation to spend their valuable time developing your Archive applications for you (indeed, they can hardly afford to spend much time on such matters in return for your QLUB membership fee). But they are under an obligation to sort matters out if your program fails to work as advertised and documented. If a problem of this nature causes you difficulty, do go ahead and ask Psion for help even if you are not a QLUB member. You will, we trust, do the same for any program that you buy. If software houses don't obtain feedback from their users about problems with their products, then they have no incentive to improve those products. The early versions of the Psion programs can certainly do with a great deal of improvement: it's up to all QL users to press to try to get it.

4

Working with Abacus

Psion's spreadsheet program, Abacus, is a powerful example of its type and a versatile program which will be useful to almost every QL owner. In this chapter we explore some of its applications. We look at its strengths and its weaknesses, suggesting some methods of circumventing the latter. We also explain how it interacts with the other Psion programs.

USING A SPREADSHEET

You are probably familiar with the basic concept of a spreadsheet, an 'electronic scratchpad', divided into rows and columns where you can store data and formulae, which will automatically make calculations and re-calculations for you. (If you are not well acquainted with the basic concepts, you will find that the Abacus manual gives a clear introduction.) Spreadsheets have developed considerably since the first versions of Visicalc, the pioneer spreadsheet, were introduced. Now it is normal to expect a good spreadsheet to offer sophisticated facilities for the formatting of numbers, to be able to support free entry of text as well as numbers, and to provide a powerful range of in-built functions. Though it has individual strengths and weaknesses, overall we consider Abacus to compare favourably with most other 'serious' spreadsheet programs for semi-business computers.

Spreadsheets have a number of major advantages, both over other popular types of programs such as databases, and over do-it-youself Basic programming. Let us outline briefly the general advantages of spreadsheets over other types of program, and in particular the advantages of Abacus over the other programs in the Psion set.

The simple data/formula design means that spreadsheets make it easy to perform simple and complex calculations, without going through the tedious business of writing a Basic program. Abacus, indeed, is streets ahead of Sinclair SuperBasic when it comes to calculations, because it works with sixteen significant figures while SuperBasic uses a rather poor eight significant figures. This factor alone means that whenever you are performing precision arithmetic it is an advantage to use the Abacus program, and not SuperBasic, for the purpose.

Your data and formulae are easily entered on a spreadsheet. Careful design of general formula and data entry means that the minimum of formalities are needed in entering data. Replication facilities cut down repetitive typing to a minimum: these are very flexible in Abacus, in contrast to Archive where it is much more difficult to handle repetitive data automatically. Abacus also has adequate line editing facilities. The data is just as easily saved, with data and formulae being stored together or separately as you wish. It is far more cumbersome to set up data files on microdrive, and save data to them, from SuperBasic.

There's no need to resort to elaborate programming in order to see your data well laid out on screen: the program does it automatically, and if the default grid layout is not ideal for your purposes it's possible to amend it quickly and easily. In contrast, amending tabular layouts, if your first choice proves unsatisfactory, is often difficult in word processors and still more so in database reporting routines. It's a slow and longwinded business in Archive, though Quill is admittedly strong on this point. Data is just as easily dumped (with equally good layout) to a printer: there's no need to program a separate routine for this purpose. Compare Abacus with Archive in this respect: it's a major task to reproduce an Archive screen display on the printer, while in Abacus it can be done in seconds.

The spreadsheet screen layout in rows and columns may seem restrictive at first, but in fact it is surprisingly versatile. It is not difficult to 'bend' the row/column layout to accommodate the more flexible formatting of a typical data report, with headings, breaking lines, emphasized totals and sub-totals.

Using a spreadsheet you can cram a lot of data on to the screen, with no need to worry about it scrolling out of view and being lost forever. The data layout is so useful that it's worth using for primarily textual data as well as for numbers and calculations. You may think of this as database territory, but spreadsheets can win out over databases in some applications. There's no limitation to a single 'record' appearing on screen at a time: you can view a wide selection of both rows and columns.

The eighty column screen is particularly desirable, but on a television you can manage well with sixty-four or even forty columns. The manual doesn't emphasise the point, but you can see even more data if you suppress the prompts and use a full screen for your spreadsheet: F2 toggles the prompts on and off and you should get into the habit of using it freely.

Any spreadsheet will 'scroll' up, down and sideways, acting as a 'window' on to a larger sheet held in memory. It's easy to move around the sheet, providing a different view through the window: the speed and simplicity with which you can do so compares favourably with the processes needed to access different sets of data on Archive, Easel or using a typical SuperBasic program. Abacus' split-window feature (which we look at in depth below) is a major plus.

Abacus's number formatting options and text justification makes it easy to lay out data neatly within the spreadsheet grid. In comparison, it is quite difficult in Archive or in SuperBasic to ensure that numbers are displayed to fixed decimal formats or to right, left or centre justify text. It's possible to try out a wide variety of formatting options and switch from one to the other quickly and easily.

Finally, Abacus is fairly well error-trapped and there is little risk of losing your data when you commit a mistake like entering an unnaceptable formula or dividing by zero. SuperBasic, on the other hand, makes it difficult to trap errors, and has no specific inbuilt error trapping commands. It is unfortunate, though, that the early versions of Archive were not a little *more* tightly protected against crashes; and equally so that a crash lands you right back into the operating system, with no fail-safe routine to enable you to recover at least some of your data. Here the program does not compare well with its non-Psion competition.

Of course there are other points at which Abacus loses ground against other types of program. The program is best at handling data with a shortish, and fairly constant, length: it's not well suited to handling long strings and, indeed, it cannot handle strings more than a screen line in length. (Lengthy text is best handled in Archive or Quill.) Though alphanumerics can be included anywhere in the spreadsheet without undue formality, it is a drawback that other symbols (like '=' and '&') cannot: you must use the clumsy 'rept' command for them.

Abacus's two-dimensional spreadsheets can only be manipulated one at a time, unlike Archive's data files which can be used in combination. Most other spreadsheets for semi-professional computers are also limited in this way. Though it's possible to merge spreadsheets, the merge and import commands are restrictive and it is difficult to compare data on two similar sheets. The 'window' command will give you two views of the same sheet, but it won't enable you to look at two different sheets.

Abacus has a limited sorting facility, but this is not comparable with the elaborate sorting facilities available in Archive and other databases. This alone means that the program is not well suited to quick searches for data. Many other spreadsheets do include a simple 'search' command, but Abacus does not and this is an even greater limitation. In contrast, the program is fine for handling numeric 'lookup' tables.

One major problem is that the total amount of data that Abacus can handle is comparatively small. The Abacus sheet is of a fixed size: sixty-four columns by 255 rows. It isn't possible for you to select your own preferred size, which might be smaller or might contain more columns than rows. This is something of a weakness. More of a weakness is the fact that – in early versions of Abacus, at least – the program operates only in RAM and in fact uses only 15K of the QL's capacious RAM to hold its data. There's none of the memory-juggling that allows powerful word processors and databases to handle files too large to be held in RAM. There is not sufficient memory space to enable you to fill every cell of a 64 × 255 spreadsheet: one claimed maximum is 760 cells of data, but we hit problems with no more than 100 cells of data and formulae. It is important to watch the 'memory' messages on screen and ensure that you do not accidentally run out of memory.

Finally, the features for 'securing' data and more particularly formulae are not good on this spreadsheet. Some spreadsheets work on the reasonable assumption that often different people will be responsible for setting up the formula oriented structure of a spreadsheet and for keying an individual set of data into it. The former is a highly skilled task, demanding specialist abilities: the latter a much less demanding task which many clerks might feel up to. On these sheets, it's possible to 'lock' formulae and/or data, to prevent it from accidental change or erasure. Type a number into a vital formula cell by accident and the formula could be lost forever: locking the cell prevents this from happening.

You can see a similar precaution in a different context in the Archive program, where it's possible either to 'open' a file in order to make changes or simply to 'look' at it. Sadly, Abacus has no 'locking' command and its sheets must therefore be altered with particular care.

In summary, Abacus is a number crunching program *par excellence*. It scores well as a display facility for the data contained, though Easel graphs have far more visual appeal. (You can, of course, use them to plot your Abacus data). It also comes into its own in a limited but useful range of applications in which data storage and presentation is of more importance than data manipulation.

ASPECTS OF ABACUS

The Abacus manual provides a generally good introduction to spreadsheet applications, therefore we've tried to concentrate on those areas which are less fully explored in the manual. The points we cover are handled in alphabetical order.

Imports and Exports

We look in detail at the cross-handling of data between Abacus and the other Psion programs in Chapter 8. 'Import' is included here too because in some circumstances it can be useful even when you don't particularly want to use your data in other programs.

'Import' has three great advantages as an Abacus command. First, the command doesn't wipe memory (unlike 'load') , so that it can function as a 'merge' to combine data from different files. Second, you have an option to specify the co-ordinates at which the data imported will appear on the spreadsheet. This feature isn't provided on the 'merge' command. Finally, 'import' will handle text: text in 'title' positions, if the file is imported from Easel, and text almost anywhere on the sheet (so long as either rows or columns are all either text or numeric) if the file is imported from Archive. This feature, too, is not provided on 'merge'.

As a consequence, 'import' is the one Abacus command that will enable you to position all the text and numeric data from two existing separate spreadsheets on the same sheet, so that you can cross-manipulate the data or simply compare it. You might want to check on the differences between this year's sales figures and last year's, for instance, or to set up a file containing both sets of figures for export to Easel. 'Import' lets you do this (subject, of course, to the memory constraints we have already mentioned). As it can be such a useful command, it will often be worthwhile creating an export file in the Archive/Easel format (the two are virtually identical) and then reading it straight back into Abacus without using the other programs at all.

Of course, the export/import sequence has its limitations, as we explain in Chapter 8. Most important of these is the fact that it will not handle formulae correctly, so it is not a substitute for a really effective 'combine spreadsheets' command. It is unfortunate that Abacus does not possess the latter.

Lookup Tables

Lookup tables are perhaps an unusual use for a spreadsheet, but they can be a handy one and it is useful to have a good 'lookup' function in Abacus. It is difficult to work out from the brief description in the manual what the function actually does, so an explanation and simple example follows.

Lookup tables are appropriate whenever the quantities to be looked up don't follow a strict mathematical formula. There's no need to use a lookup table to find out what $x/4 + 7$ is when $x = 3$: you can calculate that immediately. On the other hand, you *do* need to use a lookup table to find out how much tax you have to pay, as the tax office's figures don't follow an entirely simple mathematical pattern. A lookup table might tell you the dose of medicine to give to a four-year old, or the maximum pension contribution payable by a man of forty-four earning £12,000 a year. You will be able to think of many other examples for yourself. Some lookup tables might give you a textual answer, but Abacus will not accept text anywhere in lookup tables.

Spreadsheet lookup tables have two advantages over paper tables. First, they do the looking up for you automatically, with no risk of your reading off the wrong figure (so long, that is, as you have prepared the sheet correctly). And second, they can carry out any calculations required in order to obtain a final answer.

The simplest lookup table is a two-column one. You identify the entry to be looked up in the first column and read off the appropriate number (or text) in the second. More complex tables have several columns. You can then use two different indices to locate the exact cell you want to look up. (For simplicity we will talk about columnar tables, but you can of course reverse the references to rows and columns if you wish to use row-based tables.)

Though the manual isn't clear on this point, Abacus does (within limits) support multi-column lookup tables. There are three arguments to the lookup command:

(1)   The range: that is, the whereabouts of the table in which you look for the value given. You can describe the range either as a section of a row or column (e.g. r1:c10) or with a variable name (e.g. 'pay') that is attached to the row or column. (At least, the manual suggests the latter: it didn't work too well for us.) You can't simply use the column letter: 'c' comes up with an error message.

(2)   The offset: that is, the whereabouts in relation to the first column of the value to be returned. It's the provision of an offset value that enables Abacus to handle multi-column lookup tables. You might specify the value in the next column, or the second column along, or the third, fourth or fifth column, etc. 'Offset' is a single number like '2': it affects the choice of column, but won't affect the row position of the data looked up, which will always be the same.

(3)   Finally, the value to be looked up. Note that in Abacus lookup tables, you will in fact look up a range rather than a particular value. Abacus returns the lookup equivalent of the *lower* end of the range in which your value comes. So if you give a value of '4', and the table contains '3' and '5' but not '4', '3' will be the number used.

For both offset and value, you can of course give an expression (e.g. a cell reference or an arithmetic expression) instead of a simple number. The lookup table itself can contain values calculated from formulae if you wish.

As an example, we drew up a simple table indicating the amount of standard rate statutory sick pay due to an individual, depending upon the number of qualifying days in the week (the lookup value) and the number of days of sick pay payable (the offset value). (The figures are taken, incidentally, straight from the DHSS's sick pay tables.) We then used the 'askn' function to obtain from the user these two values. Giving an 'execute' command returns the right answer each time, in cell a6. Figure 4.1 shows the spreadsheet and formulae we drew up.

This is a self-contained lookup table, but you can of course use values obtained through 'lookup' in other formulae used in your spreadsheet.

Figure 4.1 Statutory Sick Pay: A Lookup Table Application on Abacus

	A	B	C	D	E	F	G	H	I
	SSP Daily	Qualifying			Days SSP Payable				
1	SSP Daily	Qualifying							
2	Rates	Days in Week	1	2	3	4	5	6	7
3		0	0	0	0	0	0	0	0
4	5*	1	42.25	0	0	0	0	0	0
5	2**	2	21.13	42.25	0	0	0	0	0
6	16.9***	3	14.09	28.17	42.25	0	0	0	0
7		4	10.57	21.13	31.69	42.25	0	0	0
8		5	8.45	16.90	25.35	33.80	42.25	0	0
9		6	7.05	14.09	21.13	28.17	35.21	42.25	0
10		7	6.04	12.08	18.11	24.15	30.18	36.22	42.25

(We typed out this illustration: though it was developed on Abacus, it wasn't printed straight from Abacus.)

  * formula: askn("no. of qualifying days in week")
 ** formula: askn("days SSP payable")
*** formula: lookup(B3:B10,A5,A4)
All other cells contain the text or numbers shown: no other formulae are needed.

Giving the X(ecute) command causes the program to ask for the data that will go first into A4 then into A5. This is a very useful command and you can ask for any amount of data in this way (the calculation order will determine the order of asking). The lookup answer then goes straight into A6. You can look up the table manually (the top line provides references to help you) and verify the answer if you wish.

Merge

Abacus's merge command will *not* enable you to fit two small spreadsheets (which might, for instance, contain cash flow projections or profit figures for two successive years) on to the same 64 × 255 grid so that you can use the window command to compare the figures on screen. You can only do that, unfortunately, if you design the two from scratch on the same grid or, to a limited extent, with the import command (see above). What 'merge' *will* do is to take extra data from a sheet stored on microdrive, and overlay the data on the current sheet, adding or subtracting the values in cells on the sheet being merged with the values in the corresponding cells on the sheet already in memory.

This is a tricky operation and you should bear in mind that cells containing formulae in your current sheet may be seriously affected by the merge operation. The formulae in cells with which new values are merged will be entirely lost: so unless they are trivial, save your original sheet first! It is perhaps more sensible to ensure that you merge only data cells. Do not try to add new data into formula cells without considerable forethought.

Used with care, 'merge' could be a useful tool that will enable you to use the same data with different sets of formulae or the same formulae with different sets of data. It seems a very dangerous command, however, and we advocate great caution in its use.

Note, incidentally, that the 'data' merged from the new file will be numeric only: the term does not include text. There is no way that 'merge' can be used to combine the text from two different spreadsheets. You can, however, succeed in doing just that by producing and then 'importing' an export file. A clumsy process, but possibly worthwhile in some circumstances. Again, see our notes on 'import' above.

Ordering

For some inexplicable reason, Abacus's manual presents the 'order' command as if it were useful primarily for handling merged spreadsheets. Not so: though 'order' could be useful in these circumstances, it is far more generally useful as a simple sorting facility.

'Order' will re-arrange the rows of your spreadsheet, according to the content of any specified column. Note that it won't re-arrange the columns! It is not possible to specify more than one sort field, as it is in Archive. Curiously the sorting sequence is also different from that used in Archive. Archive sorting uses the ASCII values of the characters in each field and will therefore sort all capital letters before lower-case letters. 'apricot' in an Archive sort will come after 'PEACH'. Abacus sorting is truly alphabetical and combines upper and lower-case, so that 'APRICOT' will come after 'apple' but before 'peach'. This could be much more handy in some circumstances and you may like to bear it in mind when deciding between the two programs for some borderline applications.

The spreadsheet contents can be repeatedly re-ordered, so that you can, for instance, add new data to the bottom of a column and then sort it into its correct alpha-numerical position. Doing so is much faster than it would be to open up new rows and columns in the body of the spreadsheet. You might like to toggle between, say, ordering by salesmen's surnames in column A, and ordering by their total sales in column B. (Save both different versions as export files and then reload them into Easel: it's not at all easy to re-order the columns of an Easel graph, so this operation is best done within Abacus.)

Order has one failing: and it is a whopping one! The command will *not* correct cross-references in formulae to cells that change position as the result of a re-ordering and this will mean that later changes in data will not be reflected correctly elsewhere in the sheet. It's possible to use some formulae with care on a sheet that you will be re-ordering (summing the re-ordered rows will have the same effect, for instance), but because of this very serious problem you must be very careful when using formulae in a sheet that will be subjected to this command. Note, incidentally, that other Abacus commands which affect row or column numbering (notably the grid insert/delete commands) do adjust formulae correctly, as indeed you would expect to be done on any self-respecting spreadsheet.

Percentages

The 'percentage' formatting option is an unusual one and it could catch you out at first. It *doesn't* just add a percentage sign after the value in the cell: it multiplies it by a hundred at the same time. So if a cell has 'percentage' formatting, and you enter a value of 15, it will appear as '1500%'!

The plus of this approach is that once you've taken the requisite care in entering your data the percentage calculations are performed quickly and easily, with no need to fiddle around dividing by one hundred. To get fifteen per cent of the value in A2, for example, you could enter .15 in percentage format (it comes out looking like '15%') into A3. In A4, all you would need is the formula 'A2 * A3'.

Replication

If you are familiar with other spreadsheets, you may at first look in vain for a 'replicate' command in the Abacus documentation. Replication is the usual term for the copying of data, text or formulae from one cell to another in the spreadsheet. It saves on re-typing, allows the automatic echoing of changed values throughout sections of the sheet, and depending upon how the sheet is set up it may also be more memory efficient than entering separate formulae into different cells.

Abacus does have replication facilities, but they go under a variety of different names. 'Echo' is a simple command that copies data or formulae from one cell to a range. (Note that it doesn't copy data from one range of the sheet to a different range: it echoes from one base cell only. There's no single command to do the latter.) 'Row' and 'col' are the more usual replication-type commands, copying data from a base cell along the other cells in a row or column.

'Row' and 'col' both work in some slightly unusual ways. Note that it is necessary to place the cursor in the row or column in question. It is not, however, necessary to place the cursor in a cell which already contains the data or formula to be replicated. You can copy the data or formula from any cell inside or outside the row or column. Placing the cursor in cell C4, for instance, you might use a command like:

row = b2 from d to f

to copy the data from cell b2 and related cells directly into cells in row 4 (see below). Alternatively, you can include the data or formula in the command itself, like this:

row = sum(b1:b5) from d to f

The 'row', 'col' and 'echo' commands all work on a relative basis by default: that is, cell references are relative to the position of the cell containing the formula. Relative replication is the more usual kind, so this is a reasonable assumption. (You can force absolute replication by using a $ sign before the absolute cell reference and in this way can use a mixture of absolute and relative references within the same formula.) Note, however, that the handling of relative references in the kind of statements given above is heavily dependent upon the cursor position. In a statement like:

row = sum(b1:b5) from d to f

the actual column which contains the sum of b1 to b5 will be that with the cursor in it. It won't automatically be column d, as you might assume. If the cursor is in column b when you give this statement, then column d will contain the sum of d1 to d5. If the cursor is in column a, then column d will contain the sum of c1 to c5.

Using the commands in this way, it is not too difficult to produce replication co-ordinates that skip off the edges of the spreadsheet. If column b contains the sum of a1 to a5, what is column a to contain? The program doesn't know the answer and it will come up with an error message.

Time Periods

If you put dates into your spreadsheet, Abacus will calculate the number of days between one date and the next. This might be useful information if, for example, you're calculating a total amount due based on a daily rate.

Here's the sequence of steps to take: First, put the 'start date' into a cell: we'll say into B5. You must enter it as a text string (with leading quotes), in the format 'YYYY/MM/DD' (type the slashes). In the next cell – B6 – use the 'days' function to convert this into a number of days counting from the base date. It will be a large number.

Now put the 'end date' into the next cell, in the same format: and use 'days' again to convert this into a number which will go into B8. Finally, a simple 'B8-B6' will give the intervening number of days.

Incidentally, this command seems to be very memory intensive and in using it extensively in a couple of spreadsheets we found that we ran out of memory in record time.

Titles

In many spreadsheet applications, you will find yourself giving titles to the rows and columns all across row 1 and down column A. You can certainly do so in Abacus: but the subsequent handling of the titles needs some care.

Abacus does not – as many spreadsheets do – have any command which will 'freeze' the title area of the sheet, so that titles still appear on the screen when you scroll away from the top left-hand corner. You *can* divide the screen into two windows, so that the titles in column A will still appear on screen together with the data in columns X to Z, but you can't freeze both horizontal and vertical titles at once. Trying to define a horizontal widow when you've already defined a vertical one or *vice versa,* will cancel and not supplement the original choice. We have not found any neat solution to this problem.

The window command itself is only sketchily covered in the manual: we add a longer explanation under 'windows' below.

On the other hand an advantage of Abacus is its ability to take row and column titles and use them as references within formulae: so that you can refer to 'Jan.Sales' instead of to A4. Note that you can use any *unique* abbreviation to refer to the title: there's no need to type the whole thing out in full. The program has very good facilities for 'intelligently' deciding whether titles refer to rows or columns and you can make good use of these if you want to include titles in the body of the spreadsheet rather than at the sides.

Windowing

It's a good feature of Abacus that you can window your spreadsheet, taking a look at two different sections of it at the same time. The windowing is hardly up to a full multitasking system, and it is of course a pity that the multitasking promised for the QL is not applied in the Psion programs, but windowing can still be very handy.

The window operation is only briefly explained in the manual. It's important to position your cursor carefully before requesting a window. The relative cursor position on screen is what matters, not the column in which the cursor is placed: you can easily change the former by scrolling, but you can't change the sizes of the two windows once you've set them up. (It's not difficult, though, to scrap the window and re-define it if you have made a poor choice.)

You will get a one-row or one-column window down the left or at the top of the screen if you place the cursor either in the leftmost or topmost column/row, *or* in the next column/row. In both cases, the cursor will appear in the larger of the windows. No problem: you can swap it from window to window using the F4 key. Of course you can scroll the screen only in the window in which the cursor appears, unless the two windows are synchronized to move together.

Note that though two windows can be synchronized, they are synchronized at right-angles to the window division only. In other words, if you 'window' the title column A and select 'together' movement, you can move the contents of the other window across to columns N to P without disturbing column A at all. If you move it from displaying rows 1 to 16 to displaying rows 7 to 22, however, you will see the synchronized movement.

You can simulate a view of two different spreadsheets at once if you set up one fairly small spreadsheet in one area of your large sheet (perhaps using the range a1:f20), and another one in a different region of the sheet (say, using the range aa31:af50). You can't, however, merge a sheet from memory into a vacant region of your spreadsheet: see comments on 'merge' and 'import' above.

In our early version of Abacus, we found cursor movement in windowed spreadsheets to be a tricky business which occasionally led to a complete system crash. Hopefully this problem will be resolved in later versions of the program.

One less serious difficulty which could also cause some problems is the fact that window size is absolute and not dependent upon column width. If you set up a one-column window with an initial ten-character wide column on display, then you effectively have a ten-character wide window, *not* a one-column window. Scroll over to a column fifteen characters wide, and you'll see only the first ten characters of it. (You can't see the other five characters by scrolling, either: that will nip you smartly over to the next column.)

Finally, it may sometimes be useful to remember that you can alter the variety of columns on display not only by windowing, but also by changing column widths. Reducing a batch of columns to a minimal width allows you to see other columns in full. You could, for instance, see ten-character wide columns A, B, G, H, and M on screen at once, by reducing the intermediate columns to a width of one. (Zero width is not permitted. Incidentally, the maximum width is the full screen width.) Changing column width has no effect on the data held in the affected cells, so you can do this with impunity.

5

Working with Archive

Archive is the Psion QL database program. It is perhaps the most flexible and powerful of the four Psion programs that come with the QL and is certainly the most difficult to learn to use. This introduction explains some aspects of Archive that are covered only briefly in the manual and explores some possible uses for the program.

As Archive is so complex, we cannot hope to discuss every aspect of its operation in this book. We've concentrated on supplementing the manual, and this chapter is not intended in any way as a replacement for the Archive manual.

USING A DATABASE

A database is primarily a record-keeping program. It's suitable for use in any application that involves the keeping of records of broadly similar size and type. In the introduction to Archive in the QL manual, you'll find a description of the way it sets up a structure for holding data divided into records (individual sets of data) in files (groups of sets of data). A set of files can be thought of as a *database*. Unlike many simpler record-keeping programs, Archive is capable of working with more than one file at a time.

Typical operations based around records are:
— the keeping of name and address files;

— the keeping of indexed data on stock parts, books, customer or patient files, etc.;
— the keeping of accounting records.

It's possible to use Archive in all these various contexts.

Archive and other database/record-keeping programs have two main objectives. The first is simply to store the data they contain in an orderly fashion, enabling you to retrieve data quickly and flexibly. Some similar programs use numbered records within each file, and expect the user to give the record number when retrieving data. Archive hardly uses record numbers at all (unless you design them in when setting up a file). All retrieval is done either by paging through the file, which may be indexed or randomly ordered, or by searching for a record that meets specific criteria

The second objective is to enable you to manipulate the stored data. Not all simple record-keeping programs are strong on the manipulation of data. Archive, as a programmable database, scores highly here. It's possible to print data from individual records, for hard-copy reference or for purposes such as producing mailing labels. It's possible to print reports containing tabulated data from the file as a whole (or a specified subset of it). And it's possible to perform arithmetical operations of considerable complexity. This last facility makes it feasible for you to use Archive as the basis of a simple accounting system, a stocktaking system or for many other purposes.

DATABASE, SPREADSHEET OR WORD PROCESSOR?

As the potential database applications are so wide ranging, it can be difficult for the inexperienced to be certain whether a spreadsheet, database or a word processor is best for a particular purpose. Let's re-iterate some of the strengths and weaknesses of the different types of program, with emphasis on the database.

A database handles highly structured material. Though it's possible to use Archive to handle a narrative-type card-index file, as we explain later in the chapter, the program is best suited to the manipulation of numbers and short strings of text. Use a word processor for the latter.

Databases are hot on searching and sorting. They win out over spreadsheets in these departments. They are not as well suited as are spreadsheets or graphics programs to the simultaneous display of quantities of data from different records, though you can achieve this with a carefully written reporting routine.

Databases lack the tight number formatting options of a spreadsheet, and are less capable of handling predominantly numerical material. Their range of arithmetical and logical functions is far more limited. They are more flexible in their handling of part textual, part numeric material.

CREATING FILES WITH ARCHIVE

In order to store data using the archive program, you must design and create a file to hold it. The file can be stored permanently on microdrive, though while the program is working it may be held only in RAM. There's no need to worry about running out of RAM if the file becomes too large: there's no 'memory used' message on screen as there is with Abacus and Easel and the program should automatically shuffle the file between microdrive and RAM to prevent memory exhaustion. You must, as the program warns you, provide a microdrive cartridge in drive 2 so that the program can set up file space for temporary use, even if you don't plan to save your file permanently. (In fact, the program will *always* save your file: there's no need to give a specific SAVE command. There's no 'abandon' option, and you must delete the file on the cartridge if you do not require it.)

Using Archive there's no need to concern yourself with allocating tape space to files, as there is with many disk-oriented database programs: the program handles tape allocation automatically. As QL microdrives will support only sequential files, Archive must presumably use a simple sequential file structure. (It's not an ASCII file structure, as you can see if you look at the file in SuperBasic.) We were concerned to find that the Archive manual gives no details on how large files (i.e. files too large to fit completely into RAM) are handled or on the maximum permissible size for files. It seems that the maximum permissible size is the maximum possible file size on a microdrive cartridge: up to 120K, depending upon the formatting. Unless you have additional microdrives, this will be a maximum applying to your database as a whole, if you use multiple files.

Though Archive's data storage seems to be reasonably memory efficient, the limited storage capacity of microdrive cartridges does mean that the program will not be suitable for handling very large databases, unless and until Sinclair release a hard-disk add-on for the QL. In any case, the slow access time of microdrive files would make handling very long files on the system a tedious business.

As long as you follow the recommended shut-down procedures, the microdrive file will be fully updated, and any temporary microdrive file space used by the program should be freed, at the end of each work session. It is not clear to us what happens if the program runs short of microdrive file space and this must be a very real danger when multiple files of moderate size are being updated. We were not able to test this aspect of the program because the early version we worked with consistently failed to save files correctly. As there must be a possibility of losing data in this event, it adds up to an additional reason for you to take a back-up copy of every file you create before you begin a work session that will amend its contents.

Much of the file updating, on cartridge as well as in RAM, is done automatically while Archive is working. As soon as you OPEN a file for amendment, the original version will be subject to change. It's important to take precautions if you want to retain a copy of an earlier version of a file before making changes to it. You'd do this simply by copying the file on to a different microdrive cartridge (or on to the same one, using a different name) before starting to work with it.

When a file is first created, it's automatically 'opened' for manipulation in RAM. In subsequent work sessions or after closing the file, however, it's necessary to OPEN it before working on it. Opening a file is quite different from creating it and it isn't possible to open a file that hasn't first been created. Note that it's possible to LOOK at a file that isn't OPEN. This dual level of access reduces the risk of your accidentally changing your only version of a file in ways that you didn't intend.

The name that you give a file on creating it is the name that is used thereafter for storing it on microdrive. You can't re-name a file, though you can copy the data in the file to a different file with a new name, or copy the file as a whole and give the copy a different name. However, every time you open a file you can select the 'logical' name that is used to refer to the file while you're working on it. The logical name needn't be the same as the permanent file name, and indeed it often won't be, as the program uses a standard default logical name of 'main' for the first file you open.

When you create a file, it isn't necessary to put any data into it. What you *create* is a structure, in which data can be stored. Though you'll normally want to go on and store some information, it isn't strictly necessary to do so. There might in some cases be a point in storing a file structure, under a file name, with no data. (You might then copy it and use the same structure as the basis of a number of different files, for instance.)

File creation is done only through the CREATE command and not through any other commands that may superficially seem similar, like SEDIT. Once created, a file structure can't be amended, though you can achieve the effect of amending it by copying the data in the file to a different file with a different structure (i.e. minus some fields or with new fields into which data will later be put.) This is a very useful feature.

Files are structured in terms of fields. All the data that makes up a record must be stored in a field. Each field must have a name. Fields are not given numbers in Archive, so the name of each field within a file must be unique, though it's possible (and often desirable) to use the same name for fields in different files, even if the files are to be opened simultaneously. It's sensible, of course, to use meaningful names like 'amount-owing' or 'firstname$' for field titles.

Though you will usually want to set up more, it's quite possible to use only one field in a file if you wish. A string field can contain up to 255 characters (though one screen line is a more realistic limit if you are planning to use display screens) so a one-field record would be quite a feasible structure for a file of brief notes, for instance. Alternatively, you might set up a 'card-index' file with each record containing string fields called simply 'notes1$', 'notes2$' and 'notes3$', in order to keep the file structure as unobtrusive as possible.

The maximum number of fields that you can use in a file is 255. This means that a record may not all be visible on screen at once, regardless of how the screen is laid out. The way in which the Archive screen-oriented and DISPLAY commands work mean that it's no problem creating large records if you need to.

In most databases, it's necessary to fix a maximum length for fields when you set up the file. In Archive, this isn't the case. All numbers are stored in a standard length field, and strings (when used with the DISPLAY command) can be any length up to 255 characters. Though this gives welcome flexibility, it does make it a little more difficult to validate data: to make sure that you've entered a code of the required length, for instance. The use of display screens helps a little here, but not entirely: the length of a field, chosen when you design the screen, isn't apparent when you are entering data using the screen. The program will only save the amount of data you originally specified, but it won't always prevent you from entering *more* data than that; a weak point.

Though it isn't made clear in the Archive manual, the format for the contents of a number field is restricted. While in some similar programs, a 'numeric' field can contain any combination of numeric digits that you wish, in Archive it must contain a valid single number: that is, the sort of floating point or integer number that could be stored as a number variable. You'll soon find this to be true if you follow the 'books' file example in Chapter 4 of the Archive manual. The format of an ISBN book code doesn't comply to the format of an Archive number, and the program will reject valid ISBN codes if they are entered into a number field as suggested. Of course, you can easily get round the problem by turning "isbn" into a string field.

FILE DISPLAYS

Once the file is created, you can use the DISPLAY command to display its structure, and to give you a reminder of the field names you've chosen. DISPLAY uses a very plain and inflexible screen layout, however, and for many purposes you'll find it worthwhile designing your own screen layout using the SEDIT command.

Screen displays that you design can be saved on microdrive, as can files. However, they are not saved as a part of a file: they must be saved separately. You'll see that they have a '-scr' suffix on the microdrive directory. For instance, you might have a 'cardbox__dbf' file that acts as a general purpose 'card index' file, and a 'card__scr' screen file containing a card index-type layout for use with it. It's up to you to link the files you create and the screens you wish to use with them, either by remembering to load the screens when you load the files or by using a program that links them for you.

There's no need for you to keep a one-to-one correspondence between stored files and stored screens as we'll see below. You could use several screens with one file or several files with one screen, if you design your database appropriately.

While the DISPLAY command automatically scrolls to show you the contents of every field in a record if there are too many to be displayed at once, the 'screen' commands don't do so. Instead, they work within the fixed screen size and no more information can be displayed using a single screen than will appear on view at one time. If your records are long, each screen will be able to display only a subset of the record contents. However, since there's no one-to-one correspondence between the file and the screen designs, it's possible to display the data from a file on a variety of different screens.

Note that only one screen design can be activated and stored in RAM at any one time. However, it's possible to replace the active screen by a new one within a program, so that a variety of screens can be used with the same file even within a single application module.

Often it can be a real advantage to be able to select a subset of the fields you've defined for display. You might wish to use only a few of the fields from within a multi-purpose file, for a particular application. Fields not included in your screen design can't be accessed or changed while the design is used for display purposes and this can act as a handy security precaution.

It's also possible to produce a neat multi-page display of the contents of a long record. You might wish to copy the contents of a few identifying fields such as 'names$' or 'account number' on each page, filling the remainder of the page with unique fields so that the set as a whole displays the entire record.

Since there's no automatic link between screens and files, there is no check, while you're designing a screen, that you give the correct field names for the file with which you intend to use it. Nothing will happen immediately if you nominate a space in the display for a field that doesn't appear in the file or if you mis-spell the field name. However, you'll soon find out your mistake when you try to use the screen and find that the data you intended to appear doesn't do so!

The user-friendliness of your database applications will often be improved if you design input and output screens separately.

SEDIT lets you position the display of field contents wherever you wish and it lets you specify a space on screen within which a piece of data will be displayed. It's possible to fit two short fields on to a single screen row, thus enabling a large number of fields to be displayed at once if you wish.

Note that when using SEDIT it isn't possible to define a field that's more than one screen line in length – less, of course, if you place the field title on the same line. If you go on to define a second line using the same variable name, you'll find that this second line supersedes, not adds to, the original space you defined. This puts a practicable limit of eighty characters (and often less in practice) on the length of string fields. You'll find that you can continue to enter up to two screen lines of text into a field, if the line below is blank on your screen display. However, the second line won't be saved as part of the record. This is a rather awkward feature. As we mentioned above, it makes it difficult to use the field lengths you lay out as a validation check. It also means that if you're entering semi-continuous data, you *must* ensure that you press 'Enter' at the end of each line or the data shown on screen won't be saved correctly.

Using the screen editor, you can place explanatory text anywhere on the screen. It isn't necessary to have the field names, with their restricted format and $ suffixes, appearing on screen, so that instead of preceding a field with a bald 'name$', say, you might prefer to include more precise details on the data that is to be entered. You might allow a separate line of your display for an introductory comment like 'Enter first name (fifteen characters or less)', or 'Give date in format DD/MM/YY'.

Though you can't use all of SuperBasic's design and graphics commands within Archive, you *can* use different coloured inks and papers in screens you design, in order to improve the screen appearance and to emphasize headings or important points.

One final point to note. Screen displays are dependent upon the screen mode in which they are designed. If you try to use a display that you designed in mode 1 (the mode with a split screen containing prompt areas) on a mode 0 (blank) screen, or *vice versa*, you'll find that the record data is incorrectly superimposed on the display.

SCREEN DESIGNS: SOME SAMPLES

The Archive manual is rather short on specific examples of screen layouts, so we'll help to fill the gap by suggesting how you might design some fairly general-purpose screens.

Cardbox

'Cardbox' is a general-purpose screen to be used for a 'card index' type file, containing loosely structured material. We use a 'cardbox' type file to hold details of programming notes and hints that we've found in magazines, for instance. We use another one to make subject-by-subject notes on work in progress. We've even used one as a book indexing tool, making a note of the page numbers for each index reference under the heading of the index subject.

Our 'cardbox' layout closely follows that of a standard index card. There's a simple heading, to remind you of the file you're working with. Then there's an 'index' line, corresponding to the top line of a paper card. This is 'ruled off' to separate it from the text. Finally, there's a semi-freeform area in which your notes themselves can be stored. Figure 5.1. shows the layout.

Figure 5.1 Archive 'Cardbox' screen display

(Note: there is no command in Archive that enables you to dump a screen design to the printer, so this design was copied, with additional captions, using a word processor.)

CARDBOX (red on white)

```
-----------------------------------------------------------------------------------
| ................................................................................
-----------------------------------------------------------------------------------
  ................................................................................
| ................................................................................
  ................................................................................
| ................................................................................
  ................................................................................
| ................................................................................
  ................................................................................
```

(Screen except for title is on black background. Separating rows of dashes are in green. Field display areas in white.)

This screen is intended to display data from six or more string fields, labelled N1$ . . . N6$ . . . .

To design the 'cardbox' screen:

(a)   First, put Archive into the screen mode that you want to use for the screen display: either mode 1 (with prompt areas) or mode 0 (without).

(b)   Note that there isn't a CLS command in the SEDIT set. However, if you've previously cleared the screen to an alternate colour or mode, the screen will be displayed in this colour or mode. It may also be superimposed upon text that's already on screen. The implications of this will be clearer to you when you've done some Archive programming, as we discuss below. For now, we'll assume that your screen will have the default black background.

(c)   Move the cursor to a suitable position for the heading (a little left of the middle, one or two rows from the top). Use the F3 key to select red ink on white paper, and type your heading, starting and ending with a blank space.

(d)   Change ink to green or white and paper to black. Move cursor to the left-hand side of the next row and print a row of dashes. Use F3 to make the whole of the next row a reserved space for variable N1$. Move to the start of the next row and print another row of dashes.

(e)   Change ink colour again if you wish. (Note: the manual suggests that you can select an ink colour for data to be displayed on a screen but this feature didn't work in our early version of Archive: the default colour was used for all data.) Moving the cursor to the start of each row in turn, reserve the next rows for variables N2$ . . . N6$ (or as many rows as you wish to create).

. . . and to use it . . .

Your Cardbox will work most effectively if you sort the file on the field N1$, using the 'order' command. Use this field for your index information, starting with the word you're most likely to look up. (For instance, a file of programming hints might use field contents like 'Monitor, adjustment of', 'Archive, program hints', 'Variables, System' . . . .) Use the other fields as you wish, remembering as you complete them that there's no word-processor type word wrap in Archive, and that you must press Enter when you approach the end of each line.

Customer File Input Screen

This is an example of the sort of layout you might use in a mailing application or in a simple accounting control application. We use the SEDIT layout facilities to help provide detailed prompts for use in inputting data to the file. This sample screen includes fields for customer reference number, name, address, credit limit, last update date and amount owing, but you could of course adapt these to suit your own purposes.

Figure 5.2 Archive 'Customer input' Screen

Designed for the input of data to a customer file. See the separate output file below.

CUSTOMER RECORD (red on white)

You must enter data to the fields with names in white. It is not essential to enter data to other fields, though they should be completed if possible.

Ref. No. (4 digits) ....   Last Update (YY/MM/DD)........

Customer name   ....
Address   ....
                ....
                ....
                ....

Credit Limit (£) ....
Amount Owing (£) ....

Archive doesn't have an in-built 'forced field' feature to ensure that some fields (e.g. customer reference number) are completed on every record. We go part way to making up for this deficiency in this screen by using different markings to indicate forced and other fields. (You can force field entry absolutely if you handle data entry through a program sequence, as we discuss below.) In other circumstances, you might use yet another colour code to represent fields for which no input at all is required (e.g. total fields, the contents of which will be calculated by the program). Explanatory text is included to make it clear what input is required, as you can see from Figure 5.2.

To design the 'customer input' screen:
(a)   Start again by putting Archive into the screen mode that you want to use for the screen display: mode 1 or mode 0.
(b)   In this screen, we've assumed a black background and adopted the following colour scheme:
heading: red ink on white;
'forced field prompts: black ink on white;
other field prompts: black ink on green;
remaining text, input areas: white ink on black.
Use the F3 key to amend the ink and paper colours as you lay out the screen.
(c)   Type the heading and introductory text, and then use F3 to allocate space for the variables. Note that we don't use the field names on this screen. Instead, we use more free format prompts for each field, including spaces and omitting the final '$' sign for string fields. However, the field names *are* a part of the screen design, and it's important to ensure that the actual names you type in (in response to the F3 'V' query) are correct and are the same in every file with which you will use this screen.

. . . and to use it
This is specifically an input screen, and you'll want to use it as part of an 'add new data' or 'amend data' routine. (Either include a screen-select in your program, or select the screen from the Archive prompt using 'sload'.) It is less suitable for output and below we suggest a layout for an output screen for the same file.

Customer File Output Screen

As a reminder that output screens have different requirements to input screens, we'll finish this section with a design for an output screen, for use with the same hypothetical file. This layout (Figure 5.3) might be used in a routine that selects and displays, one by one, customers with an 'amount

Figure 5.3 Archive 'Customer output' Screen

CUSTOMER RECORD (red on white)

Amount Owing (£) ......   Credit Limit (£) ....
Last Update   ......   Ref. No. ......

Customers name ....
Address   ....
                 ....
                 ....
                 ....

owing' over £500, for example.

Though screen displays of this type are useful for output purposes, remember that you can also design more general-purpose report layouts, as we will explain below.

To design the 'customer output' screen
Follow again the general outline we explained above, to select different colours, input text and define the areas for display of different field contents. This time, however, use the strongest colour contrast to emphasize the amount owing. As you page through the records selected, you'll find that this amount leaps out of the screen at you.

In our early version of Archive, as we mentioned above, selecting a colour for input or display of field contents didn't have any effect. If this feature works correctly in later versions of the program, you will be able to highlight actual field contents. If not, you will have to highlight the name of the field instead.

Note that the fields on this screen are arranged quite differently from those on the input screen, though we've displayed the same fields in each case. In some cases, you'd want to display different fields on the two screens. You might omit the customer address from this screen, for instance, and include some more accounting details.

. . . and to use it
Select this screen, manually or within a program, before carrying out the select and display routine.

AN INTRODUCTION TO PROGRAMMING USING ARCHIVE

You will only be able to make full use of Archive's facilities if you are willing to program your own applications. Archive is not unique in this: most powerful databases are programmable. However, programming a database isn't easy. First, of course, you must analyse your application in detail, working out just what you want your program to do for you. It's necessary to master the syntax of the Archive programming language to learn what you can do within it and how to use it to code your program efficiently and correctly.

Programming an application is inevitably time-consuming. If you're going to use a database regularly, though, you will find that the programming effort more than pays off. It will speed you through even the most basic update-and-search operations, streamlining the sequence of commands and increasing your ability to validate data successfully. Archive's ready-programmed facilities are quite basic and you'll find it difficult or impossible to incorporate passwords, for instance, or generate reports unless you're prepared to program. Finally, careful programming can make it possible for even junior staff to be guided successfully through complex file-update and reporting operations. While programming an application is a demanding task, using the system once the programming is complete can become child's play! However, Archive isn't quite as well suited as some programmable databases are to 'turnkey' applications and you will find it very difficult to write a successful, complex program that's completely self-contained and never returns you to the basic operating screen.

If you are familiar with Basic programming, then you will find the commands of the Archive programming language to be fairly familiar, though it omits many features of SuperBasic and includes a wide variety of special commands that are not available in SuperBasic. You may find Archive programming even easier to learn if you've programmed in the Forth language, as the modular way in which you develop Archive programs closely resembles the way in which Forth programs are written. Learning to use the language involves much more than learning the syntax of the commands: for a Basic programmer who isn't used to modularly structured programming it can be difficult at first to adapt to this rather different program design style. Once you've mastered it, though, you'll find it a flexible and straightforward way in which to work.

If you're not a programmer then you may want to look out for special purpose application programs, written using Archive, that are likely to appear for popular applications such as small company accounting and stock control. Buying these ready-programmed modules will help you to get the most out of Archive without the effort of programming yourself.

We'll look first at the strengths and weaknesses of the Archive programming language. Then we'll go on to look at ways of using it to develop both simple and more complex applications.

COMPARING ARCHIVE PROGRAMMING WITH
BASIC PROGRAMMING

Though the Archive programming language has similarities with Basic – and most obvious similarities with QL SuperBasic – it's by no means identical with it. It certainly doesn't consist of SuperBasic plus a few extra special-purpose commands. Only a limited number of commands are available within Archive and some that look like SuperBasic commands turn out to be quite different in practice, with far more restrictive syntax requirements. Though the SuperBasic manual will help you to understand how to use the Archive commands, you can't assume that all the SuperBasic variations on IF . . . THEN . . . ELSE and similar commands will be available within Archive.

Procedures are a feature of SuperBasic – but Archive procedures are rather different. Every part of every Archive program must be written as a modular unit called a procedure. Procedures can call other procedures, which call other procedures: so what you'll be writing is, in effect, a set of procedures with a group name, rather than a named program which includes some procedures. One master procedure for each application will fix the order (and conditions) in which the others are run. It's important to know which procedure is the master: you'll need to type the name of that one in order to run the set! Follow the manual's advice and call the master for each set 'Start', or use some other standard title for it.

Because Archive doesn't use line numbers, there's no hope of using GOTO or GOSUB type commands to vary the order of program execution. Instead, your program must be structured in a modular fashion (dividing it up into clearly-defined sequential sections, each with its start and end properly marked), using the high-level tools that Archive provides. Archive's structuring tools are less comprehensive than those provided in SuperBasic. They are as follows:

ALL/ENDALL, used to loop through all of the records in a file, carrying out a set of operations on each one in turn. As the manual explains, ALL is designed primarily for record scanning, not for updates that may change the length of record fields and it should be used with care. If record fields do change in length while this command is being used, the file may be corrupted.

IF . . . ELSE . . . ENDIF, a general-purpose looping tool. Note the different syntax from SuperBasic: the Archive version does not use THEN.

RETURN, used to terminate a procedure before the ENDPROC command is reached. Several RETURNS can be incorporated into a single procedure. Note however that RETURN *won't* act as an exit from a loop to its end within a procedure, like the EXIT command in SuperBasic. It will only exit from the procedure as a whole.

WHILE . . . ENDWHILE, a general-purpose loop. Note that WHILE must be followed by a numeric expression, not a string expression, and that its format is quite limited. You can't (at least, in our early version of Archive) use some promising-looking constructs like

WHILE LEN(fig$) <> 10

though you can get the same effect with a more cumbersome sequence
like this:

```
LET x = 1
IF LEN(fig$) <> 10: LET x = 0: ENDIF
WHILE x = 0 . . . .
```

. . . and of course, PROC . . . ENDPROC, the most fundamental
(and powerful) structuring commands of all.

Note that WHILE . . . ENDWHILE largely takes the place of REPeat . . . EXIT
. . . END REPeat in SuperBasic, but that its format is more restricted. In
particular, there's no option for a general-purpose exit in mid-loop, as there is
in the SuperBasic version: you can only exit at the end, or with the
special CONTINUE command. Another major omission is any FOR-
. .·. NEXT construction.

Though it's possible to handle most situations with these structuring tools,
it's often necessary to write quite complex and cumbersome code sequences,
as you can see from the sample programs in the manual. The program
commands are well suited to repetitive operations on the records in a file.
They are much less well suited to writing introductory screens for a
self-contained program sequence that prompts inexperienced users through a
sequence of database operations, and you will find programming the latter to
be a harder task than you might expect.

Other points which may catch you out at first include:

— The use of LET in assignments is *compulsory* in Archive, though it is
optional in SuperBasic. A simple 'x = 1' will be treated as an error.
— The variety of PRINT options is restricted and though you can
change ink and paper colours, you can't obtain large characters for
example. Note that though the command summary in the manual omits
to mention it, you *can* use PRINT AT to position your output. (Again,
the syntax is different from SuperBasic, where AT requires a separate
statement.) The only separator permitted is ';': the commas, apos-
trophes and intelligent spaces of SuperBasic are not supported.
— It's not possible to set up channels for output within Archive, and you
cannot use the SuperBasic PRINT#n commands in order to obtain
hard copy. Instead you must use the special printer oriented commands
LLIST, DUMP and LPRINT, which we look at in detail later in the
chapter.
— The 'escape' used to terminate the INSERT command for example,
does *not* return you to the procedure from which it was called: it returns
you to the Archive direct-entry mode. This makes it impossible to use
INSERT within a program, without subsequently exiting from it. To add
a record to a file within a program, and then return to the menu, you
need a procedure that assigns values to fields and then calls the

APPEND command.

– You can't set the system clock from within Archive, though you can subsequently read it. Set the time before loading Archive.

– There's no PAUSE command in Archive. The best way to produce a pause (e.g. while an explanatory message is displayed) is with a GETKEY() statement.

DESIGNING AND WRITING ARCHIVE PROGRAMS

Remember that an Archive program is a *set* of procedures. You don't have the option to save to microdrive just one of the procedures you have in memory: it's all, or nothing. With this in mind, you need to work carefully and methodically when writing a program.

In the Archive manual, you'll find listings for a wide variety of useful general-purpose procedures. You'll want to use procedures similar to 'getrec' (p.25), 'change' (p.26), and 'choose' (p.29) again and again, for instance, keeping to the outline and simply changing any specific details such as the field names. It's a good idea to type out a set of general purpose procedures, based on these, for all the functions you're going to want in a variety of different applications. Save the set as a whole, under a general name like 'baseprocs'.

When you're writing a particular program, you can then start by loading 'baseprocs' into memory. Delete any of the procedures that you won't be needing and use the rest as a basis for developing your new program.

Plan out your procedure structure before you begin to code it, on paper. There may be procedures that call other procedures that call still other procedures. Archive appears to be vulnerable to recursive errors (it doesn't

Figure 5.4 Structure of an Archive Program: Stock Control System
Independent procedures:

| start | | bye |

Top level: procedures which call from all lower levels:

| sale | | delivery |

Next level: procedures called by level above, calling level below:

| quantity | | query | | doorder |

Next level: procedures called by level above, calling level below:

| inquire | | doform | | cheap | | fast | | report |

Bottom level: utility procedures called by all higher levels:

| clear | | confirm |

like procedure1 to call procedure2 that calls procedure1, and so forth), so your procedures should fit into a neat multi-level structure. Figure 5.4 shows a diagram of the structure for the 'stock control' application outlined in the manual, for instance, with the high-level procedures at the top, and the lower level ones they call progressively lower down the page. You may like to use a different layout for analysis, but you'll find it a great help to have an outline diagram like this to work with.

Start by coding the lowest level of procedures. If it's feasible to do so (and it generally should be) test each one once you've coded it, using a duplicate or dummy file to work with. (That way, you don't have to worry when testing the 'delete' options!) Debug it as fully as you can – more bugs may come to light later. Then work upwards, coding progressively higher level procedures until you've completed the set.

If you make an error that crashes you right out of Archive, you'll lose any procedures that you haven't stored on microdrive. The safe method is to save your set of procedures *before* you test each new procedure. If you have made fatal errors, you can then reload the entire set from microdrive and amend the procedure before retesting. Archive (like QDOS) won't let you overwrite program files saved on disc with other files that have the same name, so you will need to give each set you save a new name, like, for example, 'testprog1', 'testprog2' and so on. Periodically go back and 'kill' the earlier files, to free space on your microdrive cartridge.

YOUR DATABASE AS A WHOLE

Let's now summarize the components that make up an Archive database. A database may contain:

   – One or more record files, each with an individual file structure and individual record contents. These will be suffixed as '-dbf' files on the microdrive cartridge. They are created using the CREATE command, accessed using the OPEN or LOOK commands, and updated during work sessions.

   – One or more screen layouts, for use with the record files. There need not be a one-to-one correspondence between the layouts and the files. Screen layouts have '-scr' suffixes. They are created using SEDIT, saved on cartridge with SSAVE, and reloaded with SLOAD.

   – One or more programs – that is, sets of procedures. These are created with the EDIT command and saved on cartridge with SAVE. LOAD loads the program into memory; RUN both loads and runs the set, provided a procedure named 'start' is included. Any other procedure can be selected by typing its name as a command.

You will normally want to keep this complete set of data on a single cartridge, though if you have additional microdrives to use, you may be able to spread it over several cartridges.

Though you can load screens, record files and programs individually as you need them, you can streamline the process by writing a procedure that opens your files and loads the screens you want to use for you. You will find outlines of this type of procedure in the Archive manual and in the program for the application we describe at the end of this chapter.

PRINTING AND REPORTING IN ARCHIVE

Archive, like the other Psion programs, supports a printer and includes a simple printer driver. On our copy of the Archive cartridge, the 'install_bas' program that is used to initialize a printer and set up a driver was not included. That's no great problem: you can set up your printer definition using Quill and copy over the 'printer_dat' file direct to Archive (deleting the original version first) as we described in Chapter 2. Though the driver is simple, you will find this useful, for instance, if you want to amend the default 'line feed/carriage return' combination to line feed only or to set up an alternative print style for use when producing Archive reports.

In theory it is possible to send control codes to a printer while Archive is running. Note that in Archive the 'ASCII code' function is not CHR$ as usual, but CHR without the $. The manual warns you to precede codes below 32 with a CHR(0) to ensure that they are sent correctly. There should be no problem with bigger code numbers. We failed miserably in our numerous attempts to set up alternate print modes on our Epson FX-80 using this method: our signals were evidently corrupted *en route* to the printer. However, the culprit may have been either our printer interface or the QL's very suspect serial port, rather than Archive itself.

As well as changing print modes, you might use this facility for example, to send form feeds to your printer during a long report or to alter margin settings. Note that you will have to re-install your printer in order to change the default eighty-column line length, though: you can't over-ride this with control codes.

Three printer commands are provided in Archive. All three automatically open a serial channel to the printer and close the channel after use, so there is no need to worry about these matters as there is in SuperBasic. The most straightforward is LLIST: it simply lists all procedures currently in memory, and acts as a simple hard copy record of programs. It isn't possible to select procedures for printing with LLIST but you could save all procedures to microdrive, delete the unwanted ones and LLIST the remainder to get the same effect.

DUMP is less straightforward. It will reproduce selected fields (or all fields, if you prefer) of all or a subset of records on the printer. The fields are tabulated, but not intelligently so, and there is no option to select the tab positions. We found output with DUMP to be very poorly laid out, and felt that this command is best avoided except as a quick and dirty method of checking on file contents while debugging procedures. In our version of Archive, the use of DUMP also corrupted the serial communications channel and the only way to send further output to the printer was to Quit Archive, then restart the program. This more serious drawback will presumably be cured in later versions of the program.

The most flexible of all three commands is LPRINT, the printer version of the screen display PRINT command. LPRINT can be used with TAB (not AT – and not, unfortunately, a decimal tab) to format printed reports. You can print either specific text (e.g. 'LPRINT "November Sales Report" ') or fields from a file (e.g. 'LPRINT author$; TAB 30; titles$') or more complicated expressions (e.g. 'LPRINT total/numrec'). With a combination of these types of statement, it's not difficult to build up a short procedure that produces a report on your file contents, laid out more or less as you wish.

The obvious omission in Archive print commands is any command that prints out either a simple display list of a record, or better still, one that dumps a screen display containing data from a record. This is unfortunate because it means that screen displays really are confined to screen applications: they have no use at all when you want to print a record. It also means that report design can't be as interactive as screen display design: it must all be done blind.

Because LPRINT is rather different from opening a serial channel and PRINTing to that, it is also difficult to print miscellaneous items such as a file directory while in Archive.

If you are anxious to produce a report containing a great deal of narrative together with material from an Archive file, you may find it easiest to export your Archive file data to the Quill program. If your report contains mainly numbers which you wish to format neatly, then an export to Abacus might be the answer. We discuss the operation and applications of file exports in Chapter 8 and will not mention them further in this chapter.

For most purposes, though, Archive's own reporting facilities will be adequate. Using the Archive programming language, you can design a routine that will print out tabulated selections of a file's contents, add headings, perform simple arithmetic on the cumulative contents of certain fields and print out its results. Because there is no inbuilt 'report' feature in Archive, you must program a procedure in order to achieve this: you can't simply design a report output form. This is perhaps the most compelling reason why every Archive user should become familiar with its programming features. Programming report layouts is very straightforward and you should be able to achieve good results with very little difficulty. We've included a simple example in the procedures for the application we outline below.

AN ARCHIVE APPLICATION:
A SIMPLE ACCOUNTING PROGRAM

We used the Archive program to set up a simple suite of accounting procedures suitable for holding and maintaining data on a small company's set of accounts. We've used this double-entry system to balance our own accounts and on the whole it works well. We're presenting our database structure and set of procedures here, as an example of an Archive application rather different to those covered in the manual.

With the early version of Archive which we tested, we did have some very serious reliability problems and we repeatedly found that the program 'lost' the contents of our files, even when the file names appeared correctly in the microdrive directory. (A good argument for a strong set of microdrive utility programs!) The package is not as comprehensive as it might otherwise have been because of this insuperable difficulty. Until these problems are resolved in later versions of the QL and Archive, we cannot wholeheartedly recommend the database we outline as a method for keeping a sole record of a company's accounts. However, we hope the procedures in the suite will give you some useful ideas and insights into how Archive can work.

This is a two-file database system and our procedures include some routines for updating jointly the two files used. The Archive manual also includes very little information on programming mathematical functions and you may be particularly interested to see how to handle the arithmetic involved in this application.

The set of procedures is not exhaustive and inevitably it doesn't include every feature that would be desirable in an accounting suite. It's a basic system, but it is designed to be open ended: you can add to it at will to produce additional features that you feel desirable, as well as adapting it as you find necessary to fit your own requirements.

The System Structure

In this system we've used two files. 'Ledger' is a file that holds details on each different coded account in our system. It's a skeleton all-in-one ledger, with one record for each customer, client and other ledger heading (e.g. cash, travel expenses, stationery and office expenses, etc.). Figure 5.5 shows the field structure for this file. You'll see that we maintain debit and credit balances and an overall balance, for each account, but do not maintain details of individual transactions in this file. Our own company accounts are simple, and we use only around thirty ledger headings: the program works well with this number, but we haven't tested it with more.

The ledger records could of course be expanded to hold client or customer addresses, details on credit limits, etc.

The second file, 'trans', holds details on each transaction: that is, each

Figure 5.5 An Accounting System Programmed using Archive: Field Structure of the 'Ledger' File

Field name:	Type of contents:	Example:
Ledgcode$	ledger code as used in 'trans'	ohex01
Name$	full name of account	overhead expenses
Udate$	date of last transaction update	11 Aug 84
Debittot	debit total	95.46
Credittot	credit total	12.21
Balance	difference of debit/credit	83.25

Figure 5.6 An Accounting System Programmed using Archive: Field Structure of the 'Trans' File

Field name:	Type of contents:	Example:
Date$	date of entry	20 Jul 84
Item$	item description	electricity bill
Ledgcode$	ledger code	ohex01
Debit	}one only contains	121.34
Credit	}number	0

ledger entry. A single transaction is *either* a debit entry *or* a credit entry. It refers to only one ledger account, so it would not normally be both, though as the file is set up you could if you wish enter both a debit and a credit to the same account. Figure 5.6 shows the field structure we set up for this file.

We do not attempt to balance each individual pair of transactions before accepting them, but as we explain below, a 'balance' routine is included to ensure that a batch of transactions *do* balance.

The transaction file would obviously grow very large over time, if it were not weeded. We do not recommend that you continue to work with an extremely large file: there is no advantage in doing so, as long as you keep adequate records for audit purposes. You might handle the size problem either by periodically saving the file contents to an archive file and starting over again with an empty file or by introducing a selective 'delete entry' routine that prints a hard copy of the data from each redundant record before deleting it.

The Procedures

A set of partially nested procedures are provided to help to manipulate the two files. We saved these as a group, under the name 'accounts'. The accounting package as a whole is then entered by LOADing or RUNNing 'accounts'.

'Start' will of course be the normal entry point to the set. 'Start' runs automatically if you 'RUN accounts'; otherwise it can be run simply by typing 'start'. This procedure then designates four 'user' procedures, giving their names so that the user will immediately be able to select and run any one of them by typing its name. One of the user procedures may call two other procedures. These are not intended to be called individually by the user, and so their names are not listed by 'start'.

Figure 5.7 shows the simple 'tree' structure of procedures that we set up. We will now describe each one in detail.

Figure 5.7 An Accounting System Programmed using Archive: The Procedure 'Tree'

Independent procedures:

> | Start |

Top level: user procedures listed in 'start':

> | Seeledg | | Addtrans | | Balance | · | Ledgrept |

Lower level: procedures called by top level:

> | Ledgup |

Bottom level: procedures called by level above:

> | Slip |

Table 5.1 An Accounting System Programmed using Archive

The Procedures Used

These procedures are reproduced in a format intended to bring out their structure. It is slightly different from the format used by 'llist'. For clarity, we've put commands into capital letters, and used lower case elsewhere

```
proc addtrans  USE "main"
               ORDER ledgcode$; A
               CLS
               LET q$ = ""
               WHILE q$ <> "q"
                   PRINT
                   PRINT "Adding a transaction "
                   INPUT "Give date (dd/mm/yy) "; date$
                   INPUT "Item description "; item$
                   INPUT "Ledger code "; ledgcode$
                   INPUT "Debit amount "; debit
                   INPUT "Credit amount "; credit
                   APPEND
```

```
                 ledgup
                 INPUT "q to quit, any other key to continue "; r$
                 LET q$ = LOWER(r$)
              ENDWHILE
              ENDPROC
```

proc balance
```
              USE "l"
              ORDER ledgcode$; A
              LET tot = 0
              ALL
                 LET tot = tot + balance
              ENDALL
              LET tot = INT((tot+0.00002)*100)
              IF tot = 0
                 PRINT AT 10,5; "Okay, books balance"
                 PRINT AT 11,5; "Press any key to continue"
              ELSE
                 PRINT AT 9,5; "total is "; tot/100
                 PRINT AT 10,5; "Problem here, books don't balance"
                 PRINT AT 11,5; "Either abort session and start again"
                 PRINT AT 12,5; "from backup tapes, or find error in"
                 PRINT AT 13,5; "transaction records."
                 PRINT AT 14,5; "press any key to continue"
              ENDIF
              LET r$ = GETKEY()
              CLS
              ENDPROC
```

proc ledgrept
```
              USE "l"
              INPUT "today's date? ";d$
              LPRINT "Ledger Report"; tab 60; d$
              LPRINT
              LPRINT "ledger code"; TAB 30; "debit"; TAB 40; "credit"; TAB
                 50; "balance"
              LPRINT
              LET dbt = 0
              LET crt = 0
              LET bt = 0
              ALL
                 LPRINT ledgcode$; TAB 30; debittot; TAB 40; credittot; TAB
                    50; balance
                 LET dbt = dbt + debittot
                 LET crt = crt + credittot
                 LET bt = bt + balance
              ENDALL
              LET dtot$ = STR(dbt,0,2)
              LET ctot$ = STR(crt,0,2)
              LET btot$ = STR(bt,0,2)
              LPRINT
              LPRINT "totals: "; TAB 30; dtot$; TAB 40; ctot$; TAB 50; btot$
              ENDPROC
```

proc ledgup
```
USE "l"
ORDER ledgcode$; A
LET code$ = main.ledgcode$
LOCATE code$
IF ledgcode$ <> main.ledgcode$
    slip
    RETURN
ENDIF
LET udate$ = main.date$
LET debittot = debittot + main.debit
LET credittot = credittot + main.credit
LET balance = debittot – credittot
UPDATE
USE "main"
ENDPROC
```

proc seeledg
```
USE "l"
SLOAD "ledger"
ORDER ledgcode$; a
FIRST
SPRINT
ENDPROC
```

proc slip
```
CLS
PRINT "main code = "; main.ledgcode$
PRINT "ledger file code = ";ledgcode$
USE "main"
LOCATE code$
DELETE
PRINT "Ledger code not recognised on transaction"
PRINT "Transaction record deleted"
PRINT "Press any key to continue"
LET r$ = GETKEY()
ENDPROC
```

proc start
```
OPEN "ledger" LOGICAL "l"
OPEN "trans" LOGICAL "t"
CLS
INK 4
PRINT AT 1,5; "Ledger Accounts"
INK 6
PRINT AT 4,0; "Uses files 'l' (ledger) and 'main' (trans)"
PRINT AT 5,0; "Add transactions using 'addtrans' only. Ledger"
PRINT AT 6,0; "and transaction files are updated automatically."
PRINT AT 7,0; "Other adjustments can be handled manually."
PRINT AT 8,0; "Ensure that all files are backed up first."
PRINT AT 10,0; "Procedures available for use are:"
PRINT AT 11,5; "addtrans – add transactions "
PRINT AT 12,5; "balance – check balance on ledger"
PRINT AT 13,5; "seeledg – view or amend ledger"
PRINT AT 14,5; "ledgrept – printed report on ledger"
ENDPROC
```

Start

As the Archive manual recommends, we've begun our set of procedures by naming one 'start'. Running the set of procedures as a whole will then automatically cause this procedure to get to work.

'Start' opens the two files which we use in our accounting system, giving both logical names. It's necessary to do this when two files are used simultaneously. 'Trans' we call 'main', the default logical name; 'ledger' we call 'l'. The procedure then clears the screen and prints, at carefully chosen intervals, the names of the four procedures which the user can select for running: 'seeledg', 'addtrans', 'balance' and 'ledgrept'. That's all it does.

We experimented at some length with 'closed' programmed systems, which remove the screen prompts, put the screen into Mode 0 (the no-prompt mode) and try to screen the user from all the normal Archive commands. Our experiments weren't altogether successful and we found it very difficult to set up a watertight 'user interface' in this way. In this suite of programs, we've made no attempt to do so and on reflection we've chosen to print the introduction to the program on the Mode 1 screen. Swapping between mode 1 and mode 0 plays havoc with your screen designs, and we felt it not to be worthwhile at this stage. Once you are a very experienced Archive programmer, you may feel that this caution is unnecessary and that the mode 0 screen (perhaps with an alternate background or ink colour) looks more attractive.

Note that 'start' can only be run once. Attempting to re-open files which are already open leads to error messages and there is no easy way to circumvent them. The list of new procedures isn't intended to be a full menu: once an option has been selected and run, the program will not return to this list. You can, of course, check on procedure names at any later stage by using the 'edit' command.

As we use different screen displays in the different procedures in the suite, we do not load a screen display as a part of the 'start' procedure. If your application used only one display, this would however be the natural point at which to load it.

Seeledg

'Seeledg' is the simplest of the remaining procedures and is entirely self-contained. Its main purpose is to set up the ledger display screen, rather than the default display list.

The procedure must of course ensure that the ledger file is current. 'Use "l" ' (the logical name for the ledger file) does this. It loads the screen display we've filed as 'ledger', which is shown in Fig. 5.8. It orders the file according to ledger code, in ascending order. It then displays the first record in the file, using the 'ledger' display.

At this point the procedure stops. Again, it is designed to be open-ended:

Figure 5.8 An Accounting System Programmed using Archive: Screen Layout for the Ledger Records

LEDGER RECORD (red on white)

Ledger Code ......
Ledger Name ....
Last Update ....
                  Debit Total   Credit Total
                  ....

Balance: ....

(All field names are in black on white. Remainder of screen is white on black)

we don't attempt to incorporate every option that a user might want to use. Once the correct file has been selected, and the display set up, the user can use the normal set of 'first', 'next', 'last' and other commands to browse through it or can go on to add and delete records.

Keeping the procedure open in this way certainly does open the possibility that a careless user will make undesirable changes to the ledger file. It certainly would not be desirable to delete a ledger record that didn't have a zero balance, for instance. However, once again we felt that it was a herculean task to cater for all requirements within a closed system. We chose flexibility over safety in this case.

Of course the 'seeledg' structure could easily be adapted to provide a 'seetrans' file, though the transaction file should not be amended without careful cross-reference to the ledger file. (One possibility would be to close 'trans' and re-open it as a 'look' file only: however, this is a time-consuming method.) A useful addition to either procedure might be an optional call to another procedure that reproduces the current file record, in its screen format, on a printer.

Addtrans

'Addtrans' adds transactions to the transaction file. It does more than this, though: it automatically updates the ledger file from the details that are added. We haven't programmed a similar 'changetrans' or 'deletetrans' procedure, but these would obviously be desirable if you do not wish to handle all amendments and corrections to your accounts by means of balancing entries.

The procedure begins, of course, be selecting the 'main' (logical name for 'trans') file for use. It then orders the file, according to ledger code (a step which isn't particularly necessary when adding transactions, but which comes in useful later) and clears the screen before confirming the choice of procedure with a simple message, 'adding a transaction'. A 'while . . . endwhile' loop, controlled by an invitation to quit the procedure, enables the user to continue adding a series of transactions. Note that it's necessary to give an initial value of q$: otherwise an error message is generated when q$ is used in the 'while' statement.

It is apparently not possible to exit neatly from the 'insert' command back to a procedure: using 'Escape' to terminate a series of inserts dumps you back, not to the procedure, but to the main Archive program. Because of this difficulty we've chosen to use 'append' rather than 'insert' to add data to the file. There is no other reason for this choice. A disadvantage of this process is that it isn't possible to use a saved screen design for adding transaactions to the file. Obviously, it would be possible to program the equivalent of an elaborate screen design, but we haven't done so here: the procedure simply asks for data for entry to each field in turn, putting each into the current field variables, and then uses 'append' to create a new record with the current field variable contents.

We ask the user for a new date for each transaction, but if your batch of transactions will normally all have the same date, you may like to adapt the procedure so that only one date entry is required.

The procedure could be improved by a confirmation routine, which enables you to abort the process if any of the field contents have been incorrectly entered. As you will see, there is a subsequent check on the ledger code, but this falls far short of perfection as far as data validation goes.

Once the new record has been created, this procedure calls another procedure, 'ledgup' which updates the ledger file. We look at 'ledgup' in detail below.

Ledgup

'Ledgup' is a procedure called by the 'addtrans' procedure we described above. It is not intended to be called directly by the user, so we did not include it in the list of procedures provided by the 'start' routine.

The purpose of this procedure is to update ledger totals from transaction details provided in the transaction file. The procedure checks to find a ledger record with the code given in the transaction record. If one is found, then the ledger will be updated accordingly. If the ledger code is not matched, then a 'slip' procedure takes over.

'Ledgup' starts by turning the ledger file (logical 'l') into the current file, and ordering it by ledger code to simplify the search which follows. As you will notice, we've done a great deal of ordering in this set of procedures. In practice, it probably isn't necessary to do quite so much: records once ordered are saved on microdrive and reloaded in their correct order, a feature not true of all database systems, so that normally the file ordering will be correct. Extra checks on the order take minimal time, however, and ensure that all the search routines will work correctly.

We put the transaction ledger code ('main.ledgcode$') into a variable called code$, and then use the 'locate' command to find this in the sort field. (Yes, the variable is necessary: the procedure didn't work without.) 'Locate', as the manual explains, will always find a record, but it may not find an exact match, so it is next necessary to see if an exact match is found. If not, the 'slip' procedure handles the appropriate housekeeping, and the update is aborted.

Four fields in the ledger record are updated: the last update date, the debit and credit totals, and the balance. This latter is not calculated from the transaction record, but is calculated simply by deducting the credit total from the debit total. Debit balances will appear as plus amounts, credit balances as minus accounts.

The four 'let' commands give the current file variables their new values and then the 'update' command changes the record which has been located so that it will contain these values.

'Ledgup' returns to a point within the 'addtrans' procedure, so it is necessary to complete its housekeeping by changing the current file back to the trans ('main') file.

Slip

'Slip' is the second nested procedure called by 'addtrans'. It, too, is not intended to be directly accessible to users and therefore it does not appear on the 'start' summary.

In order to indicate the mistake, the procedure starts by informing the user of the ledger code on the last transaction (the value still held in the variable 'main.ledgecode$') and of the ledger code in the ledger file that has been found by the 'locate' command ('ledgecode$': no logical name needed, since this is the current file). These will of course be different, as this is a condition for the slip procedure to be called.

'Slip' then returns from the ledger file to the trans file. As a safety precaution, we locate 'code$', the variable to which we assigned the ledger code in question (in the 'ledgup' procedure above). As 'code$' was taken directly from the transaction record, there is no need to check that an exact match has been made: this should always be the case. Also it seems to be the case that the active record in 'trans' will not be changed by the changes in the current file between 'trans' and 'ledger', but as Archive's manual is none too re-assuring on such points, we felt this to be a wise precaution. 'Delete' then deletes this transaction record, a necessary step since it has failed to update the ledger file successfully. The procedure ends by indicating that the record has been deleted by returning first to 'ledgup' and then immediately to 'addtrans', where the transaction can be re-entered from scratch.

Balance

'Balance' is another user-oriented procedure. It is intended that the user should check that the records have been updated correctly and that no arithmetical errors have been made, by running 'balance' after each batch of transactions have been added using 'addtrans'. (You may like to add a screen note to this effect in 'start'.) It's not a reporting procedure, simply a checking one.

This procedure uses the ledger file. The ledger file, as we noted above, is updated from the transaction file by the 'addtrans' procedure: if the ledger file balances from batch to batch, then it follows that the transaction batch must balance.

We use a 'tot' variable, and a simple ALL . . . ENDALL loop to tot up the cumulative balance for the ledger file as a whole. As we explained above, debit balances are stored as plus amounts and credit balances are minuses: the overall balance should be zero.

Here we initially hit a problem! Our first attempt to balance the books failed to work because the total was, not zero, but 0.0000003! Not an esoteric slip in entering the data, but a good old-fashioned rounding error in the computer. The variable juggling that follows is an attempt to circumvent this problem. It's not possible to designate number formats in Archive such as two decimal places (a weakness of the program), so we multiply 'tot' by 100 to turn standard two-decimal-point money amounts into integers. As there is no integer variable in the program, we use the INT function to slice off the erroneous lower decimal places, but first we add a small amount to ensure that rounding down (which INT does, of course) will not cause even bigger errors to creep in. If the only discrepancy was a small rounding error, this will then have been eradicated.

There is a slightly simpler way to produce output with a fixed number of decimal places using the function STR, which we use in the 'ledgrept' procedure below. In this procedure we found that it caused problems: a total of '–0.00', for example! On the whole, STR is best used when no further arithmetical operations are to be carried out. Note that Archive does not support SuperBasic-type variable coercion; though you can convert a number into a string, there's no way to convert a string back into a number.

A straightforward IF . . . ELSE . . . ENDIF loop is used to cater for the two eventualities: the books balance or they don't. If all is well, the procedure simply announces the fact. If there has been a mistake, the procedure gives the balance (dividing 'tot' by 100 again to produce a conventional decimal money amount). It is then up to the user, either to abort the entire session and begin again with the backup 'ledger' and 'trans' files or to search through the batch of transaction entries to try to locate the error(s).

Ledgrept

Our final user procedure is 'ledgrept', a simple reporting procedure that reports on the contents of the ledger file. We are providing just this one example of how a report might be programmed, but in practice you would almost certainly want to introduce other reports into the system as well, including perhaps a summary report on each batch of transactions or a report on debtors above a certain limit.

The report begins by obtaining the date, for reproduction in the report heading. If you habitually set the system clock before booting Archive, you could of course use this to obtain the date automatically. A simple 'Ledger Report' heading is then printed, followed by headings for each column of the report. Because of the difficulty we experienced in sending control codes to our printer from Archive, we made no attempt to underline the heading or use an alternative typeface, but to do so would add a more professional touch to the report.

The procedure uses three number variables, 'dbt', 'crt' and 'bt', in which the totals for the number fields are built up. It is necessary to initialize each of these before use. An ALL . . . ENDALL loop then prints selected details for each record in a tabular format: the details for each record across the page, with successive records down the page. The same loop is used to add up the totals. Finally, the totals are printed at the bottom of the report.

As we discovered in the 'balance' procedure, even simple addition and subtraction can produce rounding errors in Archive. Once again we tried to eliminate these. Here we did it, not by using a numeric rounding-off routine, but by using the STR function to display each variable in a fixed number-type format. (See our notes on STR above.) We included this only for the totals, as we found that the individual record balances did not suffer from the same problem. Maybe this was just luck: if so, including a similar routine before printing each balance would be a wise precaution.

Figure 5.9 shows a sample report which we produced using 'ledgrept'. (Our books don't balance, incidentally, because the program had succeeded in 'losing' several ledger records.) You will see that an obvious problem is the lack of a decimal tab. Without one, the columns of numbers look decidedly

Figure 5.9 An Accounting System Programmed using Archive: Ledger Report

```
Ledger Report                                          8 August 84

ledger code              debit       credit      balance

capt01                   0           100         -100
car01                    370.83      0           370.83
car02                    8561.3      0           8561.3
cash01                   2102.55     0           2102.55
crds01                   0           1384.99     -1384.99
dtrs01                   3629.41     0           3629.41
fees01                   0           41217.84    -41217.84
ofeq01                   5973.99     0           5973.99
ohex01                   4669.78     0           4669.78
plos01                   0           3898        -3898
rccs01                   0           0           0
vatx01                   0           2099.09     -2099.09
wage01                   23745.93    0           23745.93

totals:                  49053.79    48699.92    353.87
```

scrappy. It might prove possible to simulate one by turning all numbers into strings using STR, finding the length of the resulting strings and then padding out the start of each number with blanks. We didn't relish the task and feel that careful number formatting is best handled by exporting Archive data to Abacus, as we mentioned above.

6

Working with Easel

Easel is Psion's business graphics program. It is perhaps the easiest to use of the four Psion programs provided with the QL and we can describe it fairly briefly.

Easel is specifically designed for the display of tabular sets of figures. You can think of each set of figures as fitting into a one-dimensional number array, with the elements of the array labelled cell(0), cell(1) and so on. It's important to note that you only give *one* co-ordinate for each entry. The second co-ordinate is defined by its cell number. This means that Easel is *only* suitable for plotting discrete data with values at regular intervals. It can't be used for plotting points that fall irregularly on both the *x* and *y* axes or plotting scatter graphs, etc. It's only suitable in very limited ways for plotting equations.

Let's rephrase that differently, to be sure that you understand it. Some graphs have two axes, both marked with a scale – from, say, 0 to 50. One axis is used to measure one continuous variable – say, time or speed – and the other is used to measure another – for example distance. You can locate any point within the plotting area and define it uniquely as, say, speed 47/ distance 45 or whatever. There's no inbuilt limit to the number of points that can be plotted.

Easel graphs have only one continuously variable axis, and one discretely marked axis. You can't plot an indefinite number of points: you can only give one value for each discrete cell on the horizontal axis. So you can plot a value for January (if you use the default axis markings) as a whole: but it would be meaningless to try to plot a value for January 29, unless you change the discrete scaling and make each cell refer to a separate day. You can't plot two values for January, unless you set up a second set of figures: if you enter a new value it will replace, not supplement, the old one.

Sometimes, the cell markings will broadly resemble the scale marking of an axis, as they do when the cells are labelled January/February/March, etc. This is just one way of labelling an axis denoting time. In other cases, though, there's no scale reference behind the cell ordering. This would be the case if, say, you used each cell to indicate a different type of product, (widgets 1, widgets 2 and widgets 3) or a different sales area (France, Scotland, Italy). In these circumstances, it's quite feasible for you to re-arrange the cell ordering without detracting from the information displayed on the graph, as it never is with a genuine axis. Indeed, you might want to re-arrange it, for instance, to order the values plotted from largest to smallest.

Easel graphs, then, are particularly suitable for plotting quantities measured over monthly values or other time intervals. Alternatively, you may wish to provide a simple visual comparison of different quantities. The line option doesn't denote a true line/scatter graph capability: it's just another style of presentation for discrete, bar-type graphs. Pie charts, too, are an alternative way of presenting the same discrete blocks of data.

As there will be a number of occasions when you do need a scatter graph, we've included a simple program to generate scatter graphs in Chapter 11. Also in that chapter is a function plotting program.

INPUTTING DATA TO EASEL

Each set of data that you input to Easel – each one-dimensional number array – is given a name, which you can think of as an array name. The default name is 'figures', but you can change this and indeed must give a new name for second and subsequent sets. You can produce a set of figures, or input data to the set array, in other words:

(a)   By putting the data directly into the graph on display. You indicate the name of the set of figures you want to work with, then position the cursor to select the cell for which you want to provide a value. Typing a value then puts that value into the chosen cell.

(b)   Or by giving a formula that explains how the figures are obtained. This is a slightly more complex business and we will go on to discuss it in more detail.

(c)   Or by loading data from disk, from a saved Easel graph or as an imported file from another program. We discuss this later in the chapter.

The section on formulae in the Easel manual is a little confusing and doesn't make it immediately clear how to distinguish between the set of figures as a whole and the individual elements that comprise it. We'll try to clarify the situation, based on our experience of how version 1.0 of Easel works. In our version some of the formulae given in the manual don't work at all: later versions may of course differ. Trial and error with Easel formulae is a tricky business, since error messages are few and uninformative and occasional wrong guesses can crash our version of the program. It may be that expressions we didn't try will give useful results or that expressions we tried unsuccessfully will work in later versions of the program.

One important point to bear in mind is that you can only give *one* formula for an array as a whole. You can't write a mini-program to fill the array with numbers. You can't even use successive one-line commands to do so. Any formula you give for an array will automatically supersede all previous formulae. Formulae are not held in memory (though the data generated are, of course) and cannot be recalled for checking or editing.

You can, if you wish, identify a single element in the array called 'figures' by giving its cell number, using the CELL expression. However, you can't use an expression like 'figures(2)' or 'figures(CELL 2)' or 'figures (CELL = 2)' to refer to cell 2 of an array. On the left hand side of the equals sign, you can *only* refer to the array as a whole and not to the individual elements within it. Instead, you use a formula like:

figures = 22 * (CELL = 5)

which will put the value 22 (not 22 times 5, as you might expect: the multiplication sign doesn't work normally in this expression) into cell 5 of 'figures'. However, you can't fill a whole array in this manner: defining cell 3 in the same way would lose you the value of cell 5 (whether you'd entered it direct, or calculated it by another formula), and so on! In practice, this is mainly useful for making a single calculation if you need to do so while you're using Easel. For instance,

figures = SQR(34.5)*(CELL = 2)

will calculate the square root of 34.5 and put the answer into cell 2 of 'figures'.

Figure 6.1 Screen Dump from Easel: Speed and Stopping Distance
This graph gives the illusion of a dual-axis graph, but in fact it's a cheat: as an admission that the *x* axis doesn't work properly we've omitted any scaling. It would be possible to use the text commands to add a simple scale.

The data are, of course, purely for illustration: they do not come from real speed tests!

The caption originally read '. . . and Bicycle'. For some unaccountable reason Easel missed off the end when preparing for the dump.

Note that we've used a plain graph paper. Our two sets of figures are of course called 'car' and 'bicycle'.

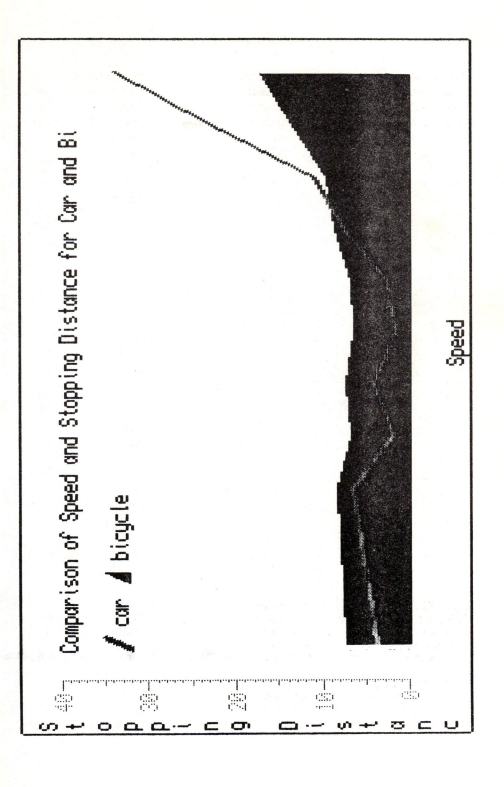

Comparison of Speed and Stopping Distance for Car and Bi

car ⚫ bicycle

Speed

There are two more generally useful ways of filling an array as a whole:

(a)   By linking the value in each cell of the array to the value in the corresponding cell of some other array which is held in RAM;

(b)   Or by using a formula which links the value in each cell to the cell number.

An example of the first of these cases is this formula, which puts values derived from array 'figures' into the new array 'figs2':

figs2 = (figures * 2) + 6

Cell 4 of figs2 will contain the value of cell 4 of figures, multiplied by two, with six added, and so on for the other cells. You can produce a wide variety of similar formulae using the fairly limited range of functions summarized on p.24 of the Easel manual.

This is an example of the second case:

figures = (CELL * 2)

Cell 4 of figures will contain the value 4*2 or 8 and so on. The Easel manual quotes a more elaborate example, using the reserved word CELLMAX, but we were sceptical about its grammar and found that it did not work.

CELLMAX itself does work as a variable that returns the number of the rightmost cell shown on screen. Note that since (in our version of Easel at least) it isn't possible to reduce the number on screen to less than twelve, CELLMAX will always have a value of twelve or more. You can't assign a value to CELLMAX directly before using it, with an expression like 'CELLMAX = 12': this will, disconcertingly, set up a new array called 'cellmax', with a value of twelve in each cell! If you want CELLMAX to have a different value, you'd first set the screen up for the new array using the NEWDATA command, and then add columns (or delete them, if your version allows you to do so) until you reach the number you require.

Note that the formula capabilities of Easel are extremely limited compared with those of Abacus or even Archive. If you want to generate a set of figures according to a complex series of formulae, it is necessary to use one of the two latter programs and then import the data to Easel.

OTHER ASPECTS OF EASEL

We've compiled some hints and ideas that may help you to make the best of the Easel program. They are listed below in alphabetical order.

Cell Labels

Though the January . . . December cell labels are useful for many purposes, there will be occasions when you want to use different labels. No alternative sets are stored in the Easel program. The sequence of commands used to delete the default labels and substitute new ones is extremely awkward. If you want to use alternative labels regularly (e.g. the days 0 to 31) then it is worthwhile setting up a 'blank' file to contain them. Starting with the usual Easel screen, delete the usual labels and work through, cell by cell, entering the new ones. Don't add any data: simply save the result (we call ours 'numaxis'). When you want to prepare a numbered graph you can then load 'numaxis' and the hard work will have been done for you.

Display Formats

Though the default selection of display formats is quite comprehensive, you can add to it considerably, by using the 'Change' command. Remember that you can select any bar/line format (0 to 6) and change the bars to lines, or *vice versa*. The Change command works on the current set of figures in every case, so if you want to change the display format for an alternate set of figures, you need to select it using the Olddata command.

Some formats have clearly 'background' and 'foreground' sets of figures. It's difficult to alter the ordering of bars in Format 1 so that the right data appears at the foreground, for example, if you originally entered the figures in a different order. You can best do so by altering the display style for the set entirely. For example, a 'filled' line will always appear in the background, an unfilled line in the foreground.

Pie Charts

A note on the colouring of pie charts. Unfortunately you can't select bordering options for piechart segments as you can for bars: solid colours only are available. From the 'select segment colour' menu, it looks as though black segments are bordered in white. However, this isn't the case in practice, as you will see if you select a black segment on a black background! There's no way of amending the background colour on pie charts, so you are advised to avoid black segment markings, unless you particularly want the effect of a 'missing slice' to appear!

SAVEing, LOADing and Merging Data

When you use the SAVE command in Easel, you don't save a single set of data. You save all the sets that are held in RAM at one time, whether they are currently on display or not, plus details on the display format set up when you triggered the SAVE command. There's no simple way to single out one array and save it, though you could of course save several sets of data, reload them, KILL the additional sets and resave the remaining one.

Incidentally, it isn't possible to merge data from different Easel files with the LOAD command. You can input new sets of data from the keyboard to add to a batch that you load, but you can't load a second file and merge its contents with the first, even if you've given different names to the data sets in each file. LOADing the new set will erase memory. However, IMPORT does not erase memory in this way and you *can* combine data from different files by creating export files and then re-importing them to the program. (We discussed a similar technique in Chapter 4, when describing the Abacus program.) If you want to import data without merging it, then it is necessary specifically to clear memory first, otherwise you may find an interesting (and unintended) combination of files on display or that you run out of memory completely.

Easel data does not take up a great deal of RAM and though the program does not mention a maximum, we found it possible to manipulate six or seven sets of figures, with around twenty figures to a set, without memory problems. Six sets is apparently the maximum that the program will display at once.

Scaling the Axes

The program offers a wide choice of cosmetic styles for vertical axis marking, but it is a little weaker in allowing the user to make a different sort of change: to rescale the data. We found it exasperating on occasion that the program would default to a vertical scale that didn't start with zero! It tends to do this, as you will notice, when the values given are quite closely grouped together, e.g. between fourteen and sixteen, or 200 and 300. In order to force a scale from zero, move to an unused column and enter the value '0' into it. If there's no unused column on screen, type '0' into a column that is in use, and then replace it with the correct value. The axis origin will remain at zero.

Similarly, you can increase the vertical scale by typing in a large 'dummy' value, and then overtyping the correct value or a '0'. You might do this if you wanted to see a scale to 100, for instance and your maximum value were less than twenty. Typing '100' does the trick.

Screen Dumps

Easel's screen dump routine works well (so long as you have a printer that is supported) and it's a pity that it isn't held as a separate program on disc so that it can be used to dump non-Easel graphics as well. Unfortunately we haven't discovered any way of doing this.

Figure 6.2 Screen Dump from Easel: Figures Developed from Formulae
These simple sets of figures were developed from two formulae, which we've included on the graph using the text facility. The first formula uses the cell value: the second uses the first set of figures *and* the cell value. The figures developed have no particular significance, so we've erased the two axis labels and added a title to indicate the purpose of the graph. Our title is on white 'paper', which looks fine on screen but rather heavy on the screen dump.

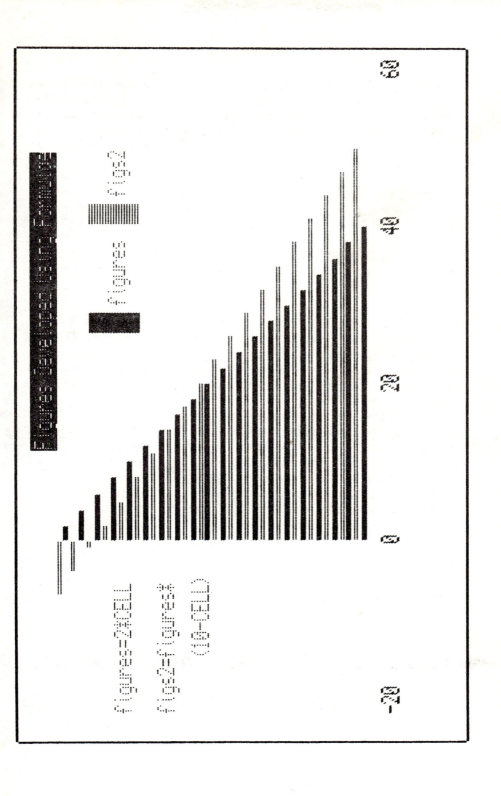

If your printer has auto-line feed, you may find that the dump emerges 'striped', with a blank line between each chunk of the picture. To correct this, you must turn off auto-line feed in your printer. (There's more on this subject in Chapter 2.) Easel doesn't have a 'printer—dat' file like the other Psion programs, so it's not possible to amend the program to make it live with the line feed.

Note that the routine does not begin with a form feed (unlike Abacus' printing routine), so align your paper carefully before calling it. If the routine is interrupted (e.g. by a paper jam in the printer) you'll find it impossible to call PRINT successfully again: quit and reload Easel to try again.

Finally, there are no routines in Easel for the printing of non-graphic data. It could be useful for you to dump a simple listing of your data if your printer is one that is not supported in the screen dump routine. You can do so quite easily by exporting your Easel file to Abacus and printing from that program.

Text

The program has very good facilities for adding text to graphs, but its default placing of text can sometimes be awkward. Use the 'Edit' command, which is well described in the manual, to reposition a title or key that is superimposed upon the graph itself. The missing section of the graph will be redrawn at the next opportunity.

If you want to superimpose a great deal of text on your graph, you may find that the result is much easier to read if you choose a 'Graph paper' (from the 'Change' command) that doesn't square up the plotting area. Graph paper 5 is a plain black background design, or you can design your own plain paper with a different coloured background. You can't, unfortunately, alter the intervals at which the grid markings are made.

When you select a pie chart, the actual value of each segment is shown next to the label. No values are shown on bar charts and it is not always easy to read values accurately from the axis. You can use the text option to label individual bars with values. Print the values either at the top of each bar or superimposed on the bar, using the 'transparent' print style. The program won't notice and correct you if you use the same colour ink as the bar colour, so check your text ink colour first. It's as well to do this once you've selected your final display style. If you later move to a different display style (e.g. horizontal bars instead of vertical) the text won't move too!

You could adapt the same idea to produce longer legends than you can fit at the bottom of the chart. Select vertical print to produce a long legend above, or superimposed on, a vertical bar.

The vertical axis is automatically labelled vertically rather than horizontally, but you may find it difficult to fit in a long axis label. You can increase the space available for the axis label, as well as the overall size of the graph, by removing the prompt area from the screen – press F2, and F2 again to restore it.

You can see some of this text manipulation at work – together with some other aspects of the Easel program – in the two screen dumps from Easel (to an Epson FX-80 printer) that we've reproduced as Figures 6.1 and 6.2.

7

Working with Quill

As you probably know already, you can use a word processor whenever you would use a typewriter. It's a tool that enables you to compose and arrange pieces of continuous – or not so continuous – text on screen, prior to saving or printing the text. The fact that your writing appears on screen, not on paper, means that you can edit and/or correct as extensively as you wish before printing the text. You can adapt or merge existing pieces of text to form new documents. You can produce multiple top copies and you can use the power of the computer to help you lay out your work perfectly, tabulating figures, justifying margins and adapting page lengths and other features.

Using a word processor is faster than using a typewriter. There's no need to watch out at the ends of lines – the computer automatically starts a new line of text for you – and there's no need to type slowly to avoid mistakes – you can work at top speed and go back to correct them afterwards. The process may seem a little artificial at first, but you'll soon adapt to the different processes involved in composing and arranging your work on screen.

Many computer users find their word processor to be the program they turn to automatically, whether they are compiling a list, preparing a report or simply making a few notes for later use. Though it's a versatile program, however, do remember that it's much easier to handle regularly structured material on either a spreadsheet or a database. Quill is a complement to the Abacus and Archive programs, as are other word processors to other spreadsheets and databases. Although there are overlaps between the uses of the three, each has obvious strengths and weaknesses.

QUILL AS A WORD PROCESSOR

As a word processor, Quill falls into the 'WYSIWYG' category. In other words, it's a 'What You See Is What You Get' program. Almost all the time, the screen display is an accurate reflection of how your printed document will look. These programs are very easy to work with, particularly for beginners: no nasty shocks when it comes to printing your work! The options built into Quill's screen display procedures mean that as well as simplifying the printing of your documents, the program makes their typing and editing as straightforward as possible. It's practicable for you to type within the margins that fit on screen, for instance, and then adjust the margin settings to wider ones before printing if you wish. You can still review the layout of your document by scrolling from side to side, switching to a different column layout if you've used forty or sixty-four column display or using the VIEW option if it is implemented in your version of Quill. (This was not the case in the earliest versions.) Though it's possible to compose or type text using wide margins and a scrolling screen, this is not easy and we find it preferable to switch margin settings in this way.

Quill goes further than many other WYSIWYG programs, in that it reflects sub- and superscripts, bold face and underlining on screen. Not all printers are capable of producing these different features and Quill will accurately reflect your printer's output only *if* your printer handles the feature in question *and* does it in a way broadly compatible with Quill's expectations. It is essential that you should set the Quill printer driver program to reflect the control codes required by your own printer. The Appendix, 'Import and Export' to the QL manual outlines the necessary steps: we looked at this subject in depth in Chapter 2.

Because of the way in which Quill is designed, it is not easy for you to make use of other special printer features using this word processor. The popular Epson FX-80, for instance (a printer that the printer drivers specifically support) provides a wide range of different print styles: condensed, emphasized, proportional, italic etc. There's no easy way of including the necessary command sequences to turn these on and off within a Quill document. If you particularly want to use a different print style, then you can do so by setting up an alternative printer driver (either replacing the default version or on a different microdrive cartridge together with another copy of the other Quill programs) and substituting the control codes required for the styles you want, for those for the basic four underline/subscript/superscript/bold options. In other words, Quill can handle four printer control codes (plus any codes used to determine the basic print style) in a single document: it's up

to you and your printer driver settings which ones they are, though they will always appear *on screen* as underline, boldface etc. If you choose codes that will work successfully in combination, you can use 'underlined boldface', for example, as yet another alternative print style. If you don't, you may have some rather peculiar-looking printout.

Figure 7.1 gives you an example of the effects you can achieve (with a suitable printer) in this way. We substituted the codes for 'emphasized print' and 'italics' for the codes for 'subscript' and 'superscript': both typestyles that we, like many users, have very little need for. As Quill doesn't 'know' that emphasized type will take up more space when printed than normal type, the program will of course not justify correctly using this kind of type and if you use full lines the print will not be reproduced correctly. Keep styles that change the character width for headings only or amend the margins so that the type will fit properly on to the printed lines.

Figure 7.1 Printer Support by Quill

PRINTER SUPPORT BY QUILL

```
        Though Quill's printer support  seems  at  first  to  be
limited, with  a little juggling you  can access most printer
features.    To produce this document  we altered the printer
driver  file  so  that  'high   script'  on   screen  became
'emphasised  type' on the printer, and 'low script' on screen
became italics on the printer.
        Our  heading  is  in  emphasised  bold  type.    Ordinary
emphasised type looks like this:
        These    are   big   letters.
        It  is best used for headings  only, and cannot be mixed
freely  with the bulk of the text, or the margins will become
hopelessly confused.
        Here's  a  paragraph  in  italic  type.    It  makes  an
attractive variant in  the  body  of  a  document.   You  can
underline it  too, though  this does  look rather  strange on
screen.
        Of  course,  you  can  select  other  alternatives  like
underlined bold type or italic bold type. Rather attractive,
this variant, isn't it.   As sub and superscript are mutually
exclusive, though,  you can't select  italic emphasised type.
What a pity!
```

When entering and editing text, Quill is very easy to use and has a good range of commands. We found it compared favourably with rival word processors. However, screen response to key presses can be slow. It's important to be cautious when using 'delete' key sequences: it's all too easy to type ahead of what is reflected on screen and delete too much text accidentally. Though the program doesn't warn you to do so, it's wise to stop typing whenever the microdrives are accessed: the program won't act on keypresses at these times.

The program is particularly slow in handling long documents, where many microdrive accesses are needed. Though Quill will handle long documents, we'd advise you to keep the maximum length fairly short. If your document will be more than, say, ten pages long, divide it in two and edit the halves separately. If you want the text to run on, you can do a final 'merge' in order to achieve this.

Quill is outstandingly good at reformatting existing text, adapting margins and tab settings. It 'remembers' the settings applicable to each paragraph, instead of working on a single group of settings at any time, as do so many programs. This means that there is no need to take special precautions when amending text that includes several different formats. We explain some special uses of the formatting commands below. If you're planning to right-justify your text, it's important to become familiar with the hyphenate command.

The QL is not particularly well equipped with function keys, in comparison with many contemporary micros and this helps to explain why there is no facility for storing frequently used words or phrases in non-alphanumeric key combinations. Many word processor users appreciate this feature on programs where it is available. In writing this chapter, for instance, I might have set up a function key or control key combination to generate the phrase 'word processor', instead of typing the phrase in full each time I want to use it. However, the QL search-replace command and its instant re-justification enable you to imitate the effect of this command, as we explain below.

Although the program includes a variety of options in its 'design' feature, it isn't possible to customize the master program so that your preferred combination is automatically selected. This can be a drawback if you always prefer tab and margin settings quite different to the defaults provided. One possible, partial solution is outlined below.

Another drawback is the fact that though the program includes a useful 'merge' option, for including existing documents within a new document, it has no facilities for producing form letters, each personalized for a different recipient. Archive and Quill will not work together to this end. It seems probable that either Psion or another software house will, eventually, plug this gap.

At the time of writing no spelling checkers were available for use on documents prepared using Quill, but it is likely that some such programs will also be made available soon. A spelling checker is a worthwhile investment, not just for poor spellers but for anyone who finds it difficult to proof-read accurately.

WORKING WITH QUILL

It is up to you to decide how to work with Quill. The program will adapt fairly well to a variety of different work styles. You might wish to draft or dictate your work in a conventional way, and then copy- or audio-type it (or have a secretary/typist do so) into the word processor, reading through and subsequently making corrections. You might prefer to compose a letter, report or the first chapter of your new novel on screen from scratch, starting perhaps with a rough outline or a few ideas and expanding, re-arranging and re-phrasing as you go. This program, like any good word processor, should handle a high level of amendments successfully: although as you make more amendments, the program will operate more slowly and be more prone to crashes.

We would certainly advise you to learn to proof-read and edit your text working from the screen, rather than from a printed draft. It's a much more flexible way of working and much lighter on paper! However, do take care to keep adequate copies of earlier drafts of your document, on a cartridge and preferably on paper as well, in case of disasters. All important documents should be backed up on different cartridges, so that if a cartridge fails you will be able to recover the document from the back-up version.

Once you are familiar with the Quill commands, you may resent the space that the 'help' menu takes up at the top of the screen. You can easily toggle it off (and on again, if necessary) using the F2 key. The ruler will remain at the top of the screen for guidance: and of course you can use commands from both Quill menus, even though neither is actually visible to you. (Precede commands from the second menu with 'O' as usual.)

The key to success with word processing is good organization. It's important for you to keep your document files methodically, arranging them in a logical order – perhaps all letters on one cartridge, all reports on a second – and backing up each one. Keep a written note of the contents of each cartridge.

Stop to think about the requirements of a document before you begin to work on it. Can you adapt any existing text to form part of the new document and thus save some typing? How do you want the document to be laid out? How are you going to handle headings and footnotes? Are there any frequently used long words or phrases for which you could use the Replace feature?

Though the word 'document' is frequently used to describe files created using Quill, a file need not be a complete physical document. It might, for instance, consist of a single paragraph which you'll want to use frequently: perhaps your address, all ready to reproduce at the top of each letter or the address of someone to whom you write frequently. It might contain the outline of an invoice or form letter, just waiting for you to type in the variable information needed on a particular copy. It might simply consist of a group of special settings, adapting the default margins and tabs to a particular need or providing standard headings and footings according to your personal style (see our comments below). In any case, give it a clearly recognizable name so that when you look at the microdrive directory, you'll identify it quickly and easily.

Let's take a specific example. Perhaps you will be writing regular personal letters using Quill. You prefer personal letters not to be right-justified, as you feel that this produces too businesslike an appearance. You need to set the right margin at sixty, to fit your notepaper and you'll start by putting your name and address at the top right-hand corner, after which you'll want to line up the address below them.

Load the Quill program and set about achieving this effect. Call up the Margins command and alter the right margin. Amend the justification. Tab across to a suitable position and type your name and address. Save your document, calling it something like 'letter'.

When you want to type a letter, you'll want to load Quill and go straight on to load 'letter'. Up will come the margin and justification settings you want. Use the cursor controls to go to the position for the date; and start to write your letter. At the end, you can Save it, if you wish to, under a new file name, perhaps including the date or a note of the recipient, or both.

Other documents, suitably arranged on different cartridges (and perhaps duplicated on a number of cartridges, for convenience – they won't take up much space) might include:

   – A report outline suitable for producing a report with numbered paragraphs. You might, say, set the indent tab to five, and the left margin to ten, so that paragraph numbers can be displayed outside the main body of the text. You might set up a footer to display the page number at the centre of the last line on each page.
   – An outline invoice for a product you sell from home – a computer program you've written and sell by mail order, perhaps. A carefully customized printer driver routine might enable you to start with a bold, centred company name in emphasized bold type. Include your address, the outline of the invoice, the standard footer details on payment terms, etc. (Though if you'd like the computer to do the arithmetic on the invoice too, you'd be better off writing a simple Basic program to do the job.) You'll then want to change the type mode to 'overwrite' rather than 'insert' when you start up Quill, so that you can easily fit the individual invoice details into your stored outline.
   – An outline for writing journalistic articles. This might set extra-wide margins, as demanded by your editor. It will select double line-spacing. It might change the justification style to left justification: many editors

find it easier to do a word count on unjustified text. You'll probably opt to include your name and the page number in a header or footer, too: why re-type them each time when the computer can remember them for you?

Note that though Quill will correctly remember margins set in the default display style when it recalls a document, it will amend margins set in a different display style (e.g. in eighty columns, when you are using a television with its sixty-four column default) back to the default settings for the current display. It isn't possible to save a display style choice with a document. Nor is it possible to save a mode (insert or overwrite) or an initial type-style selection in a document which contains no text, though type-styles used for writing parts of the text will of course be recalled successfully. Finally, margin and justification selections will *not* be recalled correctly if you merge a saved document with one you are editing, rather than loading it.

HANDLING PAGINATION

Quill is not 'intelligent' when it comes to pagination. It counts the number of lines required on each page and then starts a new one. It doesn't notice if your new page starts just after a new heading or before the last odd word of a paragraph. In order to make the page breaks appear at sensible points, you must review your text and make corrections where necessary.

The Page command enables you to force a page break. When typing your document, you'll use it wherever you are certain you want to start a new page. When reviewing and correcting, you will need to insert it wherever awkward pagination means that you need to start a new page. Work through the document methodically from the start. If you make any changes later that affect the page length, it will be necessary to review the pagination again.

You can't use the Page command to make a page a line or two longer than usual, for instance, if you find that you've just the last line of a letter carried over to a new page. Correct awkward pagination of this kind by one of the following methods:

– In a short document (e.g. a one page letter), the easiest method is often to adjust the margin settings. One character more within the margins might just squeeze your letter on to the page.
– Adjust the standard page size, using the correct option from the Design command. (Note, this option does not work correctly on early versions of Quill.)
– Adjust the upper or lower margins, again from the Design command.

The Page command can also be useful if you want to leave a blank page in a numbered text. Remember that in order to start numbering your text at a page other than 1, you can amend the 'Start Page Number' in the Design menu. However, there's no way, other than by forcing blank pages, to amend the page number in mid-document.

SOME COMMENTS ON OTHER QUILL COMMANDS

Header

Quill documents can have only one header, so it's not possible to set up alternate headers for use on odd and even numbered pages – a feature that only a few word processors have. Note that the header has to be a continuous line of text. You can only position it at *one* of the three header positions: left, right and centre. However, you can always produce the illusion of a double header, like:

Chapter 10   page 95

by positioning the header at the left, and then typing a long string of blanks in the middle of the header line.

Before setting up a header containing the page number, do remember that Quill automatically includes this in a footer! If you want a blank footer, you must specifically request it.

Justify

The Justify command may confuse you a little at first. Left- and right justification are not opposites, as you might think. Right justification is what most people think of as justification: that is, both margins justified. Left justification is ordinary, non-justified text. It isn't possible to produce text that has a straight right margin and a ragged left margin.

Search and Replace

Quill has a moderately powerful Search command. Unlike more powerful variants, it isn't case-sensitive: it's important to type the phrase that you want the program to find in the exact combination of upper- and lower-case letters that it occurs within the text. If you want to find 'Find' and 'find' for instance, you must Search twice. You'll soon discover that the command looks for any combination of the letters you give, not for whole words, so that, for instance, 'the' will also find 'together' and other words, containing the letters 'the'. To specify a word precisely, start and end your search string with a blank, like this: ' the '. Choose a combination just long enough to identify the phrase: there's no need to type the whole of a long word.

Search/Replace is useful to help you to:

    – find a particular point in your text. Quill isn't abundantly supplied with commands to enable you to page quickly through the text. If you want to get to paragraph 1.2.1, then the quickest way is to Search for

'1.2.1'. You may find it helpful to use a special symbol that wouldn't normally appear in the text, like '@' or '%', to mark points which you'll want to return to – to fill in a missing reference, maybe? You can easily delete the symbols (using Replace) before printing the final text.

– correct spellings. If you know that you're prone to mis-spell or mis-type a particular word, why not Search for the mis-spelling after you've finished typing your document? You can then replace it with the correct version.

– cut down on typing. If you'll repeatedly be typing an awkward name or long phrase – a special medical term, the name of a product or customer, the title of a character in your novel – then you might choose, instead of typing it in full each time, to simply type a special short code: a unique character you haven't used elsewhere or an easily typed abbreviation that won't appear elsewhere in the text, like 'zx' or 'qw'. Once you've finished, you can then Replace all occurrences of the code with the correct version of the phrase.

8

Combined Uses of the Psion Programs

In a truly integrated software system, all the individual programs in the system share data without difficulty. It is possible to use files saved by one type of program with any other program: often it's possible to switch from program to program without even needing to save and reload your data.

Psion's four software packages do not add up to an integrated system in this sense. Only one program will run at a time and in order to share data between one program and another it is necessary to use a special file format. However, it is not at all difficult to swap this data between the Psion programs and it is worth learning how to do so.

In this chapter we look in depth at the subject of shared data, import and export files. First we expand upon the brief general introduction given in the QL User Guide, then we present some practical examples of integrated applications.

EXPORT FILES

Archive, Abacus and Easel can all produce data in the form of 'export' files, suitable for use in the other programs. It is also easy to produce an 'export' file in Basic, if you wish to do so for some reason. Quill uses data in a different way and though it can import data it cannot export it to the other programs in the set.

A normal export file is simply a sequential ASCII file, the standard type of microdrive data file. The QL User Guide appendix that covers import and export outlines its very simple structure. The file can be read and used by any program that provides a suitable data structure (we discuss this briefly below). As well as producing an export file from Basic, you can of course read an export file created by one of the Psion programs while in SuperBasic.

The Psion programs do not usually store their data on microdrive in the 'export' format and it is not possible to mix export files and normally saved files at will. However, you can reload export files created by one of the programs within the same program. There are some real advantages to be gained by doing this. In Abacus, Export is the only command that enables you (within limitations) to combine spreadsheet data without merging cell contents. In Easel, it is the only command that allows you to merge files on microdrive with those in memory at all.

Often you will want to export data from one program, manipulate it within another program and then create a second export file for sending back to the original program.

Archive, Abacus and Easel all handle data in a broadly tabular way and it is possible to swap data quite freely between these three programs, so long as the basic rules on data layout that are outlined in the User Guide appendix are followed precisely.

WHY EXPORT FILES?

If you export a file to Quill from another program, the traffic will be one-way: you won't be able to get it back again. In effect, you will only want to do this when you want the data in the file to appear in a completed Quill document.

Quill has much more powerful editing and formatting commands than the other programs and this gives Quill a plus when it comes to manipulating your data prior to display or printing. Quill's search facilities are also good and the program is much better equipped than the others in the suite to handle special printer features. A report on data stored in Archive, produced using Quill, will often be faster to draw up and more professional in layout than the same report would be if it were produced using Archive alone. Heading and arranging a set of Abacus data using Quill is also a flexible and worthwhile process.

Exports between the other three programs might be done for a variety of purposes. Each program has its own strengths and weaknesses, and you may find that using a variety of programs enables you to get the best value out of a set of data. You might want, for instance:

> *to import data to Easel* in order to display it attractively on screen or to dump a graph to a suitable printer
> *to export data from Easel* in order to:

— to carry out arithmetical manipulations more complex than the limited set of whole-set-of-figures functions that Easel supports. Abacus will normally be your choice for this.

— or to sort it into numerical order. Archive has the best sorting facilities, but Abacus's 'order' command should also be adequate for this purpose.

— or to select a subset of it. Archive will be your choice here.

to import data to Archive in order:

— to search through it using Archive's complex search commands

— to sort it prior to further processing or as a step in a reporting procedure

— to select a subset of it

to export data from Archive in order:

— to incorporate it into a letter, report, graph or table. Any one of Quill, Abacus or Easel might be the destination.

— to carry out arithmetical manipulations more easily than Archive will permit. Abacus is the obvious choice here.

— to view records side-by-side in spreadsheet format. Abacus's data layout will often let you see more data than you can easily review using Archive itself.

to import data to Abacus in order:

— to review a large set of data quickly and easily in spreadsheet format.

— to make comparisons between sets of data, using Abacus's windowing features.

— and of course, to carry out arithmetic on the data.

to export data from Abacus in order:

— to view it in graph format on Easel or to include it in an Archive database.

— to combine it with other, separately stored, sets of data using Archive's multi-file handling capabilities.

— to sort through it, select subsets from it or search for particular data within it, using Archive.

EXPORT FILE DATA STRUCTURE

The QL User Guide appendix briefly outlines the structure of export files, and gives a short program that enables you to write one in SuperBasic. The following equally simple program enables you to read an export file:

```
10     DIM n$ (500,100)
20     OPEN_IN #6, "mdvn_filename_exp"
30     n = 0
40     REPeat get
50     INPUT#6, n$(n)
```

```
60      IF EOF(#6) THEN EXIT get
70      n = n + 1
80      END REPeat get
```

We set up a string variable array into which to read each item of data from the file. In fact an entire row or column of the file (depending upon the type of file) was read into each array element. This array has 100-character-long elements, but for a large file you would need to amend the size of it. You can check on the contents of each array element simply by printing it. You will see if you do so that each string in an export to Abacus, Archive or Easel file is tightly packed; each string intended for export to Quill, on the other hand, is padded out with spaces to emulate the spacing of the original spreadsheet or other data structure.

EXPORT FROM ABACUS

Export files from Abacus can be designed for Quill, Archive or Easel. Two different options of the 'Files' command provide for export to Easel and Archive. In fact the two should be identical and we found little difficulty in reading both Easel and Archive export files in either of the two programs. If you do run into problems, though, you will of course want to ensure that you set up the right files for the purpose you have in mind. A separate option is clearly necessary for Quill.

Abacus export files include *the data that is visible on screen* − not only in the current screen window, of course, but on whatever section of the spreadsheet you select for filing. They do *not* include formulae: they simply contain the current values generated by formulae. Numbers and text are not exported in their formatted version: so a number on screen with two decimal places won't be received at its destination in this form. It will be received as a normal floating-point number and displayed in the usual general format (or in a graphic format in Easel).

EXPORT FROM ARCHIVE

As usual, Archive does not prompt you through export and import operations as do the other Psion programs. Instead, it's prone to come up with extremely unhelpful error messages when you mistake the syntax. Hence the explanations below:

No formalities are needed to read an import file into Archive. It's simply necessary to use the 'import' command to specify the file to be read and to give an Archive filename. If you already have a file active, you must also give a logical name to the file. Archive automatically sets up a suitable file format, so there is no need to work through a 'create' sequence. 'Title' data from Easel or Abacus is automatically used as field names: Archive apparently does not mind if it fails to follow the usual one-word-only rule for field names. If the field is a string one, Archive will add the trailing '$' automatically.

In order to export a file, you must first create or open it. If you wish, you might then select a subset of it: Archive will automatically export only the selected set. Otherwise, the program will export the selected fields (or all fields, if no list is given) for every record in the file.
A statement like:

export "accsfile"; ledgcode$, debittot, credittot, balance

would produce an export file suitable for use in Abacus or Easel. Note that the first field is string in type, and all other fields are numeric: this is the only acceptable format. A statement like:

export "ledgfile" quill

would produce an export file suitable for use in Quill.

EXPORT FROM EASEL

Note that though Easel will produce export files suitable for use by either Abacus or Archive, it will not produce files suitable for use by Quill. If you initiate data in Easel that you want to use – in tabular form – in a Quill document, then your best course is first to export it to Abacus or Archive, *then* to produce an export file suitable for use by Quill.

A SAMPLE INTEGRATED APPLICATION:
A MANAGEMENT REPORT OUTLINING
CASH FLOW PROJECTIONS

To show how the program integration works in practice, we'll take you step by step through the procedures involved in preparing a management report including a cash flow projection. We prepared this example ourselves using the Abacus, Easel and Quill programs, and will point out some of the difficulties we encountered.

The figures included in the report are for illustration only, and are not intended as a serious set of cash flow figures. Nor is the model we use on Abacus intended to be a perfect cash flow model. Our aim in this chapter is to explore imports and exports, not to delve into the murky depths of financial planning!

The first step is to draw up a simple cash flow projection using the Abacus program. As the data is intended for export, you must be careful to prepare it in a suitable format, using just the top row and left-most column for text and including numbers and formulae in the rest of the sheet. Any steps that might make it unsuitable for export, such as adding underlined headings, can be performed after the export file is saved.

Our data is for a calendar year and we used the 'row = month(col()-1)' formula outlined in the Abacus manual to head each of the columns B to M with the name of a month. Column A includes a simple set of headings for the various income and expense items. January's initial cash figure is entered direct: other cash figures are 'carried over' from row 8 in the previous column. Income for January is again entered direct: the income for the other months is incremented steadily using a formula:

row = b3*110/100

with the cursor in cell c3. Cost of sales is produced in the same fashion.

Income totals are of course summed, again using a simple formula:

row = b3+b4 from B to M

with the cursor in cell B5 and so are total costs. The 'carried forward' figure is, of course, the total in row 4 less the total costs in row 7.

Figure 8.1 shows the spreadsheet layout and Figure 8.2 lists the formulae used, in the rather different notation in which Abacus prints them out.

Figure 8.1 Spreadsheet Layout: Cashflow Projection

:	A	:	B	:	C	:	D	:	E	:	F
1 :			January		February		March		April		May
2 :	carried over		2000.00		2200.00		280.00		313.00		349.30
3 :	income		1000.00		1100.00		1210.00		1331.00		1464.10
4 :	total		3000.00		3300.00		1490.00		1644.00		1813.40
5 :	cost of sales		700.00		770.00		847.00		931.70		1024.87
6 :	expenses		100.00		50.00		50.00		50.00		50.00
7 :	total costs		800.00		820.00		897.00		981.70		1074.87
8 :	carried forward		2200.00		2480.00		593.00		662.30		738.53

:	G	:	H	:	I	:	J	:	K	:	L	:	M
1 :	June		July		August		September		October		November		December
2 :	389.23		433.15		481.47		534.62		593.08		657.38		728.12
3 :	1610.51		1771.56		1948.72		2143.59		2357.95		2593.74		2853.12
4 :	1999.74		2204.71		2430.19		2678.20		2951.02		3251.13		3581.24
5 :	1127.36		1240.09		1364.10		1500.51		1650.56		1815.62		1997.18
6 :	50.00		50.00		50.00		50.00		50.00		50.00		50.00
7 :	1177.36		1290.09		1414.10		1550.51		1700.56		1865.62		2047.18
8 :	822.38		914.62		1016.08		1127.69		1250.46		1385.51		1534.06

Figure 8.2 Spreadsheet Formulae: Cashflow Projection

:	A	:	B	:	C	:	D	:	E	:	F
1 :			F1		F1		F1		F1		F1
2 :					F26		F26		F26		F26
3 :					F22		F22		F22		F22
4 :			F21		F21		F21		F21		F21
5 :					F24		F24		F24		F24
6 :											
7 :			F23		F23		F23		F23		F23
8 :			F25		F25		F25		F25		F25

:	G	:	H	:	I	:	J	:	K	:	L	:	M
1 :	F1		F1		F1		F1		F1		F1		F1
2 :	F26		F26		F26		F26		F26		F26		F26
3 :	F22		F22		F22		F22		F22		F22		F22
4 :	F21		F21		F21		F21		F21		F21		F21
5 :	F24		F24		F24		F24		F24		F24		F24
6 :													
7 :	F23		F23		F23		F23		F23		F23		F23
8 :	F25		F25		F25		F25		F25		F25		F25

```
F1      :month(col()-1)
F21     :C[+0]R[-2]+C[+0]R[-1]
F22     :C[-1]R[+0]*110/100
F23     :C[+0]R[-2]+C[+0]R[-1]
F24     :C[-1]R[+0]*110/100
F25     :C[+0]R[-4]-C[+0]R[-1]
F26     :C[-1]R[+6]
```

None of these calculations are complex or difficult to perform, but using Abacus gives you the great advantage that you can vary any or all of your assumptions about sales, income, expenses etc., and see the overall effect of the change instantly. It isn't possible to do this, of course or even to calculate the running totals from month to month, using the Easel program.

Now you need to set up export files containing this data, for use in the Easel and Quill programs. We had some difficulty at first loading the export file into Easel. The problem turned out to be the left-hand titles. Easel objected to their containing more than one word and we had to re-edit each title down to one word before it would load successfully.

Easel did not object to the quantity of data, which still left 4K of memory free. Not all the figures could be displayed at once, however. It's up to you to manipulate the available figures and the Easel display formats in order to produce a graph which brings out the most important points. We chose to display the 'carried over', 'income' and 'total costs' figures. After editing the graph to show a suitable title and axis labels, it looked like figure 8.3, which was dumped directly from Easel. Though screen dumps are not in the same class as high-quality plotter images, they do make adequate inserts into informal reports, and we have used them frequently for this purpose. If you feel that your normal printer paper lets down the presentation, you can, on many printers including the FX-80 which Easel supports, switch over to a heavier single-sheet paper for the screen dump.

When the data is read into Quill from its export file, it appears (in eighty column mode) in tabular format divided into eighty-column chunks: the headings and columns January to May in the first chunk and the remaining columns in the second, much as the spreadsheet was printed in Figure 8.1. We found this layout a little undesirable for our purposes, as we preferred to repeat the headings at the start of the second batch of columns, so we used the Quill 'copy' command to move columns November and December to a new section of the document. This is unfortunately a time-consuming operation.

Other Quill commands were used to improve the overall layout of the spreadsheet and to provide a heading and some explanatory text. We haven't provided the full text of the report, but the short section of text we have provided shows how easy it is to combine narrative with the tables imported. You can see the resulting 'report' in Figure 8.4.

Figure 8.3 Cashflow Projection: Easel Screen Dump

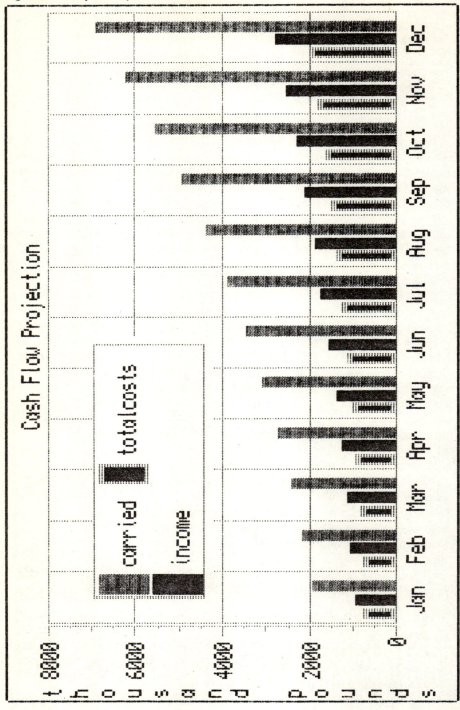

Figure 8.4 Cashflow Projection: Quill version

`Cashflow Projection for 1985`

```
Income and costs of sales are estimated to increase by 10% (cumulatively)
each month.    Other expenses estimated at £100 for the first month, and £50
thereafter.
```

	January	February	March	April	May
carried over	2000.00	2200.00	2480.00	2793.00	3142.30
income	1000.00	1100.00	1210.00	1331.00	1464.10
	=======	=======	=======	=======	=======
total	3000.00	3300.00	3690.00	4124.00	4606.40
cost of sales	700.00	770.00	847.00	931.70	1024.87
expenses	100.00	50.00	50.00	50.00	50.00
	=======	=======	=======	=======	=======
total costs	800.00	820.00	897.00	981.70	1074.87
carried forward	2200.00	2480.00	2793.00	3142.30	3531.53

	June	July	August	September	October
carried over	3531.53	3964.68	4446.15	4980.77	5573.84
income	1610.51	1771.56	1948.72	2143.59	2357.95
	=======	=======	=======	=======	=======
total	5142.04	5736.24	6394.87	7124.36	7931.79
cost of sales	1127.36	1240.09	1364.10	1500.51	1650.56
expenses	50.00	50.00	50.00	50.00	50.00
	=======	=======	=======	=======	=======
total costs	1177.36	1290.09	1414.10	1550.51	1700.56
carried forward	3964.68	4446.15	4980.77	5573.84	6231.23

	November	December
carried over	6231.23	6959.35
income	2593.74	2853.12
	=======	=======
total	8824.97	9812.47
cost of sales	1815.62	1997.18
expenses	50.00	50.00
	=======	=======
total costs	1865.62	2047.18
carried forward	6959.35	7765.29

ANOTHER EXAMPLE:
EXPORTING OUR LEDGER FILE FROM ARCHIVE

In Chapter 5, we outlined a simple accounting application using Archive, for which we set up a small ledger file. We entered Archive to read this file and export it to both Easel and – using selected fields only – Abacus.

It was only a few minutes' job to select the ledger code and numeric fields from each record and prepare the export file. We had no problems, either, in reading the file into Abacus. As there are more records than there are fields, we chose to read it column by column, like our Archive report format. Fixing the start position at A3 allowed room for a heading at the top of the spreadsheet: we included a blank line after the initial row of headings, which we re-wrote to improve their appearance.

Archive formatting of text and number tends to be primitive, but in Abacus it is easy to improve on this and we duly right-justified the column headings and converted all numbers to decimal format with two decimal places. It was equally easy to write simple formulae to total each column.

If you look closely at the result (figure 8.5) you will see that Abacus is as prone to rounding errors as is Archive, or that we imported an error from Archive. Adding the well-behaved column of numbers that made up the record balances gave us a ridiculous total of '-9.095E-13!' Displayed to two decimal figures it does look something like zero, but it still appears as minus zero, rather than the real thing. Curiously, when we panned the cursor up the

Figure 8.5 Spreadsheet Layout: Ledger Report

¦ A ¦	B ¦	C ¦	D
1¦Ledger Report"			
2¦--------------			
3¦Ledger code	Debit	Credit	Balance
4¦			
5¦bdet01	0.00	353.87	-353.87
6¦capt01	0.00	100.00	-100.00
7¦car01	370.83	0.00	370.83
8¦car02	8561.30	0.00	8561.30
9¦cash01	2102.55	0.00	2102.55
10¦crds01	0.00	1384.99	-1384.99
11¦dtrs01	3629.41	0.00	3629.41
12¦fees01	0.00	41217.84	-41217.84
13¦ofeq01	5973.99	0.00	5973.99
14¦ohex01	4669.78	0.00	4669.78
15¦plos01	0.00	3898.00	-3898.00
16¦rccs01	0.00	0.00	0.00
17¦vatx01	0.00	2099.09	-2099.09
18¦wage01	23745.93	0.00	23745.93
19¦	==========	==========	==========
20¦Totals	49053.79	49053.79	-0.00

individual balances, none of them admitted to having that awkward little bit missing: echoed at the bottom of the screen they all looked to be dead on target.

Reading a ledger file into Easel is a less obviously desirable business, but we tried it nevertheless and this, too, worked quite well. The balances in the different accounts were so widely different that the resultant graph was rather badly scaled. We found it most successful to plot only one field at a time: e.g. the balance for each account, and felt that the graph produced in this way might make a useful tool in a larger-scale accounting system.

9

Working with QL SuperBasic

QL's SuperBasic is radically different, not only from previous Sinclair dialects of Basic, but also from most other versions of the language. Though it has some similarities with other highly structured versions such as BBC Basic, it differs from these in important respects, too. Even an exerienced Basic programmer will take some time to learn the language's strengths and its weaknesses. In this chapter we take an overview of SuperBasic and explore the program structuring tools it offers in detail.

We go on in Chapter 10 to take a topic by topic look at some features of the QL which are accessible using SuperBasic. We explore the syntax and capabilities of some of the more unusual SuperBasic commands and provide a selection of sample programs which show them in operation. Chapter 11 then looks in detail at graphic programming, and provides some graphic utility programs.

This introduction is intended mainly for those who already understand the rudiments of Basic programming, and who have read the Beginner's Guide to SuperBasic included in the QL User Guide.

VERSIONS OF SUPERBASIC

As the QL was developed, a number of slightly different versions of the Basic were issued. These are known by initials (which are, incidentally, the initials of members of the development team). Typing 'PRINT ver$' will tell you which version is installed in your machine.

FB had the dubious honour of naming the first dialect to be issued with production versions of the machine. It is this version which we used throughout most of the preparation of this book. There were a large number of bugs in FB Basic, some of them blatant (try 'PRINT -2 -2', for instance, which gives the answer '0') and many of them were able to crash the machine entirely. As our problems were originally written to run under FB Basic, some of them use slightly awkward constructions designed to circumvent the bugs. This should not prevent them from running under later dialects of Basic, but we have not been able to test them under every dialect.

In the early QLs FB Basic was replaced by EPROMs when these machines were recalled for ROM refitting. All QLs should now be equipped with one of the subsequent versions of the Basic.

Subsequent versions of SuperBasic that have been released to date are (in date order) PM, AH and JM Basic. Versions up to AH certainly still contain bugs, but these should be identical to some of the bugs in FB, and our programs should not suffer because of the difference.

One command which operated quite differently in FB Basic and in subsequent dialects was AT. The order of the print co-ordinates was reversed subsequent to the FB launch. You may find it necessary to reverse the co-ordinates in our programs in order to allow for this.

We tested the programs we describe as thoroughly as possible on our QL and we found that all of them ran satisfactorily at least once. Some of the more esoteric bugs in the string slicing routines caused programs which had originally functioned well to crash on subsequent runs. It's difficult to test a program exhaustively under these conditions and it is just possible that we've overlooked one or two genuine program bugs because of the intrusion of system bugs. Where we encountered problems of this nature, we mention the fact in the text. However, if you are working with a later version of the Basic, you should have much less difficulty than we did. Similarly, you may find that some of our general warnings on Basic handling are not strictly necessary when working with later variants.

There remains the possibility that some SuperBasic syntax will be changed yet again, after this book has been written. Unfortunately there is nothing we can do about this. Your User Guide should document any changes in the Basic, though it may not summarize them in one place. Watch out for magazine articles, or information from QL user groups, that will help you to deal with any compatibility problems you come across when trying to run programs from this book and from other sources.

CONVENTIONS USED IN OUR SUPERBASIC PROGRAMS

The SuperBasic programs we've included in this book are there for one or both of two purposes. First, some of them help to illustrate the syntax and use of the more unusual SuperBasic commands. Second, many of them will, we hope, be of interest in their own right. We've tried to plug some of the obvious gaps in existing QL software, providing, for instance, file copy and directory handling programs and graphic utilities that complement rather than duplicate Easel's capabilities.

SuperBasic is an easy language to document, as it is possible to use longish and meaningful names in so many places. We've tried to do so, within reason: nobody wants to keep typing a procedure name twenty characters long and, in the shortish programs we include here, there is no need to go to such lengths. (The longer the program, of course, the more documentation is necessary.) With modular programs built around named procedures, it is not necessary to include many REMs and we have not done so. Points not clear from the program listing itself should be explained in the accompanying text.

Programs have been reproduced as they appear on screen if you type in lower case: with the compulsory part of each SuperBasic keyword in upper case, and with lower case used elsewhere. Case is generally not significant in variable and procedure names and we feel that this convention best brings out the working of the programs.

Shorter listings in the body of the text have been typeset – after a very careful proof-reading. Some longer listings have been reproduced directly from program printouts on an Epson FX-80. Though these may be less easy to read, they will be more accurate than any typeset version. In these printouts, note that the hash character (#) is reproduced as a pound sign (£). Where a pound appears in the listing, you must type a hash sign on the keyboard.

We have not followed the convention of marking the programs individually as copyright. All of the material in this book is of course protected by the copyright laws and you must use it only within the limits permissible through those laws. Feel free to copy the listings into your computer, of course, and to amend them wherever you feel you can improve on them. You are not free to reproduce them in other written material or to sell versions of the programs.

AN OVERVIEW OF QL STRUCTURING TOOLS

Writing a well structured program is a two-stage operation. First, you divide your program into clearly defined sections, which you can code – at least partially – and test individually. Next, you link the sections together in a logical manner.

SuperBasic offers two programming tools which handle the former task: procedures, and functions. It offers a variety of logical structures including

REPEAT, FOR . . . END FOR and IF . . . THEN . . . ELSE which tackle the latter problem. We'll look at the modular tools first, and at the linking tools second.

Functions

A Basic function is an operation which takes one or more variables, numbers or strings and manipulates them in some way to produce another number or string. A number of simple and not-so-simple functions are built into SuperBasic; the DEF FN command enables you to add others of your own.

The types of data with which a function deals are described as its *parameters*. When you define a function you give these parameters variable names. The parameter of the inbuilt SIN function, for instance, is a number which we can call 'n'. The specific number that the function takes is normally called its argument, though the QL User Guide calls it an 'actual parameter', as opposed to the 'formal parameter': so the formal parameter is 'n' and the actual parameter or argument might be '10'. The function takes this number and 'returns' another number, which we might call the answer: so SIN(0.5) takes the number 0.5 as its argument and returns the answer 0.4794255 which is the sine of 0.5.

In other functions, there is a less neat fit between the parameter or parameters provided and the data that is returned. The function CHR$, for example, takes a number as its parameter and returns a string. The function DATE$ needs no external parameters at all. The function RND can take a parameter range like '5 TO 10'; yet other functions may have a whole series of parameters. In each case, however, only one expression is returned. This will always be so.

When using any function, you need to:

(a)   indicate which function you wish to use, by giving its *name*;
(b)   provide suitable data for its parameters and;
(c)   indicate what is done with the data that is returned. You might either make immediate use of it (e.g. by printing or transmission) or put it into a variable.

In this sense, user-defined functions are no different from inbuilt functions. You use both in statements like:
    LET z = RND(0 to 10)
(function name RND, argument the range 0 to 10, data goes into variable z)
    LET n% = lowest(x,y,z)
(function name 'lowest', arguments variables x, y, and z (which have already obtained values earlier in the program) data goes into variable n%)
    PRINT initial(n$)
(function name 'initial', argument string N$, data is immediately printed and not stored in memory).

The distinctive thing about a user-defined function is that you must define it before using it. You so this with the DEFine FuNction . . . END DEFine commands. Once defined, the procedure can be used within the program as often as you wish, and this economy is a major argument in favour of using function definitions.

The three elements we mentioned above are just as apparent when you define a function. You *must*:

(a)   give it a name, which you provide after DEF FN (and are advised to repeat after END DEF, too);

(b)   indicate what its parameters, if any, are to be, (by listing their names in brackets following the function name) and;

(c)   return a string or number, using the RETURN command.

Within the function definition, you will normally need to use a variable in which to build up the data you will be returning. It's the name of this variable (which can be made local to the function if you wish) that you give after RETurn. This name does *not* indicate what is to be done with the data in the rest of the program: it's simply a working name within the function. Take this simple example:

```
10     DEF FN anycol
20     LOCal z
30     z = RND(1 TO 7)
40     RETurn z
50     END DEF anycol
```

This simple function, which has no parameters, is called 'anycol'. (Note that nested in it is another function, 'RND'.) You might use it to select a random colour to use on a black background. This is a trivial task for which you hardly need to set up a special function, but it provides a useful example.

You can use this function in statements like 'PRINT anycol' or 'c = anycol'. There's no need for you to remember, in using it, that the variable z is used within the function.

Incidentally, it is not essential to use a z variable, though it's often useful in the interests of clarity, especially when you have long and complex function definitions. If you wish you can RETurn a complex expression rather than a simple variable, like this:

```
10     DEF FN anycol
20     RETurn RND(1 TO 7)
30     END DEF anycol
```

Note, too, that the *type* of data that the function returns is determined, not by the working variable z (or any similar variable), but by the *name* of the function. Here's a short example which proves that.

```
10     DEF FN anycol%
20     LOCal z
```

```
30       z = RND(1 TO 7)*.3
35       PRINT "z = ";z
40       RETurn z
50       END DEF anycol%
100      FOR n = 1 TO 10
110      PRINT "colour is ";anycol%
120      END FOR n
```

Anycol% is an integer function, so it will return an integer, even though z may hold a non-integer number. As the 'n' loop calls the function anycol% ten times, you'll get output like this:

'z = .3
colour is 0
z = 1.5
colour is 2'

and so on. It's obviously good practice to make the working variable and the name of the function of the same data type, but if you do make them different SuperBasic will try to 'coerce' the data in the working variable to fit the function type. If it fails to do so, you will of course get an error message. (More on coercion in Chapter 10.)

It is important to understand the functioning of the different identifiers you use for parameters. Let's take as an example a function called 'count', with three numeric parameters. When calling the function, you might use a statement like:

count(x,y,z)

In this statement, x, y, and z are the names of ordinary, global variables which have acquired values earlier in the program. They have nothing particular to do with the function definition. Of course, there is no necessity to use variable names as parameters: you can equally well include numbers or strings directly, like:

count (5,6,7)

When defining the function, your definition will start with a 'DEF FN' statement giving the name of the function and indicating the type of its parameters. It might be:

DEFine FuNction count (a,b,c)

Here a, b and c are formal names for the parameters. They act as variable names that will be local to the procedure. You must use names (or 'identifiers' in SuperBasic terminology) in this context: here it is not possible to use numbers or strings instead. The values given in the procedure call – 5, 6 and 7, or the values in x, y and z – are *automatically* transferred to a, b and c – in that order, of course. The definition then has no more truck with x, y and z or any other variable names used in the procedure call: it uses a, b and c throughout. Indeed, it could use local variables x, y and z with quite different values, though you may feel that to do so is unnecessarily confusing!

Note that within a function definition, you can use all the usual SuperBasic commands and can print output directly if you wish. This is useful for debugging, but it's as well to use function definitions only when you want to obtain an expression, not as a general-purpose alternative to the procedures we describe below. You should certainly not include sequences within the definition which might make you EXIT from the function without providing a RETurn value. However, RETurning a value will automatically end the function and you can make use of this to simplify a listing of alternatives, as in this example:

```
10    DEFine FuNction nsize(n)
20    If n< 100 THEN RETurn 1
30    If n< 1000 THEN RETurn 2
40    RETurn 3
50    END DEFine nsize
```

We recommend that you always give the function name after the 'END DEF' statement and always specifically define as local all variables used within a function definition. It's not necessary to define as local the parameter variables (the ones in brackets after the function name); these automatically function as local variables and do not affect variables with the same name elsewhere in the program.

(Note: in some early versions of SuperBasic local variables in functions and procedures did not work correctly. Using these versions, it made and makes sense to stick to global variables.)

Use a function definition whenever you will be repeating a fixed series of manipulations on different sets of data during a program. Here are some simple examples:

(a) to find the lowest of three numbers:

```
10    DEFine FuNction lowest (x,y,z)
20    LOCal n
30    IF x < y THEN
40    n = x
50    ELSE
60    n = y
70    END IF
80    IF z < THEN n = z
90    RETurn n
100   END DEFine lowest
```

typical use:

```
110    ^x = 10: y = 1 ^x: z = 1/x
120    PRINT lowest(x,y,z)
```

(b) to find the circumference of a circle:

```
10    DEFine FuNction circum(r)
```

```
20        LOCal c
30        c = 2*PI*r
40        RETurn c
50        END DEFine circum
```
typical use:
```
100       c = circum(10.5)
```

(c) to convert a number to a fixed number of decimal places:
```
10        DEFine FuNction dec(n,d)
20        LOCal x,m%
30        m% = n*10 ^d
40        x = m%/10 ^d
50        RETurn x
60        END DEFine dec
```
n is the number, *d* the number of decimal places to be displayed. Note that we use integer variable coercion, which rounds to the nearest number, rather than the INT function, which always rounds down.

typical use:
```
100 n = 10.3456
110 PRINT dec(n,2)
```

(d) To turn a name in the format 'surname,initial,title' to a name in the format 'title initial. surname'. This would be handy to turn a list of names formatted for sorting alphabetically into a format suitable for printing on labels. It is a rather more complex function, but note that it still returns just one string (see Figure 9 overleaf).

It is good practice to group all your function definitions together in your program, either at the start or, perhaps more usually, towards the end. It makes little difference to the running of the program where you place them: they need not be numbered before the statements which call them. You might always use the range of line numbers from 5000 for functions, for example, numbering the first function definition from 5000, the second from 5100 (or 5200 if it is long) and so on. Though function calls can be nested, function definitions should not be nested: you list first one, then the next and so on.

If you build up a set of general purpose functions like those we listed above, which will have a part to play in many programs you write, then it is a good idea to save them as a separate microdrive file. You can then load the function definitions (and delete any unwanted ones) before starting to type in your program proper or you could merge the definitions with the rest of your program.

Later versions of SuperBasic may implement the system feature of 'resident' procedures and functions, machine code and/or Basic routines

Figure 9.1 Function Name

```
100 DEFine FuNction name$(n$)
110 LOCal n, s$, i$, t$, z, m$
120 n = 1: s$ = "": i$ = "": t$ = ""
130 REPeat surname
140 IF n$(n) = "," THEN EXIT surname
150 s$ = s$ & n$(n)
160 n = n+1
170 IF n> LEN(n$) THEN EXIT surname
180 END REPeat surname
190 n = n+1
200 REPeat initials
210 IF n$(n) = "," THEN EXIT initials
220 i$ = i$ & n$(n)
230 n = n+1
240 IF n>LEN(n$) THEN EXIT initials
250 END REPeat initials
260 n = n+1
270 FOR z = n TO LEN(n$)
280 t$ = t$ & n$(z)
290 END FOR z
300 m$ = t$ & " " & i$ &" " & s$
310 RETurn m$
320 END DEFine name$
330 PRINT name$("Jones,M.B.,Miss")
```

which can be loaded into a specific area of high memory before any Basic programs are run. This feature was not implemented at a high level on the version of the QL that we used.

Procedures

A procedure is a looser construct than a function and, unlike a function, it does not specifically return a value. Procedures are simply used to identify modules of your program. You might set up a procedure to hold a sequence of operations that you will be performing repeatedly in the course of a long program or you might set it up to hold a sequence that you will use once only. (Later, we'll offer some examples of both types.) In either case, the use of procedures can simplify your programming and improve your program style, making it easier for you to debug your program and for others to understand and amend it.

If you are used to older dialects of Basic that do not include procedures, you might like to compare a SuperBasic procedure with a standard Basic subroutine. The two have some obvious similarities. It's possible to call both a procedure and a subroutine from any point within a program. Once the procedure or subroutine is completed (or a return statement is encountered) program control returns automatically to the next statement in the program, making it possible to call both procedures and subroutines from different parts of the program without difficulty. (This is not true of a part of the program identified merely by GOTOs, for example.)

However, procedures have two major advantages over subroutines. First, they are named. Using a meaningful name for your procedures much improves the readability of your programs and is far less clumsy than using REMarks to identify the purpose of subroutines. We recommend names like 'title,' 'countermove,' 'graphdraw,' etc. You'll then have a statement in your program like:

50 title

instead of

50 GOSUB 500: REM title

Second, it is possible to pass parameters directly to the procedure, much as parameters are passed to function cells. Using parameters rather than normal global variables again shortens programs and improves program logic, as we shall show later in the chapter.

Subroutines, in contrast, do not have any advantages over procedures and you should get into the habit of using SuperBasic procedures wherever you would have used subroutines previously. Though SuperBasic does include GOSUB and RETURN statements, the correct use of procedures makes these redundant and you will need to use them only when converting programs originally written for other computers. Even here, swapping the GOSUB for a procedure call will almost always improve the program.

Though procedures do not specifically return values as do function calls, they do of course interact with the rest of your program. In planning your program, it is important to understand the scope of that interaction and to limit it where necessary.

As with function definitions, you can use both local and global variables within procedures. Good programming practice demands that you make use of both types. Do not fall into the habit of using solely global variables simply because they are the default type.

If the procedure is specifically designed to generate or alter a variable value and return the variable to the main program, the variable should be global. If a variable is to be used purely for 'working' purposes within the procedure, it is best to define it specifically as local. It is all too easy to duplicate often-used variables like 'x' or 'loop' accidentally and the use of local variables prevents slips caused in this way from ruining the logical flow of your program. Local variable definitions must come right at the start of your procedure definition, following the 'DEF PROC' statement.

Not sure which of these purposes a variable has? That's a sign of sloppy programming and you should review your programming habits. It's good practice to draw up a list of variable names while planning a program and to mark each one as global or as local to one or more procedures.

Unlike a function, a procedure does not return a single value, though you can get the same effect as returning a value (and, indeed, do it for a whole series of values) by using global variables within and outside a procedure.

Since no value is returned, though the function has a name like a function name, it doesn't have a type (e.g. integer or string) as does a function.

Of course, the parameters passed to the procedure will affect the way in which it works, even though they won't have a direct effect upon a value returned. You can think of the parameters as a third type of information, to set against local and global variables. It's appropriate to put global variables into parameters, rather than passing them individually to the procedure, whenever the value of the variables at the end of the procedure is irrelevant: you won't use them again or you will re-initialize them elsewhere in the program. If this is not clear now, you may find that it is made more so by the examples below.

In Figure 9.2 we summarize the proper uses of all three kinds of data: in parameters, in global variables, and in local variables.

Procedures, like functions, are handled in two stages. First you define them, giving a unique name, then you call them simply by using that name elsewhere in your program. Procedures too are defined with a sequence starting with DEFine (PROCedure, in this case) and ending with END DEFine. Again, we advise you to repeat the procedure name after END DEFine. You can exit from the procedure at any point (and return control to the next statement after the procedure name) by giving a RETurn command. RETurn is different from the function RETurn, in that it does not return any value: it simply shifts program control. It's not necessary to include a RETurn at all in the procedure definition, as END DEFine will act as an automatic RETurn and this again is in contrast to functions, where a RETurn is certainly necessary. Do ensure that you end the procedure definition with an END DEFine instead of a RETurn, or you may muddle successive definitions together.

One point of syntax may catch you out at first. When calling a function you provide its parameters *in brackets* after the function name. When calling a procedure, you may again provide parameters – but this time, you don't put them in brackets. The QL User Guide describes the brackets as 'not necessary': in fact, we found that in FB SuperBasic, they were not allowable.

Figure 9.2 Using Parameters, Global and Local Variables in Procedures

You can use any combination of local and global variables and parameters within procedures. These diagrams may help you to understand which to use where.

'x' is our all-purpose identifier (i.e. formal parameter or variable name) in these examples. The outlined boxes represent the procedure in question.

value of x in

| statements that change x | x will be a *global variable*

new value of x out

value of x in

```
┌─────────────┐
│ statements  │   x could be a global variable; should be a parameter
│  that use   │
│     x       │
└─────────────┘
```

final value of x unchanged or not important

variety of values in (or no values in)

```
┌─────────────┐
│ statements  │   x will be a global variable
│ that create │
│     x       │
└─────────────┘
```

value of x out

variety of values in (or no values in)

```
┌─────────────┐
│ statements  │   procedure not appropriate: use a
│ that create │   function call instead
│   a value   │
└─────────────┘
```

value out may go into x, y or z

x not input (may have other value elsewhere in program)

```
┌─────────────┐
│ statements  │   x will be a local variable
│  that use x │
└─────────────┘
```

x not output (will retain its original value, if any, elsewhere in program)

Using Procedures

You will find many examples of the use of procedures elsewhere in this book, and of course in program listings that you obtain from other sources. Study them: the best way to understand the power of this tool is to see it in use and then to use it yourself.

The simple examples we give here are designed mainly to make it clear how procedures are built up and how variables are used within them. We'll look at some longer examples of structured programming in the next chapter.

These are outlines rather than complete programs, with the emphasis on the procedures themselves. Line numbers are used purely for illustration: other numbers might be more appropriate in a completed program.

(a)   A self-contained procedure used to print the title to a program

It's worth using a procedure for this purpose, even though you will only call it once. The procedure call relegates all the detail of the title from the 'meat' of the program at the start and makes the overall structure of the program much easier to follow. 'Title' is the obvious name for the procedure, though you can use any similar name you wish.

The 'title' procedure should include all the details necessary to ensure that the title appears correctly: setting the screen mode, window, paper and ink colours, character size, etc. It will not include any details not directly related to the display of the title.

Your outline program will be rather like this:

```
10        REMark name of program
20        title
30        setup: next procedure that sets up screen for next part of
program
40        body of program . . . . .
1000      DEFine PROCedure title
1010      MODE 8
1020      CSIZE 3,1
1030      PAPER 5: INK 7
1040      AT 5,0: PRINT "(title of program)"
1050      CSIZE 0,0: INK 3
1060      print instructions, logo, other screen information
1070      PAUSE 1000
1080      END DEFine title
```

Of course, you will vary the individual statements to suit your own requirements.

(b)   A procedure that takes parameters from the main body of the program and then uses them internally: in this case, to draw a shape.

You might want to draw the same complex shape – or even a simple shape like a triangle, that isn't directly included in the SuperBasic graphic commands – repeatedly in the course of a program. This procedure will do it for you. All details that affect the individual shape to be drawn (within the general scope of the procedure as a whole) are passed to the procedure as parameters. For instance, they might include its co-ordinates; its orientation; its scaling; it's colour; whether it is filled or not. The procedure doesn't return any data, so that a parameter is the correct choice in this instance.

These specific statements draw a triangle, so we have called the procedure 'tridraw'. We've used absolute graphics statements, but in other circumstances relative or turtle graphics could be more appropriate. (More details on SuperBasic graphics in Chapter 11.)

```
10 Obtain values for variables used in procedure calls: e.g. by
calculation, by input from user, by reading from DATA statements
20        tridraw 10,50,60,60,70,80,2
```

```
30          tridraw x(1),y(1),x(2),y(2),x(3),y(3),5
```
. . . and other similar tridraw calls in the body of the program
```
1000        DEFine PROCedure tridraw (x1,y1,x2,y2,x3,y3,col)
1020        INK col
1020        FILL 1
1030        LINE x1,y1,TO x2,y2 TO x3,y3 TO x1,y1
1040        FILL 0
1050        if appropriate, return INK to default colour
1060        END DEFine tridraw
```

(c)   A procedure that uses global variables for both input and output. This
one is used in a simple 'bouncing ball' program. It checks the position of the
ball, and alters its direction if the ball is about to hit the sides of the screen. We
call it 'checkcoord'. As the same variables (dx and dy, the direction
horizontally and vertically) are input *and* output, it is not appropriate to put
them into parameters.
```
  10        setup (procedure to set up screen with mode 4, suitable paper
            (0) and ink (3) colours, full screen window, etc.)
  20        x = 40: y = 12
  30        dx = 1: dy = 1
  40        REPeat loop
  50        checkcoord
  60        INK 0: AT x,y: PRINT "*"
  70        x = x + dx: y = y + dy
  80        INK 3: AT x,y: PRINT "*"
  90        END REPeat loop
2000        DEFine PROCedure checkcoord
2010        IF x = 0 OR x = 79 THEN dx = –dx
2020        IF y = 0 OR y = 23 THEN dy = –dy
2030        END DEFine checkcoord
```

SuperBasic Loops

If you are familiar with older dialects of Basic, you may be used to just two
types of loop: the FOR . . . NEXT counted loop, used when the number of
repetitions is fixed in advance and an IF . . . THEN GOTO structure, used
when the number of repetitions is not fixed in advance, like this:
```
  50        statements that make up loop
 100        IF (condition for loop repeat) THEN GOTO 50
```
Sometimes it can be helpful to divide loops that are not strictly counted into
two sub-classes. There are loops with an uncertain number of repeats, when
the actual number is determined by user choice, by a random number or by
some other uncertain event. Also there are loops with a maximum number of
repeats, when this maximum may not always be performed. This latter (which

we call a semi-counted loop here) is particularly awkward to handle in conventional Basic: SuperBasic makes it much easier.

In SuperBasic a powerful variation of FOR . . . NEXT is provided, which can be adapted both to counted loops and to semi-counted ones. IF . . . THEN GOTO is available, but SuperBasic provides much better structures for loops which in conventional Basic are handled with these commands and you should never need to resort to this construction.

You may be familiar with two more sophisticated loop structures: the REPEAT . . . UNTIL structure provided in BBC Basic and in other structured languages and the WHILE . . . WEND or WHILE . . . ENDWHILE structure. The first of these is used when the operations within the loop will always be repeated at least once; the second when they may not be required at all. In SuperBasic, the REPeat . . . .END REPeat structure serves both these purposes.

FOR . . . NEXT . . . END FOR

Though SuperBasic's FOR . . . END FOR loop is superficially similar to the familiar Basic FOR . . . NEXT, it has some important differences and you should be careful in adapting programs written for other computers that use FOR . . . NEXT.

FOR has a simple 'short form' that needs neither NEXT nor END FOR: it's simply contained on one line. It looks like this:

FOR n = 1 TO 10 STEP 2: PRINT n

This is used for very simple counted loops, which will be familiar to all Basic programmers. Adding NEXT or END FOR statements at the end of the line won't trigger an error, but it can cause confusion when you are also using long-form FOR statements and is therefore best avoided.

Note that in both forms of the statement, the loop counter or identifier must be a *floating point* variable. You cannot use an integer variable. This is a pity, as the use of integer variables might have been expected to speed the Basic interpreter. It does so markedly in BBC Basic and when adapting BBC Basic programs to SuperBasic you should take particular note of this. Possibly this rule will be changed in later revisions of SuperBasic.

The 'long form' statement is more complex and needs examining closely. It too can be used to handle counted loops with more statements than can conveniently be placed on one line. It can also be used to handle a variety of semi-counted and multi-part loop structures, including some for which conventional Basic uses an IF . . . THEN GOTO type of structure.

In its long form the FOR statement takes a line to itself, and subsequent program lines are used for the statements that make up the body of the loop. The loop is terminated, *not* by NEXT, but by END FOR. Every long-form FOR loop must have an END FOR. END FOR is followed by the loop identifier (e.g. 'FOR n = 1 TO 50 . . . . END FOR n), a useful check to ensure that loops have been correctly nested. It is *not* an invitation to tangle loops!

NEXT is needed only if you wish in some circumstances to restart the sequence of loop operations *before* the end of the loop. It is *not* the equivalent of 'NEXT' in conventional Basics: END FOR is that and you should note this point in converting programs. Using NEXT at the end of loops immediately before END FOR will not cause errors, but it is not good practice and is best avoided.

NEXT increments the loop counter and returns control to the statement following FOR – unless the sequence of repetitions is complete, when it proves a little unpredictable. Instead of causing an exit from the loop, it returns control to the statement immediately following the NEXT.

It's used like this:

```
10      FOR loop = 1 TO 10
20      n = RND(10)
30      IF n = 0 THEN NEXT loop
40      PRINT n
50      END FOR loop
```

If n = 0 then it will not be printed – unless the *last* value of n is '0', when the NEXT will send program control to line 40, and it *will* be printed. If you don't want to see that final 0, then you must take account of that in your programming.

More than one NEXT can be used in the same loop if you wish, like this:

```
10      FOR loop = 1 TO 10
20      n = RND(10)
30      IF n = 0 THEN NEXT loop
40      PRINT n;
45      IF n = 5 THEN NEXT loop
47      PRINT n
50      END FOR loop
```

As well as returning control to the start of a FOR . . . END FOR loop using NEXT, you can vary the program flow in mid-loop by using the EXIT command. EXIT will leave the loop entirely and return program control to the statement following END FOR. It's bad practice in conventional Basic to exit from a FOR . . . NEXT loop with GOTO. EXIT makes it perfectly acceptable to do so in SuperBasic and this means that FOR can properly be used for semi-counted loops, where the loop counter outlines a maximum rather than a compulsory number of repetitions.

Departures from FOR loops in this fashion should be done via EXIT only. It will confuse program control if you attempt to exit from a FOR loop using GOTO or RETURN: don't do it!

Note, too, that a single EXIT statement should be able to handle your departure from an entire series of nested loops, which might include both

FOR loops and the REPeat loops we describe below. All you need to do is to follow EXIT with the identifier of the outermost loop involved. In practice, such rather unorthodox and demanding switches in program control have occasionally caused crashes in the early versions of SuperBasic, and you may feel that they are best avoided. They do little to contribute to good structured programming and should not be necessary.

REPeat . . . END REPeat

REPeat is used for non-counted loops and can be used for some semi-counted loops. FOR is a more convenient structure for proper counted loops and in SuperBasic it is often better for semi-counted loops too. You should use that statement in preference to REPeat when you can properly set up a loop counter.

The conventional REPEAT . . . UNTIL loop, as found in BBC Basic and some other languages, includes in the outline loop structure a condition under which the loop will terminate (e.g. 'UNTIL n = 10'). So, too, does the WHILE . . . WEND loop structure (e.g. 'WHILE n <> 10'). SuperBasic REPeat loops do not, and unless you particularly wish to set up an endless loop, you must include an IF condition in your loop, with an EXIT from it when the condition is met.

In fact, then, a normal SuperBasic REPeat loop has three essential statements: REPeat identifier; signals the start of the loop; IF . . . THEN EXIT identifier; END REPeat identifier; signals the end of the loop. You can of course use any forms of the IF statement. (We discuss the various forms below.)

Though there must be at least one IF . . . THEN EXIT, it does not matter where in the loop the IF . . . THEN EXIT is included and indeed there can be a whole series of such statements providing for exits under different conditions. Putting the EXIT right at the start of the loop statements provides the equivalent of a WHILE . . . WEND loop. Here's an example:

```
10      REPeat wrong
20      IF answer THEN EXIT wrong
30      PRINT "No good, try again"
40      INPUT "What's your guess"; g
50      IF g = 7 THEN answer = 1
60      END REPeat wrong
```

Putting the EXIT right at the end provides the equivalent of a REPEAT . . . UNTIL loop. Here's another example:

```
10      REPeat person
20      PRINT "I'm looking for Jim"
30      INPUT "Who are you?" ;p$
40      IF p$ = "Jim" THEN EXIT person
```

50   END REPeat person
60   PRINT "Hi there, Jim".

Putting EXITs in the middle is more flexible than anything offered by either of the other two structures. Some more complex examples are provided by programs later in the book.

Finally, note that you can use NEXT to return control to the start of a REPeat loop, just as you can with a FOR loop. See our comments on the use of NEXT, above.

Conditional Structures in SuperBasic

You should already be familiar with the simple IF . . . THEN structure, sometimes with ELSE added in, that is the most fundamental conditional tool of the Basic language. SuperBasic does of course provide a version, which we look at below. IF provides only a two-choice branch in a program: either you do this or you don't (and maybe do that); though you can produce a more complex decision point by combining a whole sequence of IFs. Some Basics provide a simple one-command multiple choice branch, with the ON . . . GOTO (and/or ON . . . GOSUB) command. Though SuperBasic includes this, it has a more flexible and powerful tool in SELECT. We look at this second conditional structure below and then go on to consider some of the unusual features of SuperBasic's logical operators.

IF . . . THEN . . . ELSE . . . ENDIF

IF . . . THEN and its variations comes in two main forms: a short form and a long form. In both forms, as the manual points out, the 'THEN' is optional. In the short form you can replace it with a colon: in the long form you simply miss it out. For clarity, we feel it is better to include THEN.

If there is a second statement following THEN or a colon on the same line as the IF statement, the short form is assumed. So these are automatically short form statements:

IF n = 6: PRINT "n = 6"
IF n = 6 THEN PRINT "n = 6"

The second statement is in standard Basic, familiar to every Basic programmer. There is no need to give an END IF after the short form statement and though you will not get an error message if you do so, you will find that you may corrupt the logic sequence in complex sets of nested loops including both form of statement. (These are best avoided anyway: stick to the long form for nested loops.)

If there is no second statement on the same line as the IF, the long form is assumed. This time you *must* terminate the loop with an END IF. The long form IF . . . THEN is extremely useful: standard Basic dialects do not provide anything similar and it does enable you to make several statements dependent on an IF without confusing your program listing.

Note that *only* the long form of IF . . . THEN . . . END IF includes an ELSE statement. You *cannot* use a statement with IF . . . THEN . . . ELSE on a single program line.

The QL manual explanation of IF . . . THEN . . . ELSE suggests that it is necessary to put 'ELSE' on a line by itself, but this isn't the case. A program sequence like this works fine:

```
50      IF n = 5 THEN
60      PRINT "n = 5"
70      ELSE PRINT "n <> 5"
80      END IF
```

Note that it isn't necessary for program control always to go as far as the END IF statement. As the example given for the longer version 1 in the User Guide shows you, you can EXIT from a FOR . . . NEXT loop that includes the IF . . . THEN sequence or RETurn from a procedure that includes it, before the END IF is reached. We feel, however, that this is a poor practice that will lead to confused programming, even if it does not lead to outright logical errors, and that it is best avoided.

One final interesting point, covered in the Beginner's Guide but not under the IF . . . THEN keyword explanation, is the fact that IF will work on a true/false basis as well as evaluating logical expressions. In this context, '0' equals false and all other values equal 'true'. Try this program, for instance, with a range of different values for 'fat':

```
10      fat = (−1,0,1,2,200)
20      IF fat THEN PRINT "Must go on a diet"
```

SELect . . . END SELect

SELect is used to force alternative choices depending upon the value of a variable. It will work either with specific values or with ranges of values, as we show below.

Note that though SELect has a menu-type action, you *cannot* use it with a string variable to determine the action to be taken on various non-numeric key presses. Nor will the FB version work with an integer variable. The program doesn't come up with an error message, but it doesn't select the alternatives properly either.

SELect works rather like ON . . . GOTO, but there's no need to use the GOTO. You simply follow the SELect statement with a sequence of alternatives, like this:

```
50      SELect ON m
60      = 5: PRINT "m = 5"
70      = 6: PRINT "m = 6"
75      PRINT "hi there"
```

```
80       = 7 TO 10: PRINT "m is between 7 and 10"
90       = REMAINDER: PRINT "m is not between 5 and 10"
100      END SELect
```

(Note: the manual outlines another, longer, version on which the alternative lines begin with 'ON m = . . . '. This didn't work correctly in our Basic and, as it has no apparent advantages over the shorter versions, we have not used it.)

The alternatives are mutually exclusive: once one has been selected, then as soon as the next '=' appears the program will send control to the statement following END SELect. There is no need to include any GOTO or EXIT statements and in this way SELect is different from an ON . . . GOTO construction. Of course, if you want program control to process all statements from the selection to the end of the sequence, then ON . . . GOTO would be a better choice.

Note that if you provide two choices which would apply to the variable value, then only the first will be used.

Each alternative can be one or more lines long: so when $m = 6$, for instance, the statements on lines 70 to 75 will be carried out. If your alternative courses of action are more than a couple of program lines in length, however, it would be much clearer to include them in procedures which are called from within SELect.

Note that though you can include a 'REMAINDER' option to allow for the failure of all selections, there is no need to do so. If no option is selected, this won't cause an error message: it will just pass program control to the statement following END SELect.

It is particularly worthwhile getting used to the 'short form' of the SELect statement, which is neater than the rival IF statement when it comes to identifying values within ranges. The example the manual gives is:

SELect ON answer = 0.00001 TO 0.00005: PRINT "Accuracy OK"

To produce the same effect using IF would mean a sequence like this:

IF answer $>$ 0.00001 AND answer $<$ 0.00005 THEN PRINT "Accuracy OK"

which is both longer and much less immediately clear.

HANDLING STRINGS AND NUMBERS IN SUPERBASIC

A general trend in the development of structured programming languages has been the movement towards very strong 'typing' of data. If you've done any Pascal programming, you will know that in Pascal (and in many other languages) you must start your program by declaring the type (e.g. integer, floating-point number, string) of each variable or constant you plan to use. Switching of data between types is generally frowned on and such operations are quite difficult to handle. Many such languages include a wide variety of data types: numbers might be divided into three or more different categories, depending upon their precision and the way in which they are stored.

SuperBasic's designers have taken a quite different approach. Typing of data is kept to an absolute minimum in SuperBasic and it's quite possible tochange the type of data very easily, through the use of 'coercion'.

Let's take an example. In order to convert a number or number variable into a string variable in many dialects of Basic, it's necessary to use a special function, STR$, like this:

LET n$ = STR$(n)

or

LET n$ = STR$(100)

In order to convert a suitable string into a number, it's necessary to use a second function: VAL is a common name for it. Yet other functions may be provided to fix or change the type of variables: DEFINT, DEFDBL and so on.

In SuperBasic, no function is needed: all you need to do to turn a number into a string is to type:

LET n$ = 100

or something similar.

Coercion is taken as far as possible in SuperBasic. Depending upon the type of name given to a variable or the type of argument needed by a function or parameter by a procedure, the interpreter will do its best to 'coerce' the data given to fit the requirements of the situation. A fuller explanation of the precise types of coercion possible is given under 'coercion' in the 'Concepts' section of the QL User Guide.

Coercion certainly makes for brief programs, but it can also make for sloppy programming and for unexpected mistakes. It's not difficult to convert a floating-point number into an integer, or even into a string, by 'accident', without consciously intending to do so. It's all too easy to include some very open ended string-into-number statements and then crash your program by inputting unsuitable data.

In short, we feel that this feature is dangerous and that it should be used only with the greatest care, in conjunction with careful planning of the variables used in a program.

The use of coercion helps to explain many of the unusual functions and operators (and unusual ways of working of familiar functions and operators) in SuperBasic. The ordinary string concatenator '+', for example, is used to add two numeric strings together, so that a new operator, '&', has been introduced for string concatenation. String slicing (treating a simple string rather like an array with one-character elements) will be reasonably familiar to users of earlier Sinclair Basics: we use it in some programs in this book. In this chapter, we look in detail at the unusual mode of operation of SuperBasic's logical operators and of its string comparisons.

Of course coercion has its plusses. With careful string-type manipulation, for example, you can make up for the lack in SuperBasic of a PRINT USING or similar number formatting command. Coercion of a floating point number into a variable is often more handy than using the INT function: it rounds to the nearest integer, instead of consistently rounding down as INT does. You will find other examples for yourself. But the practice has its minuses too. Not all of them are avoidable by the programmer. Many people feel that the use of coercion, and the wealth of data checking it entails, is one of the main factors responsible for the slow speed of SuperBasic. The interpreter does indeed work very slowly, considering the fast speed of the QL's main processor.

SUPERBASIC'S LOGICAL OPERATORS

In many Basics, the logical operators AND, OR, XOR and NOT all operate on a 'bitwise' basis, acting on the binary contents of memory locations. Bitwise operation doesn't always give the results you'd expect from comparisons, so we'll briefly run through some examples.

You can take either numbers or letters as a basis for bitwise operations, but numbers are easier, so let's use them. We'll take decimal 48, which is binary 00110000 and decimal 80, which is binary 01010000.

ANDing the two numbers produces a 1 wherever there is a 1 in both bits. So 48 and 80, in normal Basic, equals 00010000 or decimal 16. ORing them produces a 1 whenever there is a 1 in either bit, so 48 or 80 equals 01110000 or 112. XORing them produces a 1 whenever there is a 1 in one bit only, so 48 XOR 80 equals 01100000 or 96. NOTting a number, in a strictly binary way, produces its binary opposite, so NOT 48 equals 11001111, which is 207 (equals 255 − 48). Often a binary NOT operator will instead produce the negative of the number, though, so that NOT 48 equals −49 (treating 0 as the first positive number).

The AND and OR operations in particular, and occasionally the XOR operations, are particularly useful when you want to change only one bit of a register, without affecting the contents of the other bits. We give some examples of this on pages 160 and 161.

SuperBasic has bitwise operators, but they do not take the names AND, OR, NOT and XOR. Instead symbols are used for them, so that bitwise AND is '&&', bitwise OR is '||', bitwise XOR is '^^', and bitwise NOT (in fact a binary NOT, producing a negative) is '~~'.

SuperBasic *also* uses AND, OR, NOT and XOR as operators, but these work on a purely logical basis, using the two values zero (false) and one (or any value other than zero) for true. They are intended to be used for logical tests, where they produce answers broadly related to the English use of the words 'and', 'or, and 'not'. A typical use would be in statements like:

    IF a = b AND c = d THEN PRINT "YES, RIGHT ANSWERS"
    IF colour = red OR colour = yellow THEN PRINT "HOT!"
These logical operators can be used on a numeric basis, but in this case they
produce quite different answers. ANDing 48 and 80 is interpreted as ANDing
'true' and 'true', giving the answer 'true' (1). ORing 48 and 80 again provides
the answer true (1). XORing the two is interpreted as an exclusive OR of 'true'
and 'true': it produces the answer 0 (false). NOT 48 is interpreted as (not
true): i.e. false, and it too gives the answer 0.

    Notice that the result of a logical operation will *always* be either '0' (true) or
'1' (false). No other answer can result. The result of a bitwise operation, on
the other hand, could be any number equal to or less than 255 (or greater
than –256, in the case of NOT operations). As the results of the two types of
operation are so different, you must be careful to ensure that you always
choose the correct type of operator.

SUPERBASIC STRING OPERATORS

As well as its unusual bitwise and logical operators, SuperBasic includes some
unusual string operators. It is important to be clear how they work, so that the
results of string comparisons will not confuse you.

    As the Concepts section of the QL User Guide explains (under 'string
comparison') SuperBasic distinguishes between four different kinds of string
comparison. One of these (type 0) is however not used by any SuperBasic
operators, making three that you need to understand.

    We found this section of the User Guide to be both brief and misleading
and we discovered several discrepancies between how the manual suggested
string operators would work and how they actually do. We've pointed out
these discrepancies below and tried to set up a logical system of comparisons
(with a 'type number' and meaningful description) which reflects what
actually does happen in SuperBasic.

    In most Basics, all alpha (i.e. letter) comparisons work on a straight ASCII
code basis. The ASCII code for 'a', for example, is 97; the ASCII code for 'A'
is 65. As 65 is not equal to 97, then a short program like:
    10   IF "A" = "a" THEN
    20   PRINT "equal"
    30   ELSE
    40   PRINT "not equal"
    50   END IF
will print 'not equal'.

    The case of each letter in the string is an important part of the comparison:
the result of the comparison is thus directly dependent upon the case. As well
as calling this an ASCII-based comparison, we could borrow the SuperBasic
terminology and call it a 'case dependent' comparison.

In SuperBasic '=', when used as a string operator, works on this basis. So as you would expect, as happens in other Basics, the program above will come up with the answer 'not equal'.

This type of comparison normally applies to 'greater than' 'less than' and similar operators as well as to 'equals' tests. The strict ASCII coding is followed. 'A' is 'less than' 'a'. So is 'Z'. In ASCII, for example, the code for 'P' is '80', less than the code for 'a', '97'. So:

```
10    IF "P" < "a" THEN
20    PRINT "true"
30    ELSE
40    PRINT "untrue"
50    END IF
```

will in most Basics print 'true'.

You can, of course, use complete strings rather than single letters in comparisons like this. The same will hold true if you use 'PEARS' and 'apples', etc. The 'greater than' or 'less than' criterion is decided on the first different letter in the two strings, counting from left to right. 'aPples' will come out as 'less than' 'apples', on this criterion, for example.

Here, however, SuperBasic differs from the competition. While most Basics use an ASCII comparison, SuperBasic uses a case dependent comparison that is *not* ASCII based. SuperBasic '<', '<=', '>', and '>=' comparisons *are* certainly case dependent, so that:

```
10    IF "A" < "a" THEN
20    PRINT "true"
30    ELSE
40    PRINT "not true"
50    END IF
```

will print 'true', and so on for the other operators: the capital letter is always judged to be less than the corresponding lower case letter. But:

```
10    IF "P" < "a" THEN
20    PRINT "true"
30    ELSE
40    PRINT "untrue"
50    END IF
```

will print '*untrue*'! In effect, the value of letters in the string comparison are handled in a dictionary-like way, like this:

A a B b C c D d E e

and so on, meaning that SuperBasic, unlike the vast majority of Basics, can produce true dictionary-style alphabetical orderings with minimal fuss.

Non-alpha symbols such as '.' and '{' are, incidentally, handled in their code number order, using the ASCII-like code listed under 'character set' in the User Manual Concepts section, at least for those symbols we have tested.

When it comes to numbers evaluated as part of strings, SuperBasic again differs from the competition. Most Basic string evaluations treat numbers digit by digit, according to their ASCII code. In this sense, '111' is less than '22': the first digit shows it to be so. In most types of SuperBasic string comparison, if a string comprises or starts with a number, then that number will be evaluated as a whole for comparison purposes. The letters that follow, if any, and later numbers in the string are irrelevant. In a string like '111aa22' it is the '111' that is used for comparison purposes. In SuperBasic '111' is greater than ('>') '22'; '44' is less then ('<') '111'; '111aaa' is greater than' '22aaaa' and so on. Numbers as a whole are deemed to be less than letters, as the code values would suggest, so that '111' is less than 'aaa'.

SuperBasic defines this type of comparison as a 'type 2' comparison and rather unhelpfully describes it as 'case independent' in the 'string comparisons' section of the 'Concepts' User Guide. We'd call it 'case dependent'.

Another type of comparison is used for SuperBasic's unusual '==' operator. When used on numbers this means 'almost equal'. When used on strings, it acts as a 'type 3' comparison. 'Type 3' is described as 'case dependent' in the QL User Guide, but we would describe it as 'case independent'.

In a type 3 comparison, the case of a letter is genuinely unimportant. For example:

```
10      IF "aPPLES" == "Apples" THEN
20      PRINT "true"
30      ELSE
40      PRINT "untrue"
50      END IF
```

will print 'true'. This is extremely handy when it comes to evaluating input. Take that standard question, 'Do you want to run the program again?' Most Basics handle it rather like this:

```
500     INPUT "Again? ";r$
510     IF r$ = "Y" OR IF r$ = "y" THEN GOTO start of program
```

In SuperBasic, this simple version will do:

```
500 INPUT "Again? ";r$
510 IF r$ == "Y" THEN GOTO start of program
```

Of course, proper program structuring will mean that your main program loop enables you to replace the GOTO with a more elegant command sequence!

The only SuperBasic string operator which currently uses type 3 comparisons is '==', so there is no way of discovering how numbers would be handled in type 3 operations. The manual suggests that they would be handled as they are in type 2 comparisons.

The final type of string comparison used in SuperBasic is a 'type 1' comparison. This too is case independent – and this time the manual gets it right! Type 1 comparisons will, therefore, compare letters exactly as do type 3 comparisons. However, they differ when it comes to numbers. Numbers are evaluated digit by digit (like conventional Basic string comparisons of numbers) and not as a whole.

Type 1 comparison is used only for the INSTR operator, so we must use that operator to demonstrate it in action. (Many people would call INSTR a function rather than an operator, but the SuperBasic manual disagrees.) INSTR returns the position of a given substring within a given string or returns zero if the substring is not found in the string.

PRINT "11" INSTR "111AAA"

will return '1': the first two digits of '111' are matched with '11'.

PRINT "RED" INSTR "occurred"

will return '6': the capital letter string is matched with the sixth letter onwards of the lower-case string.

10

Aspects of SuperBasic

We don't have space in this book to look at every aspect of SuperBasic in exhaustive detail. In this chapter we've chosen to select a variety of particularly interesting or awkward features of the language to explore and exemplify. The features covered are in alphabetical order: the index will help you to find your way around them.

We look here at aspects of the QDOS operating system that are accessible from SuperBasic, but not at lower-level programming issues, which are covered later in the book. The main graphics commands are covered in Chapter 11.

THE CLOCK AND OTHER TIMING FUNCTIONS

Several functions are provided to allow you to manipulate the QL's internal real time clock. Note that the clock is not battery-backed and that you must use these functions to set it whenever you turn on the computer.

The most fundamental of these is SDATE. This allows you to set the time in years, months, days, hours, minutes and seconds: a list that should be exhaustive enough for anyone. Note that you must give all SDATE's parameters in numeric form: e.g. 1 not Jan. The day is the day of the month, of course, not the day of the week. Hours are given using a twenty-four hour clock. Do include every parameter: in FB Basic, failure to define a parameter could crash the computer.

If you do not set the clock using SDATE it will still contain a time, but this will, of course, be incorrect.

ADATE allows you to adjust the clock once you've set it. This should only rarely be necessary, as you are not likely to keep the computer running for long enough for the timing to become inaccurate! ADATE works in seconds, from the time currently held by the clock. You can of course also use SDATE to correct the time subsequent to initial setting.

DATE$ returns the time from the clock in a fixed string format which is described in the manual. You can, instead, get the date in a numeric format using the DATE function, but note that this doesn't provide a number that refers directly to the numbers you input using SDATE. Instead, it counts the time elapsed from the base time of the clock, the start of 1961. (Actual dates given appear to vary at random around this date.) You'll find that the least significant digit of DATE changes only slowly: it's no good for counting seconds elapsed, though you can use it to count longer intervals if you wish.

It is not explained any too clearly in the manual, but using DATE$ with a number, as if you were slicing the string, causes the interpreter to treat DATE$ rather like DATE. So 'PRINT DATE$(1)' does not return the first digit of the string DATE$: instead, it returns the DATE '1961 Jan 01 00:00:01'. (Try it!) This is not a particularly helpful function: you will probably find it far handier to perform normal string-slicing operations on DATE$, so as to extract (for instance) just the month. It's possible to do this by putting the value of DATE$ into another variable, like this:

```
10    d$ = DATE$
20    PRINT d$(6 TO 8)
```

Allowing for significant spaces, digits 6 to 8 contain the name of the month.

DAY$ is rather different, because while slicing DATE$ using a second variable will give you the day of the month, DAY$ will give you the day of the week (Sun, Mon, Tues etc.). This again works in a way which is not quite what you might expect. PRINT DAY$ gives you the current day of the week, providing you've set the clock correctly. PRINT DAY$(DATE) does the same. PRINT DAY$(1) returns 'Sun', but this is not particularly helpful, since the following little program:

```
10    FOR n = 1 TO 7
20    PRINT DAY$ (n)
30    END FOR n
```

simply returns 'Sun' seven times! DAY$(n) is actually related, in a way which is not intuitively obvious, to the floating point number held in DATE.

While we are on the subject of timing, note the PAUSE command. In many cases, this will be a more convenient alternative to an empty loop when you want to slow down program execution. Notice, though, that unlike an empty loop PAUSE will continue program execution as soon as a key is pressed.

Finally, here's a program that sets up a timer for you, using not the awkward DATE command, but DATE$ with a second variable (or rather, two second variables). It counts the time elapsed in seconds from a base time of zero, continuing (unlike PAUSE) to count as the program is executed. You could use this to time repeats of a loop, much as you can in BBC Basic with the TIME function, and this program gives a simple example.

```
10      MODE 8
20      WINDOW 512, 256, 0, 0: CLS
30      d$ = DATE$
40      REPeat loop
50      INK RND(1 TO 7)
60      AT 9,15: PRINT "CHOOSE YOUR ANSWER NOW"
70      d1$ = DATE$
80      IF d1$(19 TO 20)>d$(19 TO 20) + 20 THEN EXIT LOOP
90      END REPeat loop
100     CLS: AT 2,15: INPUT "NOW GIVE THE ANSWER
PLEASE"; a$
```

Substring 19 to 20 is the seconds part of the DATE$ string and SuperBasic coercion means that you can treat these two digits as a number, as we do in line 60. The '20' added to d$ simply counts twenty seconds; amend this number to count for any other time interval. We use the version of the AT command provided in the early FB version of SuperBasic: in later versions the row and column numbers must be switched.

COLOUR

Colour handling is yet another area in which SuperBasic's unusual commands can have sometimes unexpected results.

In order to understand how the QL handles colour, you may find it helpful to think in terms of colour registers. Three colour registers hold the paper, strip and ink colours for each window in operation. The PAPER, STRIP and INK commands are used to alter their contents. All three commands can be used with a channel number to identify the window involved, or without to affect the default channel.

All three registers in the set work in an identical fashion, with the lower three bits (0 to 2) allocated to the main colour code, the next three bits (3 to 5) to the contrast colour code, and the top two bits (6 and 7) to the stipple pattern. The codes used are summarized under 'colour' in the 'Concepts' section of the manual, so we will not repeat them here.

Note that you can select a contrast colour and stipple pattern for an ink if you wish, and write with a stippled effect. This has limited applications, but you may find it useful for special effects, especially when printing larger sized characters or when producing graphics.

Some graphic commands have a colour argument and in these the same pattern of bits are used. Selecting a colour (e.g. for a BLOCK) does not change the contents of the colour registers.

Note that though you can change the colour registers using PAPER, INK and STRIP, you don't directly affect the screen display with these commands. It's only when you give commands that directly affect the screen (e.g. printing, panning or scrolling) that the new register contents will be apparent.

When setting a colour register, you can take either of two approaches. You can set all three sections separately, by giving three arguments, or you can set all three simultaneously with one argument. The size of your first argument determines which you do: if it's over seven, then the argument will affect the entire byte.

Though you can set the main and contrast colours without affecting the stipple pattern, you can't use two arguments, one to set the two colours and one to set the stipple pattern. Your first argument will set all three sections of the register or just the first one.

Note that there's no such thing as a blank stipple pattern: all four values (0, 1, 2 and 3) refer to a pattern which shows both main and contrast colours. Of course, you can set a 'no contrast' pattern simply by designating a main colour only: e.g. PAPER 7 will do this. Designating two colours (e.g. PAPER 7,2) automatically calls up the default stipple pattern. Curiously, this isn't the '0' value pattern, but the '3' value one. You can check this by trying these short programs, which make use of two of the separate windows visible in Mode 4.

```
10    MODE 4
20    PAPER#1, 16: CLS#1
30    PAPER#2, 0,2: CLS#1
```

The statements in lines 20 and 30 both set the main colour to 0 and the contrast to 2, but in window 1 the stipple pattern becomes 0, while in 30 it remains the default 3. This version, on the other hand, produces the same colour/pattern in both windows:

```
10    MODE 4
20    PAPER#1, 16: CLS#1
30    PAPER#2, 0,2,3: CLS#1
```

Stipples are useful in mode 8 as well as in mode 4. In mode 4 they don't altogether make up for the lack of a blue element: it isn't possible to synthesize bluey colours out of red, white and green, however hard you try with stipples. In mode 8, the patterns are a little more visible, but you can still produce convincing shades of orange, grey and so on.

Though it's only possible to produce a two-shade stipple effect, you can make a screen background with more than two colours by combining a stipple with a regular line pattern drawn using graphic commands. Of course, the graphic commands use the graphic co-ordinate system (default scale 100 vertically) which lives a little uneasily with the pixel numbering system. It helps if you align the two using the SCALE command:

SCALE 255,0,0

Drawing horizontal lines across the screen at suitable intervals (e.g. 2 or 4) then works fine. Figure 10.1 lists a program that provides a simple illustration of the effect you can get. This version uses a stippled ink to make a four-colour pattern with the minimum of fuss.

If you misalign the lines with the background (as it is all too easy to do when drawing lines vertically, if you misjudge the horizontal equivalent of your scale) then you can produce some interesting irregular striped effects. Figure 10.2 lists a program which uses this variation in a simple graphic display.

The program listed in Figure 10.3 is another variation, which uses diagonal stippled lines on the same basic background to produce an attractive moire design. Figure 10.4 extends the same idea, making a very pretty 'rainbow' pattern.

Figure 10.1 Coloured Background

```
100 REMark coloured background
110 MODE 8
120 WINDOW 512,256,0,0
130 PAPER 5,1,3: CLS
140 SCALE 255,0,0
150 INK 4,2,1
160 FOR horiz = 0 TO 254 STEP 2
170 LINE 0,horiz TO 511,horiz
180 END FOR horiz
```

Figure 10.2 Marquee

```
100 REMark marquee
110 MODE 8
120 WINDOW 511,255,0,0
130 PAPER 6,2,3:CLS
140 SCALE 220,0,0
150 INK 1,4,3
160 FOR vert = 1 TO 380 STEP 2
170 LINE vert,0 TO vert,249
180 END FOR vert
190 CSIZE 3,1: PAPER 5: INK 1
200 AT 10,5: PRINT "Marquee"
```

Figure 10.3 Moire Pattern

```
100 REMark moire pattern
110 MODE 8
120 WINDOW 512,256,0,0
130 PAPER 5,1,3: CLS
140 SCALE 255,0,0
150 INK 4,2,1
160 FOR horiz = 0 TO 255 STEP 2
170 LINE 0,0 TO 375,horiz
175 LINE 375,255 TO 0,horiz
180 END FOR horiz
```

Figure 10.4 Moire Rainbow

```
100 REMark moire rainbow
110 MODE 8
120 WINDOW 512,256,0,0
130 PAPER 5,1,3: CLS
140 SCALE 255,-180,0
150 INK 4,2,1
160 FOR p = 0 TO 1.575 STEP 1.5E-2
170 rainbow
180 END FOR p
190 FOR p = 4.725 TO 6.3 STEP 1.5E-2
200 rainbow
210 END FOR p
1000 DEFine PROCedure rainbow
1010 LINE 50*SIN(p),50*COS(p) TO 150*SIN(p),150*COS(p)
1020 END DEFine rainbow
```

Using the PAPER command with pans and scrolls

A new colour of PAPER is introduced not only when clearing the screen or window, but also when panning or scrolling it. You can make use of this feature to produce some interesting graphic effects. Panning while introducing a new paper colour (even a plain one) is a little jerky, but scrolling is admirably smooth.

The listing in Figure 10.5 gives an example. It's a very loose adaptation of a well-known BBC graphics program.

Figure 10.5 Horizon

```
10 REMark horizon - graphic display
20 MODE 8
30 WINDOW 512,256,0,0
40 PAPER 4:CLS
50 SCALE 100,-75,-100
60 INK 2
70 FOR p = 1.575 TO 4.725 STEP 4.5E-2
80 LINE 0,0 TO 200*SIN(p), 200*COS(p)
90 END FOR p
100 PAPER 1
110 FOR dip = 1 TO 100
120 SCROLL 1
130 END FOR dip
```

The STRIP command

Note a mistake in the early version of the QL User Guide. This suggested that STRIP came into play when OVER 1 was selected. In fact, it's OVER 0 which is the vital command.

STRIP designates the background colour that's used for printing in this mode. In fact, the effect of STRIP seems to be just like the effect of selecting a new PAPER colour, so STRIP will only be used if you wish to preserve the paper colour while you print a contrast strip of text.

The RECOL command

A final curious feature of QL colour handling is the RECOL command, which allows you to turn pixels on screen to different colours. RECOL is oddly and confusingly explained in the early editions of the QL User Guide, so we amplify its use here.

RECOL is followed by eight parameters, which specify the new colours to be given to the eight colours available in Mode 8. Though the manual suggests that the list of parameters starts with blue, it does in fact start with black as you might expect. Here's a sample program that shows its effect:

```
10      MODE 8
20      PAPER 0: CLS
30      INK 1
40      PRINT "TESTING"
50      RECOL 0,2,2,3,4,5,6,7
```

Colour 1 (blue) is changed to code 2 (red) and the blue word on screen duly changes to a red word.

You can use RECOL in Mode 4, but only every second argument affects its use. However, you must still provide the same eight numbers.

Using RECOL repeatedly produces strange results. You might expect this program to produce a word that changes colour ten times:

```
10      MODE 8
20      PAPER 0: CLS
30      INK 1
40      PRINT "TESTING"
50      FOR switch = 1 TO 10
60      RECOL 0, RND(1 TO 7),2,3,4,5,6,7
70      END FOR switch
```

but not so! Once the blue word is re-coloured to a different colour (which we'll call *a*), it will only be re-coloured again if a change of colour is specified for *a*, *not* if a change is specified for its original colour.

One disappointing feature of RECOL is that it works very slowly. The command changes every byte of screen memory containing the colour(s) in question and you can see its operation as a visible sweeping effect down the screen if you attempt to re-colour a large area. It's best to use the command only for short amounts of text or for small areas of graphic foreground.

This makes it clear that RECOL doesn't change a key register that indicates what colour, say, the 'G' bytes in screen memory (see page 161, and the 'memory map' concept in the User Guide) will appear on screen: instead it has a direct effect on screen memory. It's a pity that it is so. The BBC's superficially similar logical colour command does work on a register basis (as does Atari's colour change command). On these machines this means that you can select any combination of colours for high resolution and you can instantaneously switch areas of the screen from colour to colour. On the BBC, you can set all colours used in a mode to the background colour before drawing 'invisibly', then animate your image by setting each colour to the foreground in turn. This isn't possible on the QL. RECOL can be used only retrospectively, *after* you've drawn your image: it can't affect the basic palette of colours available to you.

DATA HANDLING

Though the QL has apparently conventional READ, DATA and RESTORE statements, there are some unusual features to them, which we look at here.

When data are read from DATA statements, the QL will perform its normal coercion where necessary in order to fit the data to the variables provided. It's possible to put numbers between inverted commas and still read them correctly into either floating point or integer variables, like this:

```
10      FOR loop = 1 TO 4
20      READ n%
30      PRINT n%
40      END FOR loop
50      DATA "1.1", "2.2", "3.3", "4.4"
```

As string data can also be enclosed in inverted commas, it may be a good idea to get in the habit of entering all your data this way. You can then read it into any kind of variable you wish! It's possible to read numbers that are not enclosed in inverted commas into string variables, but non-numeric data *must* be enclosed in inverted commas.

SuperBasic's RESTORE feature works in an unusual way. Data is not automatically RESTOREd at the start of a normal program run, so if you try to run the program above twice in succession, you will come up with an 'out of data' error the second time. The QL User Guide suggests that this could be useful if you want to use several sets of data in the same program. We feel this to be rather doubtful: on the rare occasions when you do want to use different data sets, it would be as well to do so specifically, perhaps selecting one with a routine like this:

```
10      INPUT "SELECT A DATA SET";d
```

```
20      SELect ON d
30      = 1: RESTORE n1
40      = 2: RESTORE n2
etc.
50      END SELect
```

On other occasions when you plan to use data statements in your program, you should ensure that you put a specific RESTORE near the start of the listing.

If you wish, you can also use EOF as a RESTORE pointer, like this:

```
IF EOF THEN RESTORE
```

There are also some unusual features in SuperBasic's handling of variable and array initializing and clearing and we discuss these below.

ERROR HANDLING

One of the weaknesses of the early versions of SuperBasic is the absence of any error-trapping command. 'WHEN ERROR' appears in the list of SuperBasic keywords, but it is not implemented. This means that the onus is on the programmer to ensure that the program is as carefully error-trapped as possible. Even with careful error-trapping you can't duplicate all the functions of 'WHEN ERROR' easily, but you can go a long way in the right direction.

Here are some general hints and ideas for debugging and error-trapping your programs, making use of the features that SuperBasic provides.

Debugging Programs

When a program stops running with an error message, through a STOP command, or because the end of the listing is reached, then SuperBasic will not return to its original state. All stacks and pointers will remain intact and this means – for example – that if the program was in the middle of executing a procedure when stopped, it will remain as though in mid-procedure until you give a command that resets its status.

You can, of course, check on the current values of program variables after execution has stopped in this way, using ordinary immediate commands like 'PRINT x'. (Do not amend the program listing, if you wish to CONTinue the program from the same point.) If the program was in mid-procedure, however, local variables may be in force, and you cannot find the value of global variables with the same names in this way.

If you wish to reset SuperBasic to its original status, the CLEAR command can be used to do so. This would be particularly handy if – for example – you wanted to restart the program from a different point with a GOTO, a process which might otherwise cause errors (see also the notes below on RUN). In other circumstances, it will be helpful to continue from the status in which the program stopped. You can continue from the statement that reported the error, perhaps first using immediate commands to change a variable value so that the original error is not repeated (use RETRY for this) or from the next statement in the program (CONTinue).

Note that though CLEAR will clear variable space, it will *not* reset the system to its original state. It will not change screen colours or attributes, for instance, and it will not close open channels. You should ensure that the initial phase of your program *specifically* sets all screen attributes you want for the program (including foreground and background colours, windows, character size), or the program may run differently when repeated. (See also page 149, which presents a series of short programs to set system attributes.)

Re-running a program which OPENs channels (e.g. to a printer or microdrive) when they have been opened previously and not been closed will cause an error. So, unfortunately, will an attempt to CLOSE a channel which is not actually open: and there is no way in SuperBasic to check to see which channels are open. If you do not wish to resort to machine code to get round this problem, the best solution is to ensure that before re-running a program after an error has stopped it, you automatically run the section of the program that closes channels (normally the closing section) first. GOTO *n* (where *n* is the line number that introduces the channel-closing routine) will do so. As GOTO is strictly redundant in SuperBasic, the language also lets you use RUN for this purpose. RUN *n* is broadly similar to GOTO *n* in that it does not clear variables and arrays. For instance, take this very short program:

```
10    DIM b(9,9)
20    PRINT b(9,9)
30    PRINT "END OF PROGRAM"
```

Once you've RUN the program once, dimensioning the *b* array, you can either GOTO 20 or RUN 20 without causing an error message. (This will also remind you that number arrays are automatically filled with zeros.) Number variables in contrast are *not* automatically given a value of zero, and 'PRINT b' when you have not allocated a value for *b* will produce a '*', though not an error.

Note, incidentially, that a simple RUN (i.e. from the first line of a program) will not clear variables either. This is unusual in Basics. Try running this short program repeatedly to test this:

```
10    PRINT b
20     b = b + 10
```

First assign a value to *b* with an immediate statement like '*b* = 5'.

You can, of course, re-dimension arrays on successive runs of a program without causing any error.

As a summary of the difficulties these interacting features can cause, you may like to play around with this short listing:

```
10    testproc
20     b = 8
```

```
30       PRINT b
40       b = b + 9
50       STOP
100      DEFine PROCedure testproc
110      LOCal b
120      b = 14
140      PRINT b
150      STOP
160      END DEFine testproc
```

Try variations on RUN, RUN 20/30/40 (or any other lines), GOTO 20/30/40, CONTinue, etc., to see what different values you obtain for *b*.

Finally, note that you can clear away much of the confusion by using CLEAR, not just as an immediate statement, but at the start of each program.

Checking Input

One particular task of any programmer is to ensure that all input is acceptable. The program should not crash if the user inadvertently enters a number when a letter is required or *vice versa*. If a number or letter is outside the permissible range, the program should catch this error and request a new input.

SuperBasic again offers some useful features, not least among which is its coercion facility which enables you to convert strings into numbers (and perform other similar operations) without undue formality. Normally, for instance, this sequence will cause a problem:

```
10       INPUT "GIVE ME A NUMBER";n
20       PRINT n
```

If the user inputs a letter rather than a number, any Basic – including QL SuperBasic – will register this as an error. But in SuperBasic, you can get round the problem neatly with a procedure like this:

```
10       numget: m = n
20       PRINT m
30       STOP
1000     DEFine PROCedure numget
1010     LOCAL n$, digit, bad
1020     REPeat check
1030     INPUT "GIVE ME A NUMBER"; n$
1040     bad = 0
1050     FOR digit = 1 TO LEN(n$)
1060     IF CODE(n$(digit)) >57 THEN bad = 1
1070     END FOR digit
1080     IF bad = 0 THEN EXIT check
1090     PRINT "NOT A NUMBER, PLEASE TRY AGAIN"
1100     END REPeat check
```

```
1110      n = n$
1120      END DEFine numget
```

The number variable *n* is not local to the procedure: it is used to return the number. You can assign successive values of *n*, fetched through this procedure, to the variables you will be using elsewhere in the program.

This procedure will check an input string to see if it is a number of any permissible length, catching letters (though not, admittedly, some awkward symbols) anywhere in the string. It will reject combinations like '3W3' as well as straightforward words like 'TEN'. Note on line 1060 that the CODE function can be used with sliced strings to test each element of the string in turn: it's not confined to the first element of a string as the User Guide suggests. Code 57 is the code for nine, the highest number code. As a full stop (decimal point) has a code of 46, the routine will pass decimal numbers.

Simpler routines based on this procedure can be used to check to see if a number or letter is within a permissible range, using either LEN to check the length of a string, straightforward number comparison to check the value of a number, or CODE to see if the characters input come within a fixed range (e.g. the letters A to F).

The 'REMAINDER' part of the SELect command can also be useful in this latter capacity: see page 127.

If you've used the Archive programming language, you will have noticed the useful function which turns upper case letters into lower case, easing the task of checking for input answers. Unfortunately there's no similar built-in function in SuperBasic: though the '==' string comparison does work on a case-independent basis, solving many of your problems (see pages 130 onwards). As an alternative when the use of this command isn't appropriate, here's a second validation-type procedure which checks to see if letters are upper-case and, if so, turns them into their lower-case equivalents. You can easily reverse it if you wish, to produce upper-case letters only.

```
10        PRINT "GIVE THE ANSWER NOW"
20        turnlower: a$ = z$
30        IF a$ = "yellow" THEN PRINT "RIGHT"
40        END
1000      DEFine PROCedure turnlower
1010      LOCal c, digit
1020      INPUT z$
1030      FOR digit = 1 TO LEN(z$)
1040      c = CODE(z$(digit))
1050      IF c > 64 AND c < 91 THEN
1060      c = c + 32
1070      z$(digit) = CHR$(c)
1080      END IF
```

> 1090   END FOR digit
> 1100   END DEFine turnlower

NUMBER CONVERSION

One omission in SuperBasic is any command for the inter-conversion of hexadecimal (i.e. base 16), decimal (base 10) and binary (base 2) numbers. It's often useful to be able to convert hex into decimal and *vice versa*. Memory addresses and instruction codes all too often come in an unwanted form and you may need to use hex numbers with an assembler and decimal numbers when pokeing numbers into memory from Basic. Converting binary into decimal is useful if you want to define a new character font from Basic or to poke screen memory. Converting binary into hex can also be useful, but it's not difficult to do by hand.

Figure 10.6 Hex to Decimal Conversion

```
10 REMark hex to decimal conversion
20 REPeat loop
30 INPUT "give hex. no. (or q to end) ";h$
40 IF h$=="q" THEN EXIT loop
50 l%=LEN(h$)
60 t = 0
70 FOR z = 1 TO l%
80 IF CODE(h$(z))>=65 THEN
90 makeno
110 ELSE
120 makeint
130 END IF
140 t = t+(h%*16^(l%-z))
150 END FOR z
160 PRINT "Decimal = ";t
170 END REPeat loop
1000 DEFine PROCedure makeno
1010 h% = CODE(h$(z))-55
1020 END DEFine makeno
1100 DEFine PROCedure makeint
1110 h% = h$(z)
1120 END DEFine makeint
```

The three SuperBasic programs presented here (Figs 10.6, 10.7 and 10.8) convert, respectively, hexadecimal numbers into decimal, decimal into hex and binary into decimal. They are presented as self-contained programs, and will loop around repeatedly requesting a number from the user and printing the equivalent in the different base numbering system. You can easily adapt them as procedures for use in a longer program. Make the number to be converted a parameter you pass to the procedure; e.g. hex(n) might call the procedure named hex which converts decimal number n into a hex number.

The programs have been written to display some of the structuring features of SuperBasic and in consequence are a little longer than they might otherwise be.

Notes on the listings

Hex to Decimal Converter
Converting hex to decimal is usually tricky in Basic, because of the difficulty of switching between a hex string that might include the letters A to F as well as numbers 0 to 9, and the integer variables needed to perform the arithmetic of the conversion. Here SuperBasic's coercion feature comes in handy. We slice the string containing the original hex number and treat it like an array containing individual digits, then convert some of the digits directly into number variables.

The hex number is input to a string variable, h$. Integer variable 1% holds the length of the hex string and is used as a loop counter controlling the loop that deals with each digit in turn. In SuperBasic h$(z) indicates the zth element of the string h$: there is no need to use the equivalent of a Microsoft Basic MID$ function.

Obtaining the CODE of h$(z) distinguishes the letter elements of the hex string from the numbers. The code for A is 65, B is 66, and so on: so only digits with a code of sixty-five or more are letters. The procedure 'makeno' subtracts fifty-five from the code to turn each letter into its numeric equivalent: e.g. A = 65, less 55 = 10, the decimal equivalent of hex A.

Figure 10.7 Decimal to Hex Conversion

```
10 REMark decimal to hex conversion
20 REPeat loop
30 INPUT "give decimal no. (or 0 to end) ";d
40 IF d = 0 THEN EXIT loop
50 1% = 7
60 hex$ = ""
70 REPeat digit
80 n% = INT(d/(16^1%))
90 hexdigit
100 hex$ = hex$ & d$
110 1% = 1% - 1
120 IF 1% = -1 THEN EXIT digit
130 END REPeat digit
140 PRINT "Hexadecimal = ";hex$
150 END REPeat loop
1000 DEFine PROCedure hexdigit
1010 d = d-(n%*(16^1%))
1020 IF n% < 10 THEN
1030 d$ = n%
1040 ELSE
1050 d$ = CHR$(n% + 55)
1060 END IF
1070 END DEFine hexdigit
```

Procedure 'makeint' is even simpler and simply coerces each number element of the hex string into an integer variable.

Line 130 multiplies the decimal equivalent of each hex digit by the appropriate power of sixteen and adds the result to the 'running total' variable, *t*. We do not use an integer variable for *t*, as the value of *t* might exceed the limit for integer variables, 32,768.

Decimal to Hex Converter

This program works in reverse, putting the decimal number into the numeric variable *d* and building up the hex equivalent in the string variable h$.

The program will generate hex numbers up to eight digits in length correctly. This will cover the full range of memory address on the QL. Variable 1% initially holds the largest power of sixteen that might appear in the number, seven.

Line 40 divides the total number by successively reducing powers of sixteen, in order to obtain each digit from left to right. It might look neater to use the DIV function; however, this results in an arithmetic overflow for large numbers, while the statement we give works correctly throughout the range we handle. *n%* contains the decimal equivalent of the hex digit: it will always be fifteen or less.

The procedure hexdigit handles some general housekeeping, as well as converting *n%* into its hex equivalent. Line 1010 subtracts *n%*, multiplied by the appropriate power of sixteen, from *d*. The rest of the procedure does the converse of the 'makeint' and 'makeno' procedures in the hex to decimal program, using the CHR$ function to convert a code equivalent into a letter.

The result will be an eight-digit hex number, with leading zeros where necessary.

Binary to Decimal Converter

This is an even shorter program, which takes a fixed eight digit long binary number and produces the decimal equivalent. Line 70 multiplies each successive digit by the appropriate power of two, working from left to right; variable *a%* (total will never exceed the integer limit, so integers are used for accuracy and speed) holds the running total.

RESETTING THE SYSTEM

One slightly awkward feature of the QL is the fact that simply NEWing a program doesn't restore the default window arrangement, character sizes and so on. A change of mode will clear all windows, but not restore the default window arrangement. There's no simple RESET command, so it's only possible to restore the machine to its default screen arrangement by performing a hardware reset, which is not always a desirable choice.

The best solution is to set up a short utility procedure which will reset the

Figure 10.8 Binary to Decimal Conversion

```
10 REMark binary to decimal conversion
20 REPeat loop
30 INPUT "give binary no. (8 digits) or q to end) ";b$
40 IF b$ == "q" THEN EXIT loop
50 a% = 0
60 FOR d = 1 TO 8
70 n% = b$(d)*2^(8 - d)
80 a% = a% + n%
90 END FOR d
100 PRINT "decimal = ";a%
110 END REPeat loop
```

system in software. If you do this in machine code, you may be able to load it as a resident procedure in the way we describe in Chapter 17. It will then survive NEWs, and will only be dislodged by a reset. In Basic, it will need to be saved as a separate program and loaded from microdrive before you run it.

Here are two short programs which set up the default screen arrangements for mode 4 and 8 screens. Of course, if you do not like the default screen arrangement you could select the type of screen arrangement that you find most suitable instead. For instance, you might want to increase the depth of channel 0's window, and reduce the channel 1 and 2 windows accordingly.

```
(a)  Mode 4 (high resolution):
1000    DEFine PROCedure reset__hr
1010    WINDOW#0, 512,56,0,200
1020    WINDOW#1, 256,200,256,0
1030    WINDOW # 2, 256,200,0,0
1040    PAPER#0,0: PAPER#1,2: PAPER#2,6
1050    INK#0,2: INK#1,6: INK#2,2
1060    FOR n = 0 TO 2: CLS#n: CSIZE#n,0,0
1070    END DEFine reset__hr
(b)  Mode 8 (low resolution):
1000    DEFine PROCedure reset__lr
1010    WINDOW#1,512,256,0,0: PAPER#1,0: CLS#1
1020    WINDOW#0,512,56,0,200
1030    FOR n = 1 TO 2: WINDOW#n, 500,200,12,0
1040    PAPER#0,0: PAPER#1,2: PAPER#2,1
1050    FOR n = 0 TO 2: INK#n,7: CSIZE#n,2,0
1060    CLS#1
1070    END DEFine reset__lr
```

WINDOWS

On screen, a window equals a channel. Each screen channel open has a window attached to it and when you open more channels they too will have windows attached to them. The windows can (and will) overlap: that doesn't matter, though it may make your output messy. Note that you *can't* use the windowing feature to set up screen overlays: there's only one screen memory immediately accessible from Basic and all the windows write to the same screen. Clear any window and you'll clear the designated area entirely, including screen output produced via that channel *and* screen output produced via other channels that is in the window area. You certainly won't retrieve any earlier output in this way.

On start-up, three windows are accessible: the channel 0, 1 and 2 windows. Their functions and positions are described in detail in the User Guide, and we will not repeat them here. You can change the size of any of these windows simply by using the window command with the channel number. To make the window for channel #0 cover the entire screen, for instance:

WINDOW#0, 512,256,0,0

Other windows are opened by opening screen channels: the OPEN command, used to designate a screen channel, includes a window statement. This statement opens channel/window #3, for example:

OPEN#3, CON-50x50a0x0__32

Once you've opened other windows in this way, you can change their size by using the WINDOW command as above.

Windows can be closed by closing the channel to which they refer. You can't remove a window without closing the channel, though you can of course clear it to the background colour and make it unobstrusive.

Each window has its own set of paper and ink colours, its own screen attributes, its own cursor position. In order to alter these effects within the window, you must, of course, remember to give the correct window/channel number in your statement. To change the ink in window 3, for example, you need a statement like:

INK#3, 7

The fact that the operating system holds in memory a set of attributes for each window can be very useful. It's quite feasible, for instance, for you to set up fifteen all-screen windows, each with different attributes, for use in a complex application. Instead of constantly adjusting the cursor position or the ink colour, all you need to do is to change your channel reference in order to get a different type of output. Figure 10.9 lists a short program that uses some of these features to effect: there's a more ambitious one in our discussion of turtle graphics on page 159.

The fact that windows scroll and pan independently will often be useful. By setting up a small window to hold captions, request input or do other general

Figure 10.9 Window Demo Number 1

```
10 REMark window demo number 1
20 MODE 8
30 FOR n = 0 TO 2: WINDOW£n, 512,256,0,0
40 OPEN£3, con_512x256a0x0
50 FOR n = 0 TO 3 : INK£n,n+2
60 CSIZE£0, 2,0: CSIZE£1, 2,1: CSIZE£3,3,0: CSIZE£3, 3,1
70 FOR n = 0 TO 3: PAPER£n,0: CLS£n
80 FOR n = 0 TO 3: AT£n,0,n*3
90 FOR n = 0 TO 3:PRINT£n, "Channel ";n
```

Figure 10.10 Bermuda Triangle

```
10 REMark bermuda triangle
20 MODE 8
30 WINDOW£1, 512,256,0,0
40 PAPER£1,1: CLS£1
50 WINDOW£2,256,256,256,0
60 PAPER£2,1
70 INK£2,2
80 FILL£2,1
90 LINE£2,25,70 TO 60,50 TO 10,50 TO 25,70
100 INK£2,5
110 FILL£2,1
120 LINE£2,7,45 TO 63,45 TO 60,35 TO 10,35 TO 7,45
130 FILL£2,1
140 INK£2,0
150 LINE£2,30,50 TO 35,50 TO 35,45 TO 30,45 TO 30,50
160 FOR float=1 TO 25:PAN£2,-10
```

tasks, you can prevent this kind of screen output from corrupting the rest of your display. Channel#0, with its window across the bottom of the screen, is already well set up for many purposes; we use it in our function plotter program in Chapter 11, for instance.

Sometimes for this kind of function, it's useful to have 'invisible' windows. Figure 10.10 lists a short program that 'loses' a ship in mid-screen. Unfortunately, scrolls and pans won't wrap on the QL: your left-hand picture won't re-appear on the right, and you can't reverse the program and restore the data that's scrolled off the screen. This limits the scope of this type of activity slightly.

In other functions, of course, visible windows are preferable and it is useful to use either a different background colour or the 'border' command to differentiate them. Many graphic routines work best, for example, if you set up a square window in the middle of the screen, turning the rest of the screen to a plain background. We do this in some of the programs in Chapter 11.

A transparent border will 'freeze' the text beneath it and you can use this feature if you wish to set up a 'title' to your window. Note that the border will be just as wide horizontally as it is vertically, though! We did this in the short program reproduced as Figure 10.11. Though this technique works fine for this, for a serious textual program with a title you may find a better technique would be to print the title and then simply redefine the window to remove the title area from it.

Figure 10.11 Border Title Demo

```
10 REMark border title demo
20 MODE 4
30 WINDOW 512,256,0,0
40 PAPER 0:CLS
50 WINDOW£2,200,150,50,30
60 PAPER£2,5: CLS£2
70 CSIZE£2,3,1
80 PRINT£2, "window demo"
90 CSIZE£2,2,0
100 BORDER£2,20
110 PRINT£2, "this is a"!"demo"!"of"!"how"!"borders"!"can"!"be"!"created"!"using
"!"the"!"border"!"command."!"As"!"the"!"screen"!"scrolls"!"the"!"border"!"and"!"
title"!"remains"!"unchanged"!
999 WINDOW£2,511,256,0,0
1000 CSIZE£2,0,0
```

11

Graphics on the QL

QL SuperBasic has a wide variety of graphics commands. In this chapter we look at some of them and develop some useful programs which take advantage of their features.

As the User Guide explains, the graphics co-ordinate system is quite different from the pixel numbering system on the QL. There are several important points to note.

(1)   Commands which use the *pixel numbering system* are:
WINDOW
BLOCK
CURSOR (with two parameters)
One command, AT, uses a character row/column co-ordinate based on the pixel numbering system. Other graphic-type commands involving specific locations or distances (including the turtle graphics MOVE) use the graphics numbering system.

(2)   When specifying a window size and position, you use the pixel numbering system with reference to the entire screen. Other pixel numbering commands work on a window basis only. The graphics system always scales a specific window. (A detailed discussion of window operation, with the emphasis on text handling, is in Chapter 10.)

(3)   In the pixel system, there are 256 pixels vertically, and either 256

or 512 horizontally. The size of pixels never changes (though horizontals pixels are handled in pairs in Mode 8). So if a window has a pixel width of 150, there will always be 150 pixel positions across it. In the graphics system, an arbitrary vertical scale is set, with a default value of 100 from the top to bottom of the window in use. If the window stretches right down the screen, each scale point will equal about 2.56 pixels. The horizontal scale is such that lines are drawn to be roughly equal in both directions. So in a square window, the horizontal scale will also be (by default) from 0 to 100. If the window stretches right across the screen, there will be around 175 scale points horizontally. It's difficult to fix an exact number, because the entire screen doesn't fit on to our display!

(4)   Naturally only pixels can be plotted in either mode, so when using the graphics scaling features, the actual points plotted will be the pixels most nearly corresponding in location to the scale points given. This can give rise to unusual effects, as we showed when discussing colour masks in Chapter 10.

(5)   While the pixel numbering system starts from 0,0 in the top left-hand corner of the screen or the window in question, the graphics scaling system numbers (by default) from 0,0 in the *bottom* left-hand corner of the window.

(6)   Using the graphics SCALE command it's possible to move the position of the origin within a window. We look at this feature later in the chapter. It's not possible to alter the pixel co-ordinate system in this way: pixel position 0,0 will always be at the top left of a window.

(7)   Using graphics commands and the graphics scaling system, it is possible to designate plot points *outside* the window in use. Though such points will of course not be displayed, lines drawn from them to a point inside the window will be correctly reproduced. This is a particularly handy feature when drawing graphs, as no error will be reported if you specify a point to be plotted outside the window. In contrast, there will be an error reported if you attempt to specify an AT, BLOCK or similar command outside the pixel co-ordinate area. (However, you can use a PRINT statement that overflows the window in use.)

The User Guide makes it clear which SuperBasic commands use the graphics system and which use the pixel system or a character based on that. As the two sit rather awkwardly together, it's best not to combine them when you need to align graphics carefully. If you want to draw and fill rectangles within a complex graphic display, for instance, use LINE and FILL (graphic commands), not BLOCK which is a pixel command.

Note that it's possible to print text at any position on the screen: text characters are not confined to fixed rows and columns. Though AT works on a row and column basis, the positions of the rows and columns are relative to the window origin and are not fixed on the screen as a whole. You can use the CURSOR command to position the cursor at any specific pixel position or (using four parameters rather than two) at any specific graphics scale position.

The cursor position refers to the top left-hand corner of the next character to be printed, so a letter printed at 0,0 will appear at the top left of the window, regardless of its size.

The CURSOR command deals with a text cursor only. It cannot be used to position the graphics cursor. You can do the latter with a LINE command followed by only one pair of co-ordinates (which does not plot a point) or with a POINT command (which does plot a point). Though there are two effective cursors, the same INK colour is used for both characters and graphic lines/fills.

SCALING A GRAPHICS WINDOW

In order to look at the scaling of a graphics window, we'll draw a special graphics window in mid-screen, and add a thin black border around it to show where its boundaries are:

```
10      OPEN#3,CON_100x100a50x50_32
20      BORDER#3,1,0
25      CLS#3
```

Though we've used channel 3 for this purpose, you may wish to use a different channel number if you regularly use channel 3 for a printer for example.

You'll see immediately that though our window is 100 pixels by 100 pixels, it is not in fact square. The pixels are rather longer than they are wide. The graphics scaling (we'll use the default 100 scale) uses the vertical length of a pixel, as we can see if we try to draw a diagonal line:

```
30      LINE#3, 0,0 TO 100,100
```

Though the angle is a neat forty-five degrees (or should be, if your screen is properly adjusted), the line is far from intersecting the top right-hand corner of the window. Trial and error showed us that this statement does produce a true diagonal:

```
30      LINE#3, 0,0 TO 73,100
```

A window 73 across by 100 down is not as convenient as it may have seemed at first, so we will adapt its size to make it a square. Unfortunately the interpreter won't accept variables in OPEN CON-statements, so we first find out the necessary horizontal size with a quick immediate check:

```
PRINT 100*(100/73)
```

which gives us this revised statement:

```
10      OPEN#3,CON_137x100a50x50_32
```

This time a true square does appear. We can check its accuracy by drawing another line from 0,0 to 100,100: this time it will be a real diagonal.

Changing the scale of the window is a fairly straightforward business, but changing the origin is a little less so. The second and third co-ordinates following SCALE do not (as, like us, you may have thought initially) fix the position within the square at which the origin will appear. Instead they describe the co-ordinates which will apply to the bottom left-hand corner of the window. Let's take an example. Suppose we want to move the origin (point 0,0) to dead centre of our window. We might try:

```
30      SCALE#3, 100,50,50
```

but an attempt to check this by drawing a line from the origin to a corner of the window will soon show that we are wrong:

```
40      LINE#3, 0,0 TO 50,50
```

The line does not appear at all, since it is completely outside the window area. This is one time when the ability to plot outside the window without triggering an error message doesn't seem an unmixed blessing!

The real statement we want will describe the bottom left-hand corner as –50,–50 on our new co-ordinate system. These statements *will* draw a line from centre to corner:

```
30      SCALE#3, 100,–50,–50
40      LINE#3, 0,0 TO 50,50
```

Let's celebrate our new origin position by drawing a series of rays out from the origin towards the edges of the window:

```
30      INK (red, in either mode)
40      FOR ray = 0 TO 6.3 STEP .1
50      LINE#3, 0,0 TO 50*SIN(ray),50*COS(ray)
60      END FOR ray
```

This short program will work just as well in either graphics mode, as you can easily check for yourself.

Finally, it's useful to note that you can rescale windows without clearing them in the process and this can be a handy way of producing special graphic effects. Here's one simple program which draws a set of nested squares:

```
10      OPEN#3,CON-274x200a50x50–32
20      BORDER#3,1,0
30      PAPER#3,7: CLS#3
40      FOR s = 50 TO 250 STEP 50
50      SCALE#3,s,–(s/2),–(s/2)
60      LINE#3,10,10 TO 10,–10, TO –10,–10 TO –10,10 TO 10,10
70      END FOR s
```

The program listed as Figure 11.1 is a more complex program which uses a flower-drawing procedure. The scale is repeatedly changed at random and flowers are drawn at random sizes and positions.

Figure 11.1 Flower

```
10 REMark flower
20 MODE 8
30 PAPER 0
40 WINDOW 512,256,0,0:CLS
50 WINDOW 350,256,100,0
60 BORDER 1,7
70 FOR loop = 1 TO 20
80 s= RND(1 TO 5)*50
90 SCALE s,0,0
100 flower
110 END FOR loop
1100 DEFine PROCedure flower
1110 INK RND(1 TO 7)
1120 x = RND(s): y = RND(s)
1130 FOR petal = 0 TO 6.3 STEP .3
1140 LINE x,y
1150 ARC_R TO 25*SIN(petal),25*COS(petal),PI/2
1160 ARC TO x,y,PI/2
1170 END FOR petal
1180 END DEFine flower
```

THE ARC COMMAND

You will see that the 'flower' program (Figure 11.1) makes use of the ARC command. In the early FB version of SuperBasic which we used in writing this book, this command has two failings. First, it will only draw anti-clockwise arcs; attempts to specify minus numbers result in no arc at all, not a clockwise one. Reversing the order of the end points, however, will draw an arc bowed in the opposite direction.

Second, the accuracy of the command is very poor. In the flower program, some points fail to join up by a large margin and the same is visible if you try a simple program like this:

```
110     PAPER 0
120     WINDOW 512,256,0,0: CLS
130     WINDOW 350,256,100,0
140     BORDER 1,7: SCALE 100,0,0
150     FOR a = 0 TO 6.3 STEP .3
160     ARC 30,60 TO 50,80,a
170     END FOR a
```

Some of the lines barely travel half way to their destination, while others overshoot. Hopefully this command will be improved in later versions of SuperBasic.

TURTLE GRAPHICS

Turtle graphics commands are particularly useful for sequences that involve drawing lines at precise angles. It's not easy to get an angle of, say, 192 degrees using co-ordinate graphics: it's very easy with turtle graphics and this makes them ideal for geometric drawings and similar tasks.

Turtle graphics are also handy for sequences that involve drawing identical lines or sets of lines at different angles: e.g. for drawing spokes of a wheel, ray patterns, flower-type patterns and so on. The program listed in Figure 11.2 is an example of this type. The pattern drawn will depend upon the angle at which the turtle is turned: the user has a chance to select an appropriate angle. It's a short program, but as it requires user input we've included a simple title and introduction which makes it look longer.

Finally, Figure 11.3 lists a fun 'turtle walk' program which uses seven different turtles, each drawing with a different colour in mode 8 on a black background. Each turtle has a randomized turn angle and step length and it is fascinating to see how their paths intersect over fifty random moves. You could use the same general idea with synchronized turtles or turtles that race up or across the screen. Of course, whenever you set up a variety of screen channels you have a variety of different graphics (and text) cursors to handle: it's not necessary to use turtle graphics commands in order to get the set.

Figure 11.2 Turtle Graphics Shapes

```
100 REMark turtle graphic shapes
110 MODE 8
120 WINDOW 512,256,0,0:CLS
130 title
140 REPeat loop
150 CLS
160 PRINT "Give size of angle"
170 PRINT "(Suggested range 70 to 150)"
180 INPUT "(or 0 to finish)";a
190 IF a = 0 THEN EXIT loop
200 CLS
210 SCALE 100,0,0
220 PENDOWN
230 LINE 40,80
240 TURNTO 180
250 FOR d = 1 TO 10
260 INK RND(1 TO 7)
270 FOR t = 1 TO 10
280 TURN a: MOVE 50
290 END FOR t
300 END FOR d
310 PAUSE 1000
320 END REPeat loop
1000 DEFine PROCedure title
1010 CSIZE 3,1
1020 INK 1
1030 AT 0,3: PRINT "Turtle Shapes":PRINT
1040 CSIZE 0,0
1050 INK 7
1060 PRINT "This program draws coloured shapes"
1070 PRINT "using turtle graphics"
1080 PRINT "size of angle chosen will affect shape"
1090 PAUSE 500
1100 END DEFine
```

Figure 11.3 Turtle Walk

```
20 REMark turtle walk
30 DIM wa(7)
40 setup
50 turtles
60 walk
70 STOP
1000 DEFine PROCedure setup
1010 MODE 8
1020 WINDOW 512,256,0,0:PAPER 0:CLS
1030 SCALE 100,0,0
1040 END DEFine setup
1100 DEFine PROCedure turtles
1110 FOR t = 3 TO 7
1120 OPEN£t, con_512x256a0x0
1130 INK£t,t
1140 END FOR t
1150 FOR t = 1 TO 2
1160 WINDOW£t, 512,256,0,0
1170 INK£t,t
1180 SCALE£t,100,0,0
1190 END FOR t
1195 END DEFine turtles
1200 DEFine PROCedure walk
1210 FOR t = 1 TO 7
1220 LINE£t, 80,50
1230 PENDOWN£t
1240 TURNTO£t, RND(360)
1250 wa(t) = RND(5 TO 10)
1260 END FOR t
1270 FOR crawl = 1 TO 50
1280 FOR t = 1 TO 7
1290 TURN£t, RND(360)
1300 MOVE£t, wa(t)
1310 END FOR t
1320 END FOR crawl
1330 END DEFine walk
```

HANDLING SCREEN MEMORY

As the QL's manual tells you, screen memory normally starts at location 20000 hex. You will probably find decimal addresses more useful when programming in Basic: the equivalent is 131072 decimal. The last address of screen memory is 27FFF hex or 163839 decimal. The screen mapping takes up the same 32K bytes in both high and low resolution modes.

The QL User Guide explains the layout of the memory under 'memory map' in the 'Concepts' section. The memory is, as it explains, mapped row by row, top to bottom. When it talks of the raster scan moving right to left, however, it is presumably thinking from the back of the screen: to the viewer, the memory map is left to right on each row, so that locations 131072/3 map the top left-hand corner of the screen. The User Guide *is* right when it suggests that the bits are mapped in order on the screen: the most significant bit of each byte is to the left on screen and the least significant to the right.

Two bytes (one word) of memory are taken up to describe the colouring of each eight pixels in high resolution or four pixels in low resolution, so a total of 512*2/8 or 128 bytes are taken for each line. There are 256 lines, making the total 128*256 or 32,768 (32K) bytes. Locations 131072+128 and 131073+128 will map the start of the second row, locations 131072+(128*255) and 131073+(128*255) the start of the bottom row and so on.

There is no command in SuperBasic that returns the colour of an individual pixel and the POINT command should not be confused with the BBC Basic POINT command which does just this. (It's simply a pixel plotter.) In order to discover the colour, you will need to check video memory using PEEK or a machine code routine.

High Resolution Mapping

In high resolution, the high byte of each word (which is the one with the lower, even-numbered address) is used to map the green pixels; the low byte (with the higher, odd-numbered address) is used for the red. Turning on a green pixel (by POKEing a 1 into the appropriate bit) will display a green point on screen if the corresponding red pixel is set to 0 and a white point otherwise; likewise for a red. Setting the appropriate bits of both bytes to 1 always displays white, not yellow (red plus green): the display circuitry automatically adds in blue. Setting both to 0 will display black, giving the four colours of high resolution. Note that there's no 'logical colour' register in the QL: you can't change these default colours for others. Using the RECOL command simply changes the values in every screen memory location.

Examples

In these examples we use PEEK and POKE statements to show you how to manipulate video memory. The programs are not as simple as programs obtaining equivalent effects using graphics commands: they are designed to show how the video memory works, rather than to produce amazing displays!
(1) This short program manipulates bits to produce an intricate pattern of green and red pixels. We use pixels down the middle of the screen, not those in the corner of the screen, as these will not be visible on most displays.

Set the entire screen to black in order to see the effects clearly:

```
10      WINDOW 512,256,0,0
20      CLS
```

Turn on a zigzag chain of green pixels:

```
30      FOR mem = 131150 TO 131150 + (200*128) STEP 128*16
40      FOR pixel = 0 TO 7
50      POKE mem + (pixel*128),2 ^pixel
60      END FOR pixel
```

```
70        FOR pixel = 7 TO 0 STEP -1
80        POKE mem + (8*128) + (pixel*128),2 ^(7-pixel)
90        END FOR pixel
100       END FOR mem
```

Now interface these with a zigzag chain of red ones:

```
55        POKE mem + 1 + (pixel*128),1*2 ^(7- pixel)
85        POKE mem + 1 + (8*128) + (pixel*128),1*2 ^pixel
```

(2)   This program uses a green background, and POKEs a random pattern of red pixels to it. Once each location for a red pixel is chosen, the green pixel already lit is turned off so that the red pixel will not appear white.

The z variable is used to check if a pixel has already been turned red. This is necessary because we use a bitwise exclusive-or command to turn the appropriate bit of the green memory byte to 0: using it twice over would not work! Note the use of the 'bitwise' logical operators, && (AND), || (OR), and ^^ (XOR). (See also Chapter 9, and under 'operators' in the Concepts section of the User Guide.) It is essential to use these bitwise operators, not their more common logical equivalents which work on decimal numbers and give different results.

```
10        PAPER 4
20        WINDOW 512,256,0,0
30        CLS
40        FOR spot = 1 TO 500
50        mem = 131073 + RND(16384)*2
60        pixel = RND(7)
70        z = PEEK(MEM – 1) && 2 ^pixel
80        IF z = 0 THEN
90        POKE mem – 1, PEEK(mem – 1) ^^ 2 ^pixel
100       POKE mem, PEEK(mem) || 2 ^pixel
110       END IF
120       END FOR spot
```

Low Resolution Mapping

In low resolution, two bytes are used to map four double-width pixels. The high byte maps the green and flash characteristics of each pixel, in the sequence 'GFGFGFGF'; the low byte maps the red and blue characteristics, in the sequence 'RBRBRBRB'. As you will appreciate, combinations of the primary light colours red, green and blue produce the remaining low-resolution shades as follows:

red + green = yellow
red + blue = magenta
blue + green = cyan
red + green + blue = white

As a result, it is necessary to check the status of four different bits (or three if you ignore flash) in order to ensure that any single pixel has the colour you wish.

The 'flash' bit normally works on a character basis, flashing the foreground colour on and off while leaving the background colour constant. It's difficult to see how this translates to a bit-mapped screen. The following program was an experiment to find out: it produced an interesting, if hard to watch, effect. As turning on the flash bit byte by byte is a slow process, we've done it for part of the screen only.

```
10      MODE 8
20      WINDOW 512, 256,0,0: CLS
30      FOR stick = 1 TO 256 STEP 2
40      LINE stick,0 TO stick,100
50      END FOR stick
60      mem = 133000
70      FOR n = mem TO mem + 20 STEP 2
80      FOR o = n TO n + (128*100) STEP 128
90      POKE o, PEEK(o) ||85
100     END FOR o
110     END FOR n
```

This sample turns on every flash bit within a block of the screen, but you can produce different interesting effects by turning on some of the flash bits only, changing the '85' in line 90 to any combination of 64, 16, 4 and 1 added together. You'll see that the character orientation of the flash combines strangely with the non-character spacing of the lines we drew.

GRAPHICS UTILITY PROGRAMS

The two programs which follow are fairly complex graphic programs, designed to make use of a wide variety of the QL's SuperBasic graphic commands. They are graphic utilities, intended to complement the features of the Easel program and to help you make the most of the QL's graphic capabilities.

Function Plotter

Though Easel's routines are fine for graphing specific values, they cannot be adapted to act as a mathematical function plotter. We developed this fairly short program as a simple but useful function plotter. The program works quite well as it stands, but it is not fully error trapped. Our programming notes elsewhere in the book could provide a basis for you to improve on the error trapping aspects.

The program will plot values of x and y when y is a fairly complex function of x: e.g. $y = x/2 + 7$, or $y = x\,\hat{}\,2$, or $y = 7*x - 8$. It will not plot sines, cosines and other trigonometric functions as it stands, but it could quite easily be adapted to do so. It uses a standard scale, but it could be adapted to use different scales depending upon the values to be plotted. (The following program, 'scatter' includes a scaling routine.) It uses the high resolution mode 4 screen and will look best on a monitor, though it should be usable on a television.

We've divided the program into modules, setting up procedures to cover most of the main modules. At the top level, the program contains an introductory sequence and then a loop that can be used to repeat the function plotting without erasing previous plots. This top level calls four different procedures:

> title : sets up a title screen and displays instructions
> getfunct : obtains a function to be plotted
> axes : sets up the screen for graphics and draws axes
> xyplot : plots a function

The procedure 'getfunct' calls seven lower level procedures, each involved with a type of function:

> makex   divx
> addto   mult
> takeaway   power
> divby

Figure 11.4 shows this program structure in a tree-like fashion, with the main program outline and its set of nested procedures.

We've set up a variable list, too, which distinguishes between global variables and local variables. This is shown in Table 11.1.

Figure 11.4 Structure of the Function Plotter Program

Top level: main program (lines 10 to 170)
Lower level: procedures called by main program:

Title	Getfunct	Axes	XYplot

Bottom level: procedures called by higher level procedures:

Makex	Addto	Takeaway	Divby
Divx	Mult	Power	

Table 11.1 Variable List for Function Plotter Program

Global Variables:
Array to hold *y* values:	ynum(151)
Repeat variable:	r$
Repeat loop:	morefunc

Local to procedure Axes:
Loop counter to mark axes:	axis

Local to procedure Getfunct:
Repeat loop:	build
Select loop:	n
Repeat variable:	r$

Local to lower level procedures:
Loop counters:	m,x
Input variable:	z

Notes on the Program Structure

It's not difficult to type in from scratch a function definition and then proceed to plot the function defined. The hard part comes when you try to make a program like this self-contained. There's no simple Basic statement that will input a function definition. We've chosen a rather different approach.

The program sets up an array which we call 'ynum', which holds 151 different values of *y*: one value corresponding to every value of *x* from −75 to +75, which is the range we've chosen to plot. As we develop a definition of *y* as a function of *x*, we then proceed to put values into this array.

A menu is used to help the user develop function definitions. We've tried to make this clear, but it may take some practice before you get the hang of it. All *y* values start at 0 and if you wish to make *y* a function of *x*, you must choose a function which specifically incorporates *x*. 'x' (useful when adding, subtracting, or multiplying), 'x/', '/x', and 'x ^' all do this. Choice of one of these initializes the ynum array so that each number equals the corresponding value of *x*, treated in the chosen way. To these functions you can then add other functions which don't specifically incorporate *x*: +, − or *. A sequence of menu choices might, for instance, be:

    0 x
    5 * :   asks for value, e.g. x*6
    1 + :   asks for value, e.g. x*6 + 5
or:
    6 x ^:   asks for value, e.g. x ^3
    2 − :   asks for value, e.g. x ^3 − 3

Once your menu choices are complete, the ynum array will hold every value of *y* to be plotted, and the program can go on to plot the function.

We've chosen to use numbers rather than letters to designate the menu choices because we can then use the SELect command to handle the menu. It would be possible to use letters and convert the letter chosen to a code which SELect can handle, but this is a clumsier approach. However, it could become a neat way of trapping against the error that comes up if the user inputs a letter instead of a number.

All this menu display and asking is handled at the bottom of the screen, by the simple expedient of using the preset channel 0. There's no need to open the channel: we simply PRINT, INPUT and CLS using the channel number. The material will scroll upwards and eventually off the top of the channel 0 window. The graph can then remain undisturbed in the top two-thirds or so of the screen.

Notes on the listing:
The complete listing is given in Figure 11.5.

Main program (lines 0 to 170): Nothing too unusual here. The program calls the procedures which handle the title, get a function, plot axes and perform an *x-y* plot. 'Axes' clears the screen. If more functions are to be superimposed on the graph, the screen must not be re-cleared, so a REPeat loop is set up to handle subsequent 'getfunct' and 'xyplot' routines. This is not a counted loop: the user can repeat the function plotting on the same graph as often as he or she wishes.

Note our handling of the 'another function' question. r$(1) simply takes the leftmost character of r$.

Axes procedure (lines 1000 to 1150): We use the SCALE command to set the cartesian origin to the centre of the screen. All subsequent line plot

Figure 11.5 Function Plotter

```
10 REMark function plotter
20 DIM ynum(151)
30 MODE 4
40 WINDOW 512,256,0,0
50 PAPER 0
60 title
70 getfunct
80 axes
90 xyplot
100 REPeat morefunc
110 INPUT£0, "another function? ";r$
120 IF r$="" THEN GO TO 110
130 IF r$(1) <> "y" AND r$(1) <> "Y" THEN EXIT morefunc
140 getfunct
150 xyplot
160 END REPeat morefunc
170 STOP
1000 DEFine PROCedure axes
1010 LOCal axis
1020 PAPER 0
1030 INK 7
1040 CLS
1050 SCALE 100,-75,-50
1060 LINE -75,0 TO 75,0
1070 LINE 0,-30 TO 0,50
1080 CIRCLE 0,0,1
1090 FOR axis = -70 TO 70 STEP 5
1100 LINE axis,-1 TO axis,1
1110 END FOR axis
```

```
1120 FOR axis = -30 TO 50 STEP 5
1130 LINE -1,axis TO 1,axis
1140 END FOR axis
1150 END DEFine axes
2000 DEFine PROCedure getfunct
2010 LOCal build, n, r$
2020 REPeat build
2030 CLS£0
2040 PRINT£0, "available functions"
2050 PRINT£0,"0 x  1 +  2 -  3 x/  4 /x  5 *   6 x^"
2060 INPUT£0, "select one now (you can choose more later)";n
2070 SELect ON n
2080 =0: makex
2090 =1: addto
2100 =2: takeaway
2110 =3: divby
2120 =4: divx
2130 =5: mult
2140 =6: power
2150 END SELect
2160 INPUT£0, "any more to add? ";r$
2170 IF r$ <> "y" AND r$ <> "Y" THEN EXIT build
2180 END REPeat build
2190 END DEFine getfunct



2900 DEFine PROCedure makex
2910 LOCal m
2920 FOR m = -75 TO 75
2930 ynum(m+75) = m
2940 END FOR m
2950 END DEFine makex
3000 DEFine PROCedure addto
3010 LOCal z,m
3020 INPUT£0, "add what? ";z
3030 FOR m = 0 TO 150
3040 ynum(m) = ynum(m)+z
3050 END FOR m
3060 END DEFine addto
3100 DEFine PROCedure takeaway
3110 LOCal z,m
3120 INPUT£0, "subtract what? ";z
3130 FOR m = 0 TO 150
3140 ynum(m) = ynum(m)-z
3150 END FOR m
3160 END DEFine takeaway
3200 DEFine PROCedure divby
3210 LOCal z,x
3220 INPUT£0, "divide by what? ";z
3230 FOR x = -75  TO 75
3240 ynum(x+75) = x/z
3250 END FOR x
3260 END DEFine divby
3300 DEFine PROCedure divx
3310 LOCal z,x
3320 INPUT£0, "what divided by x? ";z
3330 FOR x = -75 TO 75
3340 IF x <> 0 THEN
3350 ynum(x+75) = z/x
3360 ELSE
3370 ynum(x+75) = z/.1
3380 END IF
3390 END FOR x
3400 END DEFine divx
3500 DEFine PROCedure mult
3510 LOCal z,m
3520 INPUT£0, "multiply by what? ";z
3530 FOR m = 0 TO 150
3540 ynum(m) = ynum(m)*z
3550 END FOR m
3560 END DEFine mult
3600 DEFine PROCedure power
3610 LOCal z,x
```

```
3620 INPUT£0, "power of what? ";z
3630 FOR x = -75 TO 75
3640 ynum(x+75) = x^z
3650 END FOR x
3660 END DEFine power



5000 DEFine PROCedure xyplot
5010 LOCal skip,x
5020 INK 3
5030 skip = 1
5040 FOR x = -75 TO 75
5050 IF ynum(x+75)>50 OR ynum(x+75)<-30 THEN skip=1:  NEXT x
5060 IF skip = 0 THEN
5070 LINE TO x,ynum(x+75)
5080 ELSE
5090 LINE x,ynum(x+75): skip = 0
5100 END IF
5110 END FOR x
5120 END DEFine xyplot
6000 DEFine PROCedure title
6010 CLS
6020 INK 7
6030 CSIZE 3,1: AT 5,0: PRINT "FUNCTION PLOTTER"
6040 INK 5
6050 CSIZE 0,0
6060 AT 0,10: PRINT "Scale is fixed on graph"
6070 PRINT "X axis from -75 to 75; Y axis from -30 to 50"
6080 PRINT "Select functions to be plotted from menu"
6090 PRINT "Remember to choose function 0 (x) if function does not include x"
6100 PRINT "You may plot multiple functions"
6110 PAUSE 500
6120 CLS
6130 END DEFine title
```

commands subsequently use this origin. The command sets up a vertical scale of 100: in fact we don't use the bottom section of the window we set up, because the channel 0 window will disturb the display here. The co-ordinate at the bottom left-hand corner of the main window will be –75, 50.

The CIRCLE command (line 1080) simply marks the origin. The axes are marked off at regular intervals, but not numbered in this program.

Getfunct procedure (line 2000 to 2190): The whole body of this procedure is made up of a REPeat loop, which allows the user to build up complex functions involving a series of menu choices. The loop includes a SELect ON structure and calls to other procedures.

Divx procedure (lines 3300 to 3400): The 'division by x' procedure is slightly more complex than the other 'function build' procedures, because of the need to avoid division by zero. Note that if x equals zero, we divide instead by .1. It isn't likely that this will lead to a continuous graph, but that is no problem as we allow in the xyplot procedure for discontinuous plotting when values exceed the scale limits.

Xyplot procedure (lines 5000 to 5120): Note the use of the 'skip' variable. This isn't used simply to skip a point that's off screen (line 5050 does that), but to 'flag' the fact that a point has been skipped, so that the graph line will start from, not draw to, the next point that is plottable. The LINE statement in line 5070 draws from one plottable point to the next; the alternative LINE statement in line 5090 simply moves the cursor to a plottable point and turns off the 'skip' flag.

Scatter Diagram

Our second graphics utility is for a scatter diagram, another function that the Easel program won't fulfil. This program will plot up to 500 different points for which the user gives x,y co-ordinates. Unlike the previous program, this one will scale automatically: and we include a routine for labelling the ends only of each axis, as an indicator of the scale used.

In this version, the co-ordinates of the points to be plotted are input by the user and are not saved with the program. If you input a large quantity of data, you will, of course, want to save it. You could do this either by including the data in DATA statements in the program itself or by OPENing a new microdrive file as part of the input routine and PRINTing all the data to this. Your own use of the program will determine which of these alternatives is most appropriate: neither is at all difficult to program.

Table 11.2 Variable List for Scatter Diagram Program

Global Variables:	
Array to hold points:	pt(500,1)
Array pointer:	n
Max and min x and y values:	maxx, maxy, minx, miny
Local to procedure Getpts:	
Loop counter:	loop
Point co-ordinates:	x,y
Local to procedure Setscale:	
X and Y ranges:	xrange, yrange
Loop variable:	loop
Local to procedure Axes:	
String variable to hold maxx:	s$
Length of s$:	1
Local to procedure XYplot:	
Loop variable:	loop

Notes on the Program Structure

The program listing is given in Figure 11.6. Again we've used procedures for all the main sections of the program. The brief initial section, to line 90, calls each procedure in turn. Only one set of points can be plotted at once as the program stands, so there is no loop in this section. If you wish, you could

Figure 11.6 Scatter

```
10 REMark scatter
20 CLEAR
30 DIM pt(500,1)
40 title
50 getpts
60 setscale
70 axes
80 xyplot
90 STOP
1000 DEFine PROCedure title
1010 MODE 4
1020 WINDOW 512,256,0,0
1030 PAPER 3: CLS
1040 INK 7: CSIZE 3,1
1050 PRINT "Scatter Graph"
1060 PRINT: CSIZE 0,0
1070 PRINT "Enter points by giving pair of co-ordinates for each"
1080 PRINT "Up to 500 points can be entered"
1090 PRINT "Program will scale and plot points automatically"
1100 PAUSE 500
1110 PAPER 0
1120 CLS
1130 END DEFine title
2000 DEFine PROCedure getpts
2010 LOCal loop,x,y
2020 n = 1
2030 REPeat loop
2040 PRINT "Give co-ordinates of point, x then y (0,0 to stop) "
2050 INPUT "x co-ordinate? ";x
2060 INPUT "y co-ordinate? ";y
2070 IF x = 0 AND y = 0 THEN EXIT loop
2080 pt(n,0) = x:  pt(n,1) = y
2090 n = n + 1
2100 IF n > 500 THEN
2110 PRINT "500 points selected; no more available"
2120 EXIT loop
2130 END IF
2140 END REPeat loop
2150 END DEFine getpts
3000 DEFine PROCedure setscale
3010 LOCal xrange,yrange,loop
3020 n = n-1
3030 maxx = 0:  maxy = 0
3040 minx = 0:  miny = 0
3050 FOR loop = 1 TO n
3060 IF pt(loop,0) > maxx THEN maxx = pt(loop,0)
3070 IF pt(loop,0) < minx THEN minx = pt(loop,0)
3080 IF pt(loop,1) > maxy THEN maxy = pt(loop,1)
3090 IF pt(loop,1) < miny THEN miny = pt(loop,1)
3100 END FOR loop
3110 IF minx>0 THEN minx=0:  IF miny>0 THEN miny=0
3120 xrange = maxx - minx:  yrange = maxy - miny
3130 IF xrange>1.4*yrange THEN
3140 range = xrange/1.3
3150 ELSE
3160 range = yrange*1.1
3170 END IF
3180 SCALE range, minx, miny
3190 END DEFine setscale
```

```
4000 DEFine PROCedure axes
4010 LOCal s$,l
4020 PAPER 0: INK 7: CLS
4030 WINDOW 480,256,0,0
4040 BORDER 1,3
4050 LINE 0,miny TO 0,maxy
4060 CURSOR 0,miny+(range/25),6,0: PRINT miny;
4070 CURSOR 0,maxy,6,0: PRINT maxy;
4080 LINE minx,0 TO maxx,0
4090 s$ = maxx:  l = 10*LEN(s$)
4100 CURSOR minx,0,0,12: PRINT minx
4110 CURSOR maxx,0,-1,12: PRINT maxx
4120 END DEFine axes
5000 DEFine PROCedure xyplot
5010 LOCal loop
5020 INK 5
5030 FOR loop = 1 TO n
5040 POINT  pt(loop,0),pt(loop,1)
5050 END FOR loop
5060 END DEFine xyplot
```

adapt the program so that two or more sets of points can be superimposed, with different colours used to differentiate the sets.

The five main procedures, 'title', 'getpts', 'setscale', 'axes' and 'xyplot' are all independent, and none of them calls any other procedure.

Notes on the Listing:

Getpts procedure (lines 2000 to 2150): Again, we use a REPEAT loop, but this time it structures a semi-counted loop with *n* used as a control variable. An alternative would be to use a FOR ... END FOR structure, which is acceptable in SuperBasic for semi-counted loop. The exit from the loop in either case will come in one of two cases: when the maximum number of repetitions is completed or when the user signals that there is no more data.

If you wish to direct the data to a microdrive file, you should OPEN-NEW the file before the start of the loop, and CLOSE it again after the loop. Inside the loop itself, a simple 'PRINT#n, x;y' will then direct the data to the file.

Note that 'n' is not a local variable. It is used later in the program to control various other loops which are counted through the filled variables only in array point.

Setscale procedure (lines 3000 to 3190): The setscale procedure is quite complex, as we wanted to make the maximum use of the screen area for plotting, while ensuring that all values and captions would appear correctly on the screen. Note, incidentally, that while you can line draw outside the screen using graphic commands, you cannot use the 'CURSOR' statement to print outside the screen area without generating an error message. With graphic scaling, it's difficult to be sure in both dimensions which points *are* fully on screen, as we found in developing this procedure.

The first part of the procedure is a straightforward loop that finds the maximum and minimum values of *x* and *y*, and stores them in variables (which are not local: they are used in the 'axes' procedure too). As the program is set up, negative values are acceptable and indeed the program works better with a mixture of positive and negative values.

If all values are positive, then the minimum value to be plotted will be zero on both axes. It's necessary to provide for this, as the axes are drawn through point 0,0. We haven't allowed for all values being negative, but it might be as well to do so if you expect that you may plot entirely negative values.

Lines 3130 to 3170 determine if the x range or the y range is to be used for plotting, so as to ensure that the whole of both ranges will appear on screen. We add in a 'safety factor' as well: the program works better with this.

SCALE is used to set the range and the bottom left-hand corner will take the minimum x,y value.

Axes procedure (lines 4000 to 4120): While the introductory routines use a full-screen window, the actual graph plotting routines use a slightly thinner window. On our monitor, the right-hand edge of the picture isn't visible, and the left-hand edge only just creeps in. Reducing the window makes the whole of the plot visible. To improve the appearance, we draw a border round this newly defined window.

The axes are drawn straight, but we've used some juggling to ensure that the axis labels (at the ends only) fit correctly on to the screen. Three different methods are used in lines 4060 and 4100/4110 (the first partly for demonstration purposes, as the latter method would do here): in all cases we are setting the cursor position and then moving it to allow for the fact that the cursor describes the point at the top left hand corner of the first character to be printed. Note the four arguments required with the CURSOR command, in order to align it with the graphics co-ordinates. The command works a little unpredictably: y values on the pixel co-ordinate system seem to work from the bottom of the screen, not the top, so it's necessary to add and not subtract a relative y value in order to move the cursor off the bottom of the screen. We've moved the cursor up twelve pixels to allow for the ten-pixel depth of a character.

We use '1' to hold the length of the 'maxx' value (converted into a string), as this may be a long number and we need to ensure that it will fit on the screen.

Xyplot Procedure (lines 5000 to 5060): Nothing unusual in the programming here, but note that we've chosen to use POINT to plot the individual points. At high resolution, the points plotted are small and though they look fine if a large number appears on the graph, the graph looks a little weedy with only a few points. An alternative would be to use the CURSOR . . . PRINT commands and print, say, an asterisk to mark each point. It's necessary in this case to amend the cursor position so that the centre of the asterisk (and not its top left-hand corner) is in the correct position; and it may be necessary to change the scaling slightly in order to ensure that extreme value points are plottable.

12

Inside the QL

In the remainder of this book, we will be concentrating on a lower-level look at the QL's capabilities. We'll begin by taking a look inside the QL's casing, and finding out in detail what the machine consists of.

THE MAIN CIRCUIT BOARD

Figure 12.1 sketches out the layout of the QL's main circuit board, and labels the main components. This layout is that followed in early models of the QL; it may be changed slightly in later models. It's the layout you'll see if you unscrew the case of your QL and look at it from the front with the main ports at the back, as if you were about to type on it. We'll look at each major component in turn.

Processors

The QL contains two processors. The main processor is a Motorola 68008 and the second processor an Intel 8049.

The Motorola 68008
You will see the Motorola 68008 processor marked on the bottom left-hand side of Figure 12.1 It's a large chip which operates at an impressive speed of 7.5 MHz.

Figure 12.1 Internal Layout of the QL

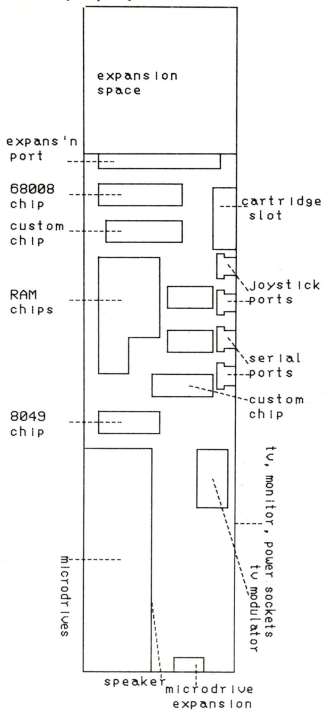

An entire family of chips with slight differences make up the Motorola 68000 family, of which the 68008 is a member. The 68000 itself is becoming well known as the main processor in many upmarket personal computers, including the Apple Macintosh and Lisa machines, Torch machines etc. It runs the well-known Unix operating system.

We can't explain every detail of the 68008's operation in this chapter, but we hope to give you enough information to enable you to understand how the chip compares with other processors, including the 68000, and to see in outline how it can be programmed. This information is all of great interest to machine-code programmers. To users of application programs and to Basic programmers, it may also be interesting but it is not essential. If you are not familiar with processor architecture and with machine-code programming, you may find some of the information we give hard to follow. Skip this section if you wish: it is not essential to your understanding of most of the rest of the book.

The instruction sets of the 68000 and 68008 are identical, so for almost all purposes the two processors 'look' the same to machine code and assembly language programmers. If you're a low level programmer, you'll find books centring on the 68000 to be a good introduction to 68008 programming, too.

Central to both chips is an impressive complement of registers. There are seventeen thirty-two-bit registers. Thirty-two-bit length means that the registers are capable of holding bytes (eight bits), words (sixteen bits) and long words (thirty-two bits) of data. (When less than a long word is being manipulated, the remaining bytes of the register are simply not used and instructions which manipulate the bits of the register are modified accordingly so that they affect only the part in use.) You'll see the different data lengths reflected in SuperBasic's PEEK and POKE commands.

In comparision, the popular eight-bit chips found in many home computers, the 6502 and the Z80, have respectively four and seven eight-bit registers. (Some of these can be used in pairs to make sixteen-bit registers, but there's no way of simulating a thirty-two-bit register on either chip.) It's obviously why the 68008 packs so much more power. Of course, register length is not the only measure of a processor's power, but it is of enormous help when it comes to handling complex arithmetic and for a number of other purposes.

The quantity of registers on the 68000 and 68008 means that memory accesses need to be less frequent and sequential operations can be speeded up, since transfers of data between internal registers are many times faster than transfers of data from RAM to the processor. The processors work in a 'pipelining' fashion, on three successive program instructions. A simple serial processor fetches, decodes and executes each program instruction in turn. The 68000 and 68008 proceed to fetch and decode two more instructions while the first is still being decoded and executed. So long as program execution is sequential (i.e. not branching to a subroutine or procedure) it will be much faster than a simpler processor.

The 6502 and Z80 have program counters (specific registers used to hold memory addresses) only sixteen bits long. This limits the range of memory they can address directly (i.e. without paging techniques) to 64K locations: hence the maximum of 64K combined ROM and RAM found on most home computers. The 68000 and 68008, in contrast, use a thirty-two-bit program counter. However, not all of the bits in the program counter can be used to designate addresses, because of the limitation in size of the address bus (the communication channel from the processor to the memory). On the 68000, there's the equivalent of a twenty-four-bit address range, enabling the chip to address 16Mbytes (i.e. 16,000 Kbytes) of memory. Here the 68008 differs: it has only the equivalent of a twenty-bit address bus, giving it the ability to address one Mbyte (1000 Kbytes) of memory. This impressive quantity of memory directly available to the processor (more than fifteen times the amount available on the Z80 or 6502) is a major advantage of the 68008, as we shall see when we come to discuss RAM. Of course, though the 68008 *can* address 1 MB, there is no need for 1 MB of memory to be available to it and indeed there will normally be rather less.

Another difference emerges when we look at the data bus: the bi-directional channel that transfers data between the processor and memory and peripheral devices. The 68000 has a sixteen-bit data bus, enabling it to transfer a word (two bytes) of data at a time. (Long words can be transferred by two successive data transfer operations.) On the 68008, the data bus is reduced to only eight lines, meaning that only one byte of data can be handled at once. The 68008 can, of course, handle long words sequentially, but this limitation does mean that it takes twice as long for data transfer as does the more powerful chip. Both chips dedicate output pins to the address and data buses: different pin functions are not multiplexed (i.e. handled in strictly timed sequence on the same pins) as they are on some processors.

Opinions differ as to whether the size of registers, the size of the data bus or some other measure, should be used to determine the 'bit-rating' of a chip. Some commentators use register size and by this criterion both 68000 and 68008 are thirty-two-bit chips (as Sinclair claims in its promotional material). Others use the data bus as the vital measure, and in this way the 68000 emerges as a sixteen-bit chip, and the 68008 as a mere eight-bit. Though it is obvious that the 68008 has temendous advantages over conventional eight-bit chips such as the Z80, it is certainly true that its limited data bus reduces the computer's overall speed of operation.

The major reason for the differences in bus size between the 68000 and the 68008 is the different number of pins available on the two chips. Processors with a large number of pins (i.e. connections to the rest of the computer's circuitry) are expensive to produce, to test and to use. Most cheap microprocessors limit their pin allocation to forty or forty-two. The 68000 uses an expansive sixty-four pins, while the 68008, with the help of its reduced size registers, cuts this number to forty-eight. Figure 12.2 shows how the two chips differ in pin allocations.

We follow the standard conventions for pin labelling in these diagrams. Arrows are used to indicate the direction of data flow, to or from the processor, or both (e.g. the data bus) or neither (grounded pins). A horizontal line above a signal name indicates that the pin is 'active low': i.e. that a low voltage is its significant state. (Other pins are either active high or may have two different active states.)

Figure 12.2 Motorola MC68008 Pin Assignments and Motorola MC68000 Pin Assignments

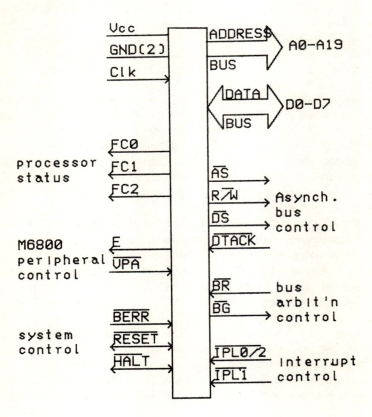

Motorola 68000
Pin Assignments

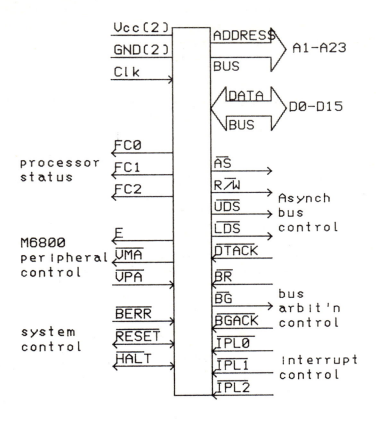

At the top right of each diagram, you'll see the allocation to the address bus: twenty pins for the 68008, twenty-four for the 68000, as we mentioned above. Immediately below are the pins that connect the processor to the data bus: eight for the 68008, sixteen for the 68000.

The other pins are various types of control signals, and we've divided these up into groups.

Processor Status signals: FC (Function Code) 0, 1 and 2 identify the type of bus activity being performed.

M6800 Peripheral Control signals: these signals are provided to enable the 68000 and 68008 to make use of the family of peripheral devices originally designed for use with the simpler 6800 processor. E(nable) is a clock signal, designed to help interface these processors, designed primarily for asynchronous data transfers, with the 6800 peripherals designed for synchronous data transfer. VPA stands for 'valid peripheral address' and is a signal sent by the 6800-type devices to the processor. VMA is 'valid memory address' and is sent to the peripheral device, on the 68000 only. The 68008 is better suited to handling 6800-type peripherals than is the 68000 and this is reflected in the lower number of signals required.

System Control signals: there are three of these. BERR (bus error) is a signal to the 68000 when an external device has not given a required acknowledgement to a read or write operation. HALT and RESET are both input and output signals, used – as you might expect – to halt operations in, or reset, the recipient device. The fact that the processors can output these signals enables them (in theory: little use of this is made in QDOS) to control other parts of the computer system via halts and resets, without the processor itself being affected.

Asynchronous Bus Control signals: four of these on the 68008, five on the 68000. AS is an address strobe; DS a data strobe, which becomes two signals, UDS (upper data strobe) and LDS (lower data strobe) when handling the larger data bus on the more complex device. R/W is a read/write control and DTACK a data transfer acknowledge signal. This last is an input: the recipient device must generate a suitable signal during every read and write operation or (as mentioned above) a bus error will be signalled.

Bus Arbitration Control signals: three on the 68000, only two on the 68008. BR is a bus request (input); BG a bus grant (output), while BGACK is a grant acknowledge input provided on the 68000 only.

Interrupt Control signals: interrupt request signals (input to the processor from the interrupting device) which are used to determine the priority of the interrupt request. The three interrupt signals (reflected in the status register, see below) provide seven different status levels. Three signals are used on both processors, but IPL0 and 2 are multiplexed on the 68008.

As you will appreciate, the different number of pins on the two chips means that there is no question of simply removing the 68008 from your QL and replacing it with a more powerful 68000. Though the machine *can* be enhanced, the enhancements must be achieved in different ways.

Registers in the 68008
Figure 12.3 shows the register complement of the 68008, which is, as we mentioned above, identical to that of the 68000.

The first eight registers, labelled D0 to D7, are data registers. (They can also be used as index registers.) As we mentioned above, these are thirty-two-bit registers. Byte values occupy only the lowest eight bits (0 to 7); word values the lowest sixteen bits (0 to 15) and long word values the entire register. It's not possible to store two (or more) separate byte or word values within the same register.

The next nine registers (making up the complement of seventeen we

Figure 12.3 Motorola MC68008 Registers

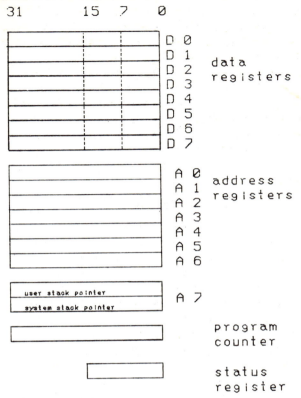

mentioned) are labelled A0 to A7 and are address registers. A7 has some special features and we look at A0 to A6 first. Again these are thirty-two-bit registers and they are normally used for full thirty-two-bit values. They can all be used as software stack pointers (i.e. to point to the next free location on a 'stack' set up by software in RAM) or as base address registers (i.e. to point to the base of a reserved area of RAM, which might, for instance, contain a table of values).

In fact A7 is a set of two registers, which are specifically designated as stack pointers, though one of them, the system stack pointer, can act as a conventional address register and has a variety of other uses. The processor can operate in two base 'states', 'supervisor' or 'user' (which we consider below) and the processor state will determine which stack pointer is operative. Because only one pointer can be operative at any time, the two pointers can share a single address.

The program counter is also a thirty-two-bit register. Finally, the status register has sixteen bits, only ten of which are normally used for flag operations.

If you look up the CALL command in the SuperBasic keywords section of your QL manual, you'll see that following the address of the machine code routine called up by the command, there is provision for thirteen pieces of data. These data are placed in the data and address registers in sequence. So in fact, the thirteen data items could each be up to a long word in length.

The two-byte status register is in fact divided into two halves. The lower byte is known as the 'user byte' and indicates conditions that (like an arithmetical 'carry' or 'overflow') are related directly to program operations. The upper byte is the 'system byte', and contains data on system states (e.g. whether the system is in supervisor or user mode). It is far less easy for the machine code programmer to alter bits in the system byte and they can only be altered when the system is in supervisor mode. (Movement into or out of supervisor mode automatically sets the 'mode' bit.) Figure 12.4 shows what functions the different bits in this register perform.

Figure 12.4 68008 Status Register

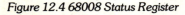

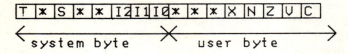

```
15 14 13 12 11 10 9  8  7  6  5  4  3  2  1  0
```

```
C    Carry
V    Overflow
Z    Zero
N    Negative
X    Extend

I0/I1/I2    Interrupt Mask
S           Superior State
T           Trace Mode

*            Unused Bit
```

System States

As we mentioned above, the 68008 has two modes of operation, called 'supervisor' and 'user'. 'User' is the standard mode, in which most programs execute and in which many operating system functions can be performed. In user mode, accesses are controlled, so that the effect which any one program can have on the system as a whole is strictly limited. This is an essential precaution if the system is to be used for multitasking.

'Supervisor' mode removes the limitations imposed in user mode and enables the programmer/operating system to have access to all resources while performing essential 'housekeeping' tasks. It is essential to move into supervisor mode before performing operating system tasks that are 'atomic': that is, that are to be completed in one go, without intervention from any other job. A special operating system 'trap' moves the system into supervisor mode, setting the appropriate bit of the status register and switching stack pointer operation to the 'supervisor' stack (which is, incidentially, limited to sixty-four bytes).

These system states will only be important to you if you plan to program in assembler or machine code. For more information, you may find it useful to read Chapter 15, which deals with the QDOS operating system in more detail.

Interrupt and Exception Handling
When dealing with most microprocessors, the word 'interrupt' is used to refer to a state that alters the usual processor operating pattern. Normally only a limited range of 'events' such as a request for service from a peripheral device, a system error or reset, can cause interrupts. In the 68000 and 68008, the general concept of interrupt handling is extended to create a wider concept that is normally described as 'exception handling'. Exception handling in these processors covers a very wide range of events, including some which are generated internally (that is, from the execution of program instructions inside the processor) rather than externally (for example, via a peripheral interrupt).

When an exception occurs, program operation does not follow the normally ordained sequence. Instead, program control is diverted to a 'vector table' (near the start of the memory) which provides the start address for a special exception handling program. Some of the positions in this table are filled with the addresses of routines that handle genuine interrupts and system errors. Other positions are left to be filled either by the addresses of operating system routines or by the addresses of user programs.

It's possible to send program control to a routine via this vector table through the use of the 68000/8's 'trap' instruction. We will see in more detail how this works when we consider the QDOS operating system in Chapter 15.

The Intel 8049
The second processor, the Intel 8049, is located towards the bottom right-hand side of Figure 12.1.

This second processor is used to control the keyboard, generate sound from the QL's internal loudspeaker and act as an RS-232-C serial communications receiver. It does *not* control the video display, a function of second processors in many dual-processor machines; and the lack of a dedicated video display chip is evident in some display intensive QL operations.

Intel's 8049 chip is of the same family as the better-known 8048. Like the 8048, it is a composite chip containing small amounts of ROM and RAM as well as banks of eight-bit registers and processor functions. It's designed specifically as a device controller. It doesn't have the address bus and data bus of a general purpose microprocessor: instead, all programs and data are held in the internal ROM and RAM. The pins freed by the disappearance of these buses are dedicated instead to a selection of input and output ports.

It's thanks to the presence of the 8049 that sounds made by the QL do not 'tie up' the main processor: they can continue while program operation moves on to later statements. However, the chip doesn't have the impressive sound-generating capabilities of dedicated sound chips.

You will also recognize the hand of the 8049 in SuperBasic's unusual KEYROW command.

Few programmers will wish to make use of the 8049's facilities on a low level and for most low-level programming purposes you can ignore its presence.

Custom Chips

The two QL processors are supported by two custom-designed control chips. The use of these custom chips means that the computer has none of the usual selection of processor support chips found with the 68000 and similar processors. All peripheral functions, including the real-time clock, are handled by the custom chips.

One custom chip is marked towards the top of Figure 12.1, and towards the left-hand side; the other is towards the bottom right of the diagram.

One custom chip handles the QL display and its memory allocation; the other provides a real-time clock which controls the microdrives and the local area network and handles RS-232-C transmission. (Unfortunately, this clock is not backed up by a battery: you have to reset it each time you turn on the computer.) Note that serial reception and transmission are handled separately: transmission by the custom chip and reception by the 8049.

Display handling by the custom chip presumably includes control of aspects such as the screen scrolling and panning and the windowing features. Unfortunately, we have no details on the low-level handling of these features.

QL Firmware

The QL's operating system, like its Basic, is provided in ROM form in the computer, so there is no need to load the operating system from microdrive on powering up. Two ROM chips (EPROMs in the earliest versions of the computer) are used to hold the QDOS routines and the Basic interpreter. QDOS takes up 32K; the Basic interpreter 16K. The two ROMs are located towards the top of the diagram, near the left-hand side.

Inbuilt RAM

The QL comes with 128K of RAM on the main circuit board. Sixteen identical chips to the right of the main processor make up this complement.

OTHER INTERNAL COMPONENTS

In Figure 12.1, you can see how the circuit board fits into the space inside the QL's casing. To its left is an empty space, into which an expansion RAM board (providing an additional 512K of RAM, taking the total up to 640K) should eventually fit. The expansion port is internal to the computer, but it's possible to gain access to it by removing the plastic plate on the left-hand side of the box. While RAM expansions may be internal, chained peripheral devices linked to the main board by an expansion module will obviously be external to the computer. To its right is the circuitry for the two inbuilt microdrives and the UHF (colour television) modulator. Nestling under the microdrives (where the ventilation slots appear on the casing) is the computer's piezo-electric speaker. The power supply is of course provided separately.

EXTERNAL PORTS

The peripheral expansion port, as we mentioned above, is inside the QL, though you can gain access to it via the plate at the left-hand side of the computer. On the right-hand side, next to the Reset button, is another removable plate. This hides another expansion port which will enable up to six additional microdrives to be chained to the computer.

The QL's other ports are all at the back of the computer. They are quite well described in the QL User Guide and we will make only a few comments about them.

The ROM Cartridge Slot

In very early versions of the QL, this slot was occupied by a third EPROM containing the final section of the QL's firmware. A later upgrade fitted all the firmware into the two internal ROM sockets. All QLs should now have internal firmware: if you own an early model which has not been upgraded, we urge you to return it to Sinclair Research for upgrading. As well as being more convenient, the ROM version of the operating system has better features than did the early EPROM versions.

The cartridge slot will normally be used to hold utilities (e.g. assemblers and language compilers or interpreters) and application programs in ROM form. If you look at the QL's memory map (page 199) you'll see the 32K of memory allocated to the ROM expansion. These programs are durable, quick and easy to use. Though they can be expensive, it is certainly worthwhile buying heavily-used programs in this form.

Next to the ROM slot are two joystick ports labelled CTL1 and CTL2. As the manual betrays, these are not fully implemented: it will be necessary to buy an adapter in order to use conventional joysticks with D-type connectors with the computer. No joystick adapters were available at the time of writing. The ports may also be used by various other control devices such as game paddles and light pens.

The two RS-232-C serial ports (labelled SER1 and SER2) are differently configures, as the User Guide explains. Any RS-232-C compatible device designed specifically for use with the QL should work with one specific port: the device should tell you which one to use. Note that these ports, too, have unusual connectors similar to those provided on modern British plug-in telephones. You will need to use a cable specifically designed for use with the QL.

The baud rate for RS-232-C communications can (and indeed, must) be programmed using SuperBasic's BAUD command. Both ports must be set to the same baud rate.

The RS-232-C ports are used for external communications using a modem, for connecting serial printers and plotters and various other serial devices. The QL does not have an inbuilt parallel printer port and the Psion programs assume that the serial port will be used for a printer. You can use a Centronics parallel printer successfully if you use it with an external interface that connects to one of the RS-232-C ports. It's possible that some interfaces for parallel printers will use other ports instead. In this case, you may have difficulty with the Psion programs and other commercial programs that assume a serial printer, though you should be able to program your printer successfully yourself using Basic and machine code (and any other languages that your QL supports). There are more details on printer interfacing in Chapter 2.

'UHF' is the connector to an UHF television aerial socket, and 'RGB' is the monitor connection. It's described under 'monitor' in the QL User Guide and you will see that a composite video line is provided as well as RGB signals, so that the computer can be used with either a monochrome or an RGB monitor. Unfortunately, the QL screen image is poorly adapted to both television sets and conventional RGB monitors: the full 512 x 256 pixel image will overflow the screen on both. If you are buying a monitor specifically for use with the QL, we advise you to obtain one that has been adapted to provide a full picture. Such monitors will be advertised as QL-compatible. If you already have a monitor, you should be able to obtain an almost full picture by adjusting the internal and external controls.

The wiring of monitor cables varies from computer to computer and again you will need to buy a cable specifically designed to work with the QL. Sinclair provide a rather expensive cable with a QL-compatible plug on one end: you need to fit a suitable connector to your make of monitor on the other. We found it cheaper to have a cable made up by a local electronics dealer. The information in the User Guide under 'monitor' and the handbook for your particular monitor, provides all the necessary information on wiring.

Commercial software should make use of the QL's windowing facilities to ensure that the active screen image does not overflow a television screen, but it may not do so for monitors, particularly as more QL-oriented monitors become available. You can do the same yourself by setting a window size to less than the maximum.

Though the QL boot routine asks you to designate a television set or a monitor, this question simply determines the screen mode to be used: it doesn't affect the signals sent via the UHF and RGB ports. You can press 'F2' for television while using a monitor if you want a forty-column screen, and *vice versa*.

The two local area network ports are identical. We discuss their use in detail in Chapter 16.

THE KEYBOARD

The QL keyboard has conventional keys topping a membrane mechanism. When you press a key, it in turn presses down on a moulded plastic sheet. A spike moulded below the key then presses down on an electronic circuit printed on another plastic sheet, making a connection with another circuit beneath.

Though the keyboard looks conventional, this arrangement does mean that it is important to press the keys dead centre in order to make the necessary electrical connections. You must be particularly careful in pressing the large Enter key: hitting it edge-on will often not register a key press. With reasonable care, though, it is possible to touch type fast and accurately on the QL keyboard.

The keys auto-repeat, but it's not possible to program the repeat period.

None of the QL's sixty-five keys can be programmed to return a variable character string. Each key returns a fixed code, which may be modified if Control, Shift and/or Alt are pressed at the same time. You'll find a complete list of codes under 'Character Set' in the Concepts section of the QL User Guide. The codes used are broadly compatible with the standard ASCII code. This means that you can't program the function keys to return strings (e.g. 'PRINT CHR$(') while you are actually typing in programs, as you can on some computers; they can only be used within application programs.

13

Using Files and Microdrives

In this chapter we look at the way in which programmers – and particularly Basic programmers – can use the QL's microdrives. In order to do so, we look also at some general points involving file structure. We then present two utility programs to help you handle the maintenance and backup of your microdrive files.

DATA CHANNELS BETWEEN THE
COMPUTER AND THE MICRODRIVES

In order for any data to pass between the computer and the microdrives, two conditions are necessary. It's necessary for a *channel* to be open between the two devices and *filespace* (identified by a file name) needs to be available on the microdrive, for the storage of data.

A channel is simply a line of communication. Opening a channel has a secondary function, however: it activates the device driver (in this case, the microdrive operating system) that will handle the communications. (We also discussed device drivers in Chapter 2, when talking about printers.)

Some input and output commands automatically open channels between the computer and the microdrive. 'SAVE' and 'LOAD' work in this way. There's no need for you to use the OPEN command to create a channel; the SAVE/LOAD commands do the job. The completion of the command will then close the channel just as automatically.

When you use other commands such as PRINT, it's necessary specifically to open your channel first. OPEN is the command to do so. It is followed by a unique channel number within the range 0 to 16. You'll normally want to use a channel number that isn't in use for other purposes. For instance, channels 0, 1 and 2 are used for screen output and you may use specific channel numbers regularly for your printer, for other RS232 communications, networking, etc. The channel number is followed by the device name: MDV__n in this case, to designate one of your microdrives. You'll also need to give a filename which will be used to refer to the data on the microdrive.

When using the microdrive operating system, there's no need for you to 'reserve' filespace on the microdrive cartridge. The operating system will automatically allocate space (assuming there *is* some free space available) as you need it. However, you *must* not only give a filename, but also indicate whether you're reading data *from* an existing file or writing data *to* a new file. Note that you don't do both at once. It isn't possible to update a file on microdrive selectively or to add to an existing file except by reading in the old version, making the necessary changes or adding the new sections and writing back the new version. OPEN__IN is the statement that opens an existing file for reading; OPEN__NEW (*not* OUT, as you might expect) the one that opens a new file for writing to.

These are examples of complete OPEN statements:

    OPEN__IN #9, MDV1__data

opens an existing microdrive file (on microdrive 1) called 'data' for input, using channel 9.

    OPEN__OUT #8, MDV2__newdata

opens a new microdrive file, to be called 'newdata', on microdrive 2 for output, using channel 8.

To update a single file you need to use both these types of statement.

TYPES OF FILE ON MICRODRIVE

The microdrive operating system does not support random access files, where you can gain access immediately to any section of the file. All files are sequential in type: you save or load first the first piece of data, then the second and so on.

You can use microdrives from Basic to store four different kinds of file:

    (1)   Files containing Basic programs, a type of ASCII coded data file. The entire file is loaded or saved by giving a single command. It is saved using the SAVE command and loaded using LOAD, MERGE, LRUN or MRUN. All these commands automatically open and close the necessary data channels: their arguments contain the microdrive number and the name of the file.

(2)   Files containing ASCII coded data that does not consist of Basic programs: e.g. data used in a database application, a word processor document, data used in a spreadsheet. Such files are created using an application program (including the Psion programs supplied with the QL). The files are both loaded and saved one data item (i.e. one number or string) at a time, in sequence. Each item is saved to microdrive using PRINT# (followed by the number of the appropriate data channel); it is loaded using INPUT or possibly INKEY$. It is up to you to OPEN and CLOSE data channels as necessary.

(3)   Files containing the data of a machine code program. The program must first be loaded into an appropriate area of RAM, using a suitable loader. The area of RAM containing the program is saved byte by byte (in decimal form, not coded) using the SEXEC command to specify its start address, the length of the program and the data area it will require. EXEC or EXEC-N (EXEC-W in some versions of QDOS) are then used to reload and run the program. These commands open and close data channels for you: like SAVE and LOAD, they· are followed by the microdrive number and the file name(s).

(4)   Files consisting of non-coded data that does not comprise an executable program. This data too will normally come direct from a section of the QL RAM and the SBYTES command is used to identify the section to be saved (which might, for instance, be screen memory). Like EXEC, it is followed not only by details of the start address and length of the memory section, but also by a microdrive number and file name: there is no need to specifically OPEN a data channel. LBYTES is the corresponding input command. Note that these commands work, like LOAD and SAVE, on the file as a whole: you can't input selective bytes from a file.

FILE HEADERS

Each file starts with a header that contains information about the file. If you save a file from SuperBasic, using one of the standard SuperBasic commands mentioned above, then this header will be written automatically by QDOS. However, you may find it helpful to know what it contains.

The first sixty-four bytes of the file are reserved for the header information, as follows:

00 to 03:	file length
04	file access (in QDOS v. 1.03, = 0)
05	file type:
	data files: 0
	Basic programs: 0
	executable machine code programs: 1

06 to 0E:	type dependent information: for executable programs, the first four bytes give the default size of the data space required
0E to 10:	length of file name
10 . . .	actual file name (up to thirty-six characters)
34 . . .	date information (some of which is not implemented in early versions of QDOS).

File pointers are normally set so as to point to the first position in the file *after* the header, and the file will actually start sixty-four bytes before the position indicated by the pointer. In other words, the header will normally be invisible to you when you manipulate files in Basic. If you want to use the header information, you'll need to manipulate the computer or microdrive's memory accordingly.

THE MICRODRIVES

Now we look briefly at the construction of microdrives and their cartridges, before going on to see how filed data is stored on the cartridge.

A microdrive unit is basically a special type of mini-cassette player, designed to play only the tape found on microdrive cartridges. It has a slot into which the cartridge is fitted, a drive motor to turn the tape, two sets of read/write/erase heads and necessary control electronics.

You may be surprised to discover that there are two read/write/erase heads in the unit, when the tape being read is a continuous loop. In fact, the tape has two parallel data tracks, both on the same side. Bits of data are stored alternately on each track and tend to overlap slightly, so that bit 2 might start on the lower track before bit 1 has finished being written on the upper and so on. This arrangement is designed to speed the operation of the system: it doesn't normally concern the user. It's generally easier and more straight-forward if you think of the data as being stored in a simple sequential one-track order.

Each tape cartridge contains a single, continuous loop of tape around 200 inches long, and about 1/16 inch wide. (So each track is rather less than 1/32 inch wide.) The tape has a single 'splice' to join its ends: it's the presence of this splice that ensures that not every sector of the tape is usable, since some sectors on the formatted tape will cover the splice area. A pinch wheel mechanism feeds the tape from the centre of its single spool: once it has passed the heads it is taken up on the outside of the spool.

There's no hard 'format' on the tape itself. All formatting (i.e. dividing the tape up into areas and preparing it to hold data) is done in software, using the FORMAT command. It's because formatting is a software operation that the same microdrive cartridges can be used on the Spectrum and on the QL. Only after formatting are the two types of cartridge incompatible.

Note that QDOS doesn't include any built-in check to see whether a cartridge contains data, before it carries out a FORMAT command. It's up to you to ensure that you format only blank cartridges or cartridges whose data contents you no longer wish to keep.

MICRODRIVE DATA STRUCTURE

The tape in microdrive cartridges is divided by the formatting routine into sectors. Each sector is capable of holding at least 512 bytes of data. microdrive tape speed is not absolutely constant, the sectors are actually formatted with a fairly large (ten per cent) margin of error, to ensure that the block of data will always fit.

As you will know from the SuperBasic FORMAT command, this command gives a name to the tape cartridge as a whole, and returns the total number of sectors and number of 'good' (i.e. acceptable for data storage) sectors on the tape. The total number will vary slightly, not just from tape to tape, but from one format to another on a single tape, depending upon a variety of factors including speed variations. It should be in the range of 225 sectors, plus or minus five per cent. (So each sector is in fact a little under an inch in length.) It is normal for there to be a small number of bad sectors on a formatted tape, even a new tape: as we mentioned above, these may be caused by the tape splice, for instance.

It isn't possible to obtain read/write access to a single byte of data. Instead, read and write operations must cover a sector as a whole: so to change the contents of one byte, the entire block (the term for the sector contents) must be re-written. Each sector can contain data relating to a single file. It's not possible to store data from more than one file in a single sector, and this is one factor which puts an effective limit on the number of files that a cartridge can hold.

Small markers known as sector headers are recorded at intervals on the tape by the formatting routine. The routine also records dummy data on the tape between the headers, as a check to ensure that all the tape is in an acceptable condition. The sector headers are not affected by subsequent read/write operations and remain in place until the cartridge is reformatted.

Four different elements are recorded on each tape:

(i)   A 'preamble' or 'sync' block of data, used to synchronize the read/write heads so that they recognize byte boundaries.
(ii)   Data, including:
    (a) The sector header (see below)
    (b) The block header (again, see below)
    (c) The block of a file, including the file header outlined above
(iii)   A checksum, an error-checking device used to help ensure that data is recorded correctly and that read errors are identified.

(iv)   Specific gaps, both to separate the sector header from the sector contents and to fill the space between the end of one sector contents and the header of the following sector.

Sector Headers

The sector header consists of fourteen bytes of data. First is a flag (byte FF, to indicate that this is the start of the header). Next comes the sector number. The sectors are numbered in descending order, down to zero. Ten bytes contain the characters of the tape name: that is, the name you choose to give the cartridge as a whole when formatting it. If the name is less than ten characters long, this name is padded with blanks. Finally, there is a sixteen-bit random number.

The Block Header

The block header is separated by a six plus two byte preamble from the actual block contents and can be read separately from the block if required. It consists of a one byte file number or flag, followed by a one byte block number. The file number indicates the number of the file to which the block belongs: e.g. six blocks of data might be used to hold a long basic program and they would all be identified by the same file number, which is cross referenced to the file name in the cartridge directory. Special file numbers are reserved for the microdrive map ($F8) and to indicate vacant or bad blocks ($FD). The block number simply sequences the blocks within a file: so block 0 of the file will contain bytes 0 to 511, block 1 bytes 512 to 1023 and so on.

The Microdrive Map

Sector 0 of the tape is used to hold the sector map. It is referenced as file number $F8, block 0.

The map consists of 255 pairs of bytes: each pair comprising the file number and block number for a sector, in sequence. A vacant sector is given file number $FD and a bad sector file number $FF. The last byte holds the number of the most recently allocated sector.

The Directory

The microdrive map should not be confused with the tape directory, which is itself a file and can be read and manipulated as one. The directory is always given the file number 0. It consists of copies of the headers of every file on the medium, in numerical order, starting with its own header. If a file is deleted, the file length and the name length in the copy of its header are cleared.

Allocation of sectors to individual files is complex and is governed largely by the need to allow for the finite stop/start time of the microdrives. If a file is more than one block long, then twelve sectors are skipped between successive blocks. The first block is positioned twenty sectors after the most recently allocated sector on the tape.

DEALING WITH MICRODRIVE ERRORS

It isn't possible within SuperBasic to review microdrive contents other than through the normal file directory procedures. Utility programs written in machine code can, however, handle aspects such as retrieval of damaged file contents. It's possible to buy such programs, if you are not confident of writing your own.

Microdrive errors can be of various kinds. Read and write operations may cause 'soft' errors, which can be circumvented by a repeat of the operation. Tape failures may cause 'hard' errors, which cannot be circumvented. A hard read error will make an entire file inaccessible: it is for this reason that it is desirable to make at least one backup of every important file. The formatting routine will mark for non-use sectors which are suspected of physical deficiencies: however, later degradation of the tape may cause hard errors in sectors which passed the initial format check.

You may like to note that an automatic verify operation is included in the SuperBasic block-writing commands for saving all types of file. The data is verified on the next pass of the tape, ensuring that it is still present and correct seven seconds after the initial write. It is not necessary – or possible – to command a separate Verify of saved data.

Should you suffer from read errors, note that errors are likely to be minimized if you read files on the same drive as you wrote them on. Writing to drive 1 and reading from drive 2 or *vice versa* may cause marginally adequate files to become unreadable.

HANDLING THE MICRODRIVE DIRECTORY

Though the directory is an ordinary microdrive file, as we mentioned above, and can in some ways be manipulated as an ordinary file, it's easier to handle it via the DIR(ectory) command. The DIR command automatically outputs selected data from the directory, in a fixed format: first the cartridge name, then the numbers of free and available sectors, then the names of each normal file on the cartridge. Much of the information in the directory file, including useful data such as the length of each file, is not output by the directory command. If you want to gain access to this information, you will need to write your own machine-code routine (or buy a utility) that accesses and manipulates the directory contents.

Often, though, you'll be happy with the information the directory provides: you may just wish it was presented more attractively! The default QDOS directory scrolls rapidly down the channel 1 screen, making it difficult for you to read the first entries if the directory is more than twenty items long. The program listed in Figure 13.1 is designed to make the directory use rather easier and more versatile.

Figure 13.1 Directory Utility Program

```
10 REMark file directory program
20 WINDOW 512,256,0,0
30 CLS
40 AT 0,5: PRINT "Directory Utility"
50 getdir
60 set = 0
70 display
80 REPeat choice
90 FOR menu = 1 TO 6
100 SELect ON menu
110 =1: AT 13,10: PRINT "F    forward";
120 =2: AT 14,10: PRINT "B    back";
130 =3: AT 15,10: PRINT "D    delete program";
140 =4: AT 16,10: PRINT "L    load program";
150 =5: AT 17,10: PRINT "R    run  program";
160 =6: AT 18,10: PRINT "X    exit program";
170 END SELect
180 END FOR menu
190 AT 19,10: INPUT r$
200 IF r$ == "X" THEN EXIT choice: END IF
210 IF r$ == "F" THEN nextlot: NEXT choice
220 IF r$ == "B" THEN backlot: NEXT choice
230 IF r$ INSTR "LRD" = 0 THEN NEXT choice
240 AT 20,0: CLS 2
250 AT 21,1: INPUT"file name ";x$
260 IF r$ == "L" THEN ldr: EXIT choice
270 IF r$ == "R" THEN lrn: EXIT choice
280 IF r$ == "D" THEN DELETE "mdv"&m%&"_"&x$
290 END REPeat choice
300 DELETE "mdv"&m%&"_f$"
310 STOP
320 DEFine PROCedure getdir
1000 DEFine PROCedure getdir
1010 LOCal a$, loop
1020 AT 2,5: INPUT "Which microdrive? ";m%
1030 IF m%< 1 OR m%>2 THEN GO TO 1000
1040 DIM d$(100,20)
1050 OPEN_NEW £5,"mdv"&m%&"_f$"
1060 DIR£5,"mdv"&m%&"_"
1070 CLOSE £5
1080 OPEN_IN £5,"mdv"&m%&"_f$"
1090 INPUT £5;n$;l$;
1100 n = 0


1110 REPeat loop
1120 n = n + 1
1130 INPUT£5;a$;
1140 d$(n) = a$
1150 IF EOF(£5) THEN CLOSE £5: EXIT loop
1160 END REPeat loop
1170 END DEFine getdir
```

```
1200 DEFine PROCedure ldr
1210 DELETE "mdv"&m%&"_f$"
1220 LOAD "mdv"&m%&"_"&x$
1230 END DEFine ldr
1240 DEFine PROCedure lrn
1250 DELETE "mdv"&m%&"_f$"
1260 LRUN "mdv"&m%&"_"&x$
1270 END DEFine ldr
2000 DEFine PROCedure display
2010 LOCal base, show
2020 CLS
2030 AT 4,0: PRINT, "Cartridge ";n$
2040 AT 4,40: PRINT l$;
2050 base = set*24
2060 FOR show = 0 TO 5
2070 AT show+6,0:  PRINT d$(base+(show*4))
2080 AT show+6,20: PRINT d$(base+(show*4)+1)
2090 AT show+6,40: PRINT d$(base+(show*4)+2)
2100 AT show+6,60: PRINT d$(base+(show*4)+3)
2110 IF base+(show*4)+3 > n THEN EXIT show
2120 END FOR show
2130 END DEFine display
3000 DEFine PROCedure nextlot
3010 IF (set*24)+23 < n THEN
3020 set = set + 1
3030 ELSE
3040 PRINT "no more sets"
3050 PAUSE 500
3060 END IF
3070 display
3080 END DEFine nextlot
4000 DEFine PROCedure backlot
4010 IF set > 0 THEN
4020 set = set - 1
4030 ELSE
4040 PRINT "first set currently on display"
4050 PAUSE 500
4060 END IF
4070 display
4080 END DEFine backlot
```

FILE DIRECTORY PROGRAM

Figure 13.1 provides the listing for a file directory program which doubles as a simple 'file update' utility. (There's a list of variables in Table 13.1.) It doesn't back up files: below we provide a separate program to do that.

The DIRectory can be input, not just to a screen channel, but to any channel that you open. It's possible to send a directory listing to a printer, for instance, without its appearing on screen at all. This program reads the directory, not to the screen, but to another microdrive file which we call 'f$'. It's then possible to read f$ item by item (as it is not possible to read the directory immediately) into a memory array: d$, with up to 100 items (you may need to increase this if you regularly put a very large number of small

Table 13.1 Variable List for Directory Utility Program

Global variables:

Array for directory entries:	d$(100,20)
Set of entries for display:	set
Menu choice loop variable:	choice
Menu display loop variable:	menu
Actual choice from menu:	r$
File name for menu choice:	x$
Name of temporary file:	f$
Data on cartridge name and stats:	n$, l$
Microdrive number:	m%
Number of last directory entry:	n

Local to procedure Getdir:

Input variable from microdrive file:	a$
Loop variable:	loop

Local to procedure Display:

First entry in set:	base
Loop variable for entry displays:	show

files on your cartridges) of up to twenty characters each. (Note: the first two items in f$, the cartridge number and usage statistics, are read instead into separate string variables, n$ and l$.)

Once in the array, the directory items can be neatly presented on screen. For this purpose we use a full-width window in Mode 0. (It's not difficult to adapt the program to mode 1). We've used the default channel #1 as the screen channel, so there is no need to include a channel number in screen-oriented statements. Channel #5 is used as an input and output channel for the f$ file. Change this channel number to another suitable one if you use it regularly for some other purpose.

We divide the contents of d$ into blocks of twenty-four file names which can be presented four across and six deep. It's possible to page through the different blocks, so that all file names can be displayed.

The bottom of the screen is used for a short menu, which includes not just the 'page through' options but options to delete files or to load and/or run files. Any number of files can be deleted; loading a file automatically exits the program. The three exit routines (via loading a new file, running a new file or a simple exit) all provide for deleting the temporary directory file and closing the channel used.

FILE COPY PROGRAM

QDOS does not provide any backup utility for entire microdrive cartridges: it only includes a single file COPY command. It takes time to type this repeatedly in order to back up most or all of the files on a cartridge. This utility

Figure 13.2 File Copy Program

```
10 REMark file copy program
20 MODE 4
30 WINDOW 512,256,0,0:CLS
40 CSIZE 3,1
50 PRINT "file copy program"
60 PRINT: CSIZE 0,0
70 PRINT "Put source cartridge in drive 1"
80 PRINT "and destination cartridge in drive 2"
90 choice
100 getdir
110 clone
120 PRINT "copy program complete"
130 STOP
1000 DEFine PROCedure choice
1010 LOCal loop
1020 REPeat loop
1030 INPUT "Copy all files (a) or selected files (s)? ";r$
1040 IF r$(1) == "s" OR r$(1) == "a" THEN EXIT loop
1050 END REPeat loop
1060 END DEFine choice
1100 DEFine PROCedure getdir
1110 LOCal d$, d1$
1120 PRINT "Accessing microdrive..."
1130 OPEN_NEW £4, "mdv2_temp"
1140 DIR £4, "mdv1_"
1150 CLOSE £4
1160 OPEN_IN £4, "mdv2_temp"
1170 INPUT£4, d$; d1$;
1180 PRINT d$; d1$
1190 END DEFine getdir
2000 DEFine PROCedure clone
2010 LOCal loop, a$, q$
2020 REPeat loop
2030 IF EOF(£4) THEN shutdown: EXIT loop
2040 INPUT£4, a$: PRINT a$
2050 IF r$ == "s" THEN
2060 INPUT "copy file? ";q$
2070 IF q$(1) <> "y" AND q$(1) <> "Y" THEN NEXT loop
2080 END IF
2090 COPY "mdv1_"&a$ TO "mdv2_"&a$
2100 PRINT "file copied"
2110 END REPeat loop
2120 END DEFine clone
2130 DEFine PROCedure shutdown
2140 CLOSE £4
2150 DELETE "mdv2_temp"
2160 END DEFine shutdown
```

program cuts down the typing for you. It can be used for selected files or for an entire cartridge. In either case it copies files from drive 1 to drive 2, using the same names for both source and destination files. The destination cartridge is *not* re-formatted in this routine. The program does not check existing file names on the destination cartridge, and these must not, of course, duplicate the names of the source files or the program will end with an error.

Note that the CLONE files on the Psion microdrive cartridges are not substitutes for this program. They are special purpose programs and not general purpose copy utilities.

Once again we use a temporary microdrive file to hold the contents of the directory. This file is placed on drive 2, so that it will not be copied itself! This time, though, there is no need to read its contents into an array. They are simply read item by item into the same variable (a$, except for the file name and statistics) and then dealt with in sequence.

The program does print 'Accessing microdrive' initially when a long wait will be caused by repeated microdrive accesses. Later access delays will vary in length depending upon the user's choice of files to be copied, and no message is printed at this stage in the program.

14

QL Memory Management

The QL's memory map has two distinct aspects. First, there are physical aspects to the memory map: the allocation of memory to hardware functions, which is not open to change by the average user. Second, there are software aspects: the way in which the QDOS operating system allocates memory for different purposes. The first aspect involves both ROM and RAM; the second concerns primarily RAM.

HARDWARE ALLOCATION OF MEMORY

Figure 14.1 shows the hardware allocation of memory. You'll note that this map is slightly different from that given under 'memory' in the 'concepts' section of the QL User Guide.

In the User Guide, memory divisions are given in hex. For Basic programmers, it's easier to work in decimal – not least because there's no function in SuperBasic that allows you to enter hex numbers directly in a SuperBasic program. Therefore, we've included both hex numbers and decimal equivalents on this map.

You'll see that of the megabyte of memory that can be directly addressed by the 68008 processor, the first 20000 hex (131,072 decimal) addresses or 128K, are allocated to ROM. This includes both the 48K bytes of the inbuilt system ROM (addresses 0 to 0C000 hex, 49,152 decimal) the expansion

Figure 14.1 Hardware Allocation of Memory

hex.	decimal		
FFFFF	1048575		
		(reserved)	expansion i/o
C0000	786432		
		(reserved)	add-on RAM (512K)
40000	262144		
		96 KB RAM	main RAM
28000	163840		
		32KB RAM	screen RAM
20000	131072		
		(reserved)	expansion I/O
1C000	114688		
		(i/o)	input/output addresses
18000	98304		
		(reserved)	expansion i/o
10000	65536		
		16KB ROM	plug-in ROM
0C000	49152		
		48KB ROM	system ROM
00000	0		

ROMs that can be added via the cartridge slot and various input/output and expansion i/o ROMs. The next batch of addresses are allocated to the inbuilt 128K of RAM, which we consider below. If the RAM is expanded by using a half megabyte RAMpack, then the next batch of addresses will be dedicated to the expansion RAM. At the very top of memory is a second area reserved for use by expansion i/o devices.

SOFTWARE ALLOCATION OF MEMORY

The allocation of RAM to different purposes by QDOS is largely automatic, though it is possible to influence RAM allocation in some ways and, of course, to reserve sections of RAM for specific purposes. Figure 14.2 shows the outline of the RAM memory map. You'll note that RAM fills from both top and bottom addresses, leaving a remaining area of varying size in the middle.

QDOS does not support 'memory management', the movement of blocks of data around memory in order to maximize the space available. Instead, chunks of memory are reserved for specific purposes. Once reserved, they remain in use for that purpose only until the reservation is cancelled by a second command. This means that data and programs can normally be referred to (in machine code) by giving specific (physical) memory addresses. In contrast, the position in memory of system variables will vary as the block allocations are made and it is often difficult to access these with standard POKEs as can be done on many other micros. The position in memory of a Basic program may also vary.

The first chunk of RAM (addresses 20000 to 27FFFF hex, 131,072 to 163,839 decimal) is dedicated to the screen memory. Later in this chapter we look at the allocation of screen memory. This is 32K, providing a full memory map for the hi-res. screen. Note that there's no less demanding screen mode available on the QL: 32K is a standard allocation to the screen. We looked in depth at the arrangement of screen memory in Chapter 11.

The QDOS version 1.03 memory map provisionally allocates the next 32K for a 'second screen': another memory-mapped screen that can be substituted for the first, allowing the user to keep two screens full of data in memory simultaneously and swap between them instantly without re-drawing. There's no command in Basic to allow swapping of screens and there are no provisions for drawing or printing to the second screen, though it would be possible to POKE data to this section of memory. At present, it is best to regard this second screen as 'unimplemented', though machine code programs may make use of it.

Following screen memory at the bottom of RAM comes an area devoted to system tables and the system variables. The 'system tables' are various tables of data involved with resource management. System variables, as you

Figure 14.2 RAM Memory Allocation

System name

SV-RAMT-1		
	resident procedures	(fills downwards)
SV-RESPR		
	transient programs	(fills downwards)
SV-TRNSP		
	Basic command interpreter data (inc. Basic programs)	fills downwards & moves with changes in size transient program area
SV-BASIC		
	filing subsystem slave blocks	soaks up spare memory
SV-FREE		
	channel data and other 'heap' items	(fills upwards)
SV-HEAP		
	resource management tables and system variable data	
	display memory	address &2800 if single screen is in use

Note that while the variable names used for the memory divisions can be useful for reference purposes, they are *not* recognized by the Basic interpreter. You cannot discover the address of a division by a command like 'PRINT SV-HEAP'. The partial exception here is RESPR: see the keyword definition for RESPR in the QL User Guide.

probably know, are memory locations in which essential pieces of systems information (e.g. on memory allocation, on screen status, on i/o status, etc.) are kept. We look later at the addresses of vital system variables and at ways in which you can read and write to them.

Another area of memory immediately above this is also reserved for system purposes. It keeps data on channels opened, and holds other 'heap' items. Working storage for the input/output system is allocated within this area of RAM; other transient programs (i.e machine code programs loaded temporarily into RAM) may also reserve workspace in this area.

Now let's look at the top of RAM. Right at the top is a space reserved for resident procedures. Resident procedures should be distinguished from the transient procedures that you incorporate into your Basic programs. They are more fundamental procedures that form a part of the extended SuperBasic language and RAM is automatically reserved for them on system boot. Though these procedures are held in RAM and not in ROM, you can call them just as if they were Basic commands with definitions stored in ROM. We'll discuss how these procedures can be created in later versions of QDOS in Chapter 15.

Below the resident procedure space is a space reserved for transient programs. QDOS will normally reserve space for these machine code programs and some QDOS functions are specifically designed to handle this task.

It's possible to store data in the transient program area, but it is necessary to handle them in special ways, so that to QDOS the data form an inactive 'job' (i.e. program).

Next comes an area that will be more familiar to you. It contains your SuperBasic programs and related workspace: e.g. space for holding arrays and variables set up by your programs. Like the other RAM allocations, this area will be expanded by QDOS as necessary to give sufficient room for your programs. With 128K minimum RAM to play with, you are unlikely to suffer from a shortage of memory for your Basic programs on the QL.

A central area of memory will be left over, of varying size depending upon the uses to which your QL is being put. QDOS automatically allocates this area as 'slave blocks' to the filing subsystem. In other words, the contents of blocks written to or read from microdrive will be duplicated in this area. (See Chapter 13 for details on how data is stored on microdrive.) This means that the spare RAM in the QL can automatically act as a 'silicon disk', providing instant access to data intended for secondary storage. If you add a RAMpack to the machine, the area free for this purpose will of course increase and you should see a marked improvement in the speed with which programs handling microdrive accesses (and reading from the 'silicon disk') run.

It is important to note that the *only* fixed address in this RAM memory allocation is the address of the top of the main display memory: 28000 hex, 163,840 decimal. *All* other significant addresses may change from-program to program.

Note too that the names used to define the boundaries of the different areas of RAM are *not* recognized in SuperBasic or indeed by QDOS. It isn't possible, then, simply to ask the computer to 'PRINT FRE' or the equivalent. Instead, operating system procedures must be followed for finding out whatever you may need to know about vital RAM addresses. We'll look at some of these procedures in the next chapter.

SUPERBASIC DATA STORAGE

Information about names used in a SuperBasic program is stored in four different areas: the name table, the name list, the variable value area and the arithmetic stack. The exact location of these four areas in memory is variable, as we explained above.

Variables and arrays are handled indirectly by SuperBasic. The name table is the first reference, to which each variable reference (i.e. variable name or array reference) in the program points. Each entry in it is eight bytes long and consists of: a description of the name usage, e.g. string, floating point, integer, loop index, function or procedure name; a pointer to the name list and a pointer to the variables values area. Note that the name table doesn't contain the name itself, as used in the program. It contains merely a brief reference to it. The actual name – which may, of course, be quite long – is held in the name list, which contains a note of the length followed by the name itself.

The variable value area is a heap – that is, an undifferentiated block of memory – in which entries are allocated in multiples of eight bytes.

Different types of variable take up different amounts of space, and though you will often find that lack of memory is no problem on the QL, you may find it useful to know how the variables are stored. The different kinds are stored as follows:

> *integer:* 2 bytes
> *floating-point number:* two byte exponent plus four byte mantissa. It's obvious why integers work faster!
> *string variable:* data on the number of characters, followed by the actual characters. Space allocation is rounded up to an even number.
> *integer array:* array header (length varies depending upon number of dimensions) plus two bytes for each element
> *floating-point array:* header plus six bytes for each element
> *string array:* this is stored as an array of characters. The maximum length of the string is rounded up to the nearest even number.

SYSTEM VARIABLES AND SIMILAR INFORMATION

As we mentioned above, the address of system variables and much other vital information may change depending upon memory allocations that are performed by QDOS. The information provided below should be used with this in mind.

The basic system variables will, if only one screen memory is in use, start from a base address of $28000, the top of screen memory. Among the addresses you may find useful are:

$28004	base of common heap area
$28008	first free space in common heap area
$2800C	base of free area
$28010	base of basic area
$28014	base of transient program area
$28018	first free space in transient program area
$2801C	base of resident procedure area
$28020	top of RAM (plus 1)

All these items are one long word (thirty-two bits) in length.

$2808A	auto-repeat buffer
$2808C	auto-repeat delay
$2808E	auto-repeat 1/frequency
$28090	auto-repeat count
$28096	sound status
$280AA	flashing cursor status

These items are a short word (sixteen bits) in length.

You can access the status register in the 68008 chip (see Chapter 12) using the address $18063. Three bits in this register have special uses in the QL:

bit 1 blanks the display
bit 3 sets (or cancels) the 256 mode
bit 7 sets the screen number

Most of the screen characteristics that, in many computers, would be held in system variables are in the QL held in 'window data blocks'. A separate set of characteristics is held for each window that has been defined (or, in other words, for each screen channel). It is necessary to use operating system commands (see Chapter 15) in order to discover the location in memory of each data block. Among the addresses *within the block* that you may find useful are:

$22	cursor position (word)
$26	cursor increment (word)

$43	cursor flag (byte: 0 = suppressed, any other value = visible)
$49	fill mode (byte: 0 = off)
$5C	(long word) pointer to fill buffer
$64	various attributes, bit by bit as follows:
0:	underline
1:	flash
2:	transparent background
3:	XOR characters/graphics
4:	double height
5:	extended width
6:	double width
7:	graphics positioned characters

15

QDOS in Depth

QDOS is the QL operating system. Some aspects of QDOS are apparent to the Basic programmer: you'll recognize certain keywords in the QL User Guide that have the legend 'QDOS' to categorize them. In this chapter, we will be concentrating on aspects of QDOS that are *not* immediately apparent to the Basic programmer. This material should be interesting mainly to low level programmers, but the short machine programs that we present towards the end of the chapter can be keyed in by those who are not familiar with low level programming.

We do not attempt to provide a full introduction to low level programming on the QL in this book. This chapter is intended mainly to give you a taste of how QDOS and the QL in general work and what they can do.

Though 'DOS' is the recognized abbreviation for a *disk* operating system, QDOS is of course not primarily a disk operating system, but a microdrive one. The system automatically handles file creation and similar tasks on microdrives. It will also handle general purpose input and output, but it does *not* contain a conventional floppy disk controller.

A number of versions of QDOS are in existence: some pre-production and several different ones on early production versions of the QL, especially those with EPROM rather than ROM system software. The version on which we base our comments is version 1.3; later or earlier versions will have more or less significant differences, which, unfortunately, we are unable to cover here.

Many operating systems act as an independent 'program' under which other programs 'run'. CP/M, for instance, stands for 'Control Program/ Monitor' and we speak of applications programs as running under CP/M. QDOS works in a rather different way. It consists of a set of procedures, which may be called up by programs. It does not provide a particular operating environment in which applications programs work, though some of its resource allocation tasks are performed semi-automatically. There's no need for a machine code program to use QDOS's resources at all, though programmers will normally wish to make use of the facilities provided by QDOS. The Basic interpreter uses QDOS functions and when writing programs in Basic you will certainly be making use of QDOS, probably without even realizing it.

The facilities that QDOS can provide are very strongly determined by the facilities provided by the 68008 chip. You may find it helpful to re-read the section in Chapter 12 that describes the 68008 and its workings, before attempting to tackle the rest of this chapter.

QDOS BOOTSTRAP ROUTINE

The QDOS bootstrap routine is run automatically whenever the system is cold-booted: i.e. by switching on power for the first time or by pressing the Reset button on the right-hand side of the case. It performs the following steps in sequence:

(a)   The system variables (specific memory locations the contents of which are important to the correct operation of the computer) are initialized to their default values.

(b)   A RAM test is performed, to ensure that the rest of RAM is functioning correctly. You will see this reflected in a random coloured pattern on the screen.

(c)   The memory address C000 hex is checked by the system. If a plug-in ROM is present, this address will contain a characteristic long word and, in this case, the ROM at this address will be treated as a plug in Basic/device driver.

(d)   The expansion slots are checked, to see if any device driver circuitry is present.

(e)   The code invoked by (c) and (d) may lead to control of the system being assumed by a plug-in device, in which case the bootstrap operation is effectively complete. If this is not the case, the operating-system next checks to see if there is a device (see notes on devices below) named 'BOOT' or file on microdrive 1 called 'BOOT'. If either of these is found, then the file will be loaded and run as a Basic program, which will then take command of the system.

You will see procedure (e) in operation when you press F1 with a Psion software cartridge present in drive 1. The program on the cartridge will be booted automatically. You can simulate the same process yourself, if you wish, by saving a 'boot' file that you have programmed yourself.

QDOS JOBS

The basic unit of QDOS operation is the 'job'. Everything that is done by the processor is seen in terms of a 'job': quite simply, a task that is to be completed. Jobs have different priorities, based upon three different states.

> *active*: i.e. capable of running and taking a share – not necessarily the lion's share – of system resources. All active jobs have different priorities.
>
> *suspended*, i.e. capable of running, but currently in suspension: e.g. waiting for another job to complete, some input/output operation or a time delay to expire.
>
> *inactive*: not capable of running.

In some cases, a job's priority is determined by its contents. In other cases, the priority can be determined – or changed – by the programmer. Once the job priority is fixed, QDOS will automatically handle the allocation of processor time and resources to that job.

You can think of a job as being a program: as it usually is, on some scale, though it's possible to treat data files as 'jobs' under some circumstances. It is a series of instructions, capable of being acted upon. However, it is not the case that only one job can be held in the computer at any one time. Though only one SuperBasic program can be stored at a time in RAM, a wide variety of lower-level jobs, active, suspended and inactive, can be held in RAM. In other words, a job might be a simple QDOS function, a machine code routine or a complete high-level program. You can even think of the command interpreter as being a job, though in this case it has some special characteristics.

Depending upon its nature, a job might be executed in one go or might share processor time with assorted other jobs. It is in this sense that the QL is a *multitasking* computer.

USING QDOS RESOURCES

In order to understand how QDOS routines are invoked, we need to understand some of the components of the QDOS environment. Among the most fundamental are the *system vectors*. There are two relevant system vectors: the manager and the input/output subsystem. Each have a variety of applications.

A system vector is an aspect of the system that normally functions automatically. The manager manages processor resources, the i/o subsystem manages input and output operations. When you want to invoke a special routine, you make a *call* that 'traps' the vector, interrupting its automatic functioning and substituting the operation that you request. It's as if you're saying to the system manager, 'hang on a minute, drop what you're doing and come and help me with this job over here'.

A call is indeed a job – as we defined 'job' above – to the operating system and, as such, it has a priority of its own. System calls must be executed in a special 'supervisor mode', in which QDOS will not allow any other job to take over the processor. In other words, supervisor mode gives the call top priority. Calls to the manager vector are 'atomic', and will be processed to completion in this way; calls to the i/o subsystem and scheduler calls are only partially atomic and they may relinquish the processor after their primary function has been achieved.

A call needs to provide three different types of information:

– A *trap number*, or trap vector, which indicates which vector is to be trapped by the call. The numbers are:

Trap #0: enters supervisor mode, necessary for jobs that must not be interrupted by competing jobs.

Trap #1: call to the manager vector.

Trap #2: calls to the i/o subsystem for the allocation of channels, devices and files.

Trap #3: calls for serial i/o.

Trap #4: used for interfacing with the Basic command interpreter.

– A *parameter* which indicates what action is to be taken. For example, in Trap #5, parameter 2 gives information on a job, while parameter 4 removes a job from the transient program area.

– Optionally, further parameters which provide data needed for the execution of the call.

The initial parameter is passed to QDOS by writing it to register D0. Additional parameters are passed by writing them to other registers in the processor. Parameters cannot be passed by writing them to RAM locations: registers are used throughout.

Many calls will result in the production of information by the system. This information too is conveyed by putting it in the processor's registers. In this case, D0 is used to send error messages: it should be checked to ensure that the call has been successfully handled. Other registers are used to return other parameters.

CREATING A JOB

As we saw above, a job consists of a set of instructions and/or data that is held in the transient program area. Now we look at the processes involved in creating a job.

A job is created by the following process.

First, a system call is used to reserve space within the transient program area. The space reserved must be sufficient for the job instructions, for its stack and its working memory. The 'job owner' (i.e. the job under which this new job will run, if any) is indicated, the length of code, data space and the start address for the instructions are also indicated. The call returns a job identification number.

Second, the instructions and data that make up the job, including any data that need to be placed on the job stack, are put into memory using a loader program or similar procedure.

Third, the processor registers are initialized to contain necessary data about the job's reserved space and the job is activated.

SCHEDULING JOBS

As a number of jobs can be active at any time, it's important that there should be a clear system for setting priorities. The job scheduler handles the priority ratings, according to the system outlined below.

A set of jobs in memory, each with a different priority rating, is known as a 'job tree'.

When a job is activated, it starts to achieve a priority rating. The job scheduler steadily increments the priorities of all jobs that are active but are not actually being executed. The one with the highest priority rating is then permitted to execute.

It is also possible to make execution of one job dependent upon the completion of another. A special flag for each in the job control area can be used to indicate if another job is dependent upon completion. The identity number of the job that is waiting for this one to finish is also given.

As well as simply activating a job, it is possible to set a specific priority or to force over-ride of the current job in progress so that a new one can be executed.

USING MACHINE CODE TO ACCESS QDOS
FACILITIES: CHANGING THE FONT

At the time of writing this book, no assemblers had been made available for the QL. The only way to program the computer on a low level was by writing direct machine code, using a loader program to load the machine code instructions and data into memory. This laborious method of programming makes the writing of large scale application programs a real feat of endurance, but it's not unrealistic for an amateur programmer to write short machine code routines to access QDOS facilities that are not supported at a high level. In the remainder of this chapter, we'll outline how this can be done and present a simple machine code utility.

We can't describe 68008 instructions or discuss QDOS utilities in detail in this book. If you wish to write your own machine code routines you will need to obtain Sinclair's documentation of QDOS (or a book which explains QDOS in much more depth) and a book describing 68000/68008 machine code.

The QDOS feature which we've chosen to explore is the facility to create an alternative font in RAM, to replace or supplement the default character set which is stored in ROM. In fact, there are two character sets held by the operating system, but there are no high-level commands at present to enable you to switch between them, let alone to define your own characters.

Trap #3, a call for serial output, is the one which we need in this instance. Routine 25 (i.e. the routine called when 25 is put into register D0) 'sets or resets the fo(u)nt'. It's necessary to provide as parameters the identity number of the channel for which the font is to be used and the base addresses of the new one and of its backup. QDOS should automatically combine two fonts. A character chosen will automatically be reproduced from the first font, if the memory block designated contains a valid character description in the correct position. If it doesn't, then the corresponding character from the second font should be used. If this, too, is lacking, then the lowest valid character from the second font should be used. This feature should mean that it's possible to insert just a few new character definitions into a RAM-based font, using the ROM font as an automatic backup for other characters. However, it didn't work as we expected in the program we outline below.

We'll create the 'new font' code as a new procedure, which can effectively be added to the existing SuperBasic procedures and called (once loaded) like any other resident procedure.

Font Structure

A standard character definition on the QL is six pixels across by ten pixels down. The number of pixels actually used on screen will, of course, depend upon the character size selected. Of these sixty pixels, the *top row* must be blank. There's no provision for entering data for this row, so it is not possible to produce a solid block of colour using character definitions. One column is also left blank, so that in fact nine rows of five pixels are defined. In memory, nine bytes are used for each character, with bits 6 to 2 inclusive being used to store the data. Figure 15.1 may make this clearer.

The font is structured on the assumption that an initial batch of codes will

Figure 15.1 Character Matrix on the QL

```
This is what a typical character looks like:
```

```
(This isn't an actual character from the QL font,
just an indication of the area available.)
When defining the character, byte 1 will indicate the top row
(not counting the blank row)
like this:
     7 6 5 4 3 2 1 0
     0:0 0 1 1 0:0 0

Bits 7 and 0 are unused; bit 1 represents the blank column
 to the right of the character
Byte 2 will indicate the next row, like this:
     7 6 5 4 3 2 1 0
     0:0 1 0 0 1:0 0
```

consist of 'invalid' characters – ASCII control codes, for instance. The default 'first valid character' comes at code IF: 31 in decimal, the start of the standard ASCII font. The font definition starts with a code to determine which will be this first valid character and then indicates how many characters are to be included in the font. After this, the actual character data is provided for each character in the code block to be defined. So from the start address of the font, the data entered will be like this:

00 code of lowest valid character (one byte)
01 number of valid characters – 1 (one byte)
02 to 0A nine bytes of pixels to define the nine definable rows of the first character.
0B to 13 ditto for the second character, etc . . . .

The definition of the default font stretches from $20 to $7F in ROM. If you PEEK these locations, you will be able to see its structure.

Creating and Loading the Machine Code

Here's a simple program that can be used to create and load the code you will be producing, and (with slight adaptations) other machine code routines you may devise or come across.

```
10    base = RESPR(200)
20    add = base
```

```
 30       REPeat put__code
 40       READ a$
 50       POKE__W add, dec (a$)
 60       IF EOF THEN EXIT put__code
 70       add = add + 2
 80       END REPeat put__code
 90       SBYTES MDV1__FONT__MC, base, 200
100       STOP
```

In line 10, we use the RESPR command to reserve space in memory (in the resident procedure area, which is not affected when Basic programs are NEWed) for the new code. It will return the base value of the reserved space, which goes into the 'base' variable. We then read the data of the program repeatedly and POKE__W (long word) it into the reserved space. A user defined function 'dec' is used to convert the hex data that will be read into the decimal data required by the program. The 'add' variable which controls this REPeat loop is incremented by two, since we are using sixteen-bit words rather than bytes. Line 90 saves the section of memory we've POKEd, using a suitable microdrive file name, for future direct use.

Here's the 'dec' function:

```
500       DEFine FuNction dec(z$)
510       LOCAL hex$, t
520       hex$ = "0123456789ABCDEF"
530       val = 0
540       FOR t = 1 TO LEN(z$)
550       val = val*16 + (Z$(T) INSTR hex$) - 1
560       NEXT t
570       RETurn val
580       END DEFine dec
```

We'll be loading nine short sections of machine code which make up our 'new font' utility. We'll give the coded data for each, and explain in outline what each does.

Table
This section contains the data required for the loader (see below) to add a new procedure to the set of resident procedures. In the table must be given the name of each new procedure and/or function, and its execution address. In this case we're adding only one new procedure, so there is just one entry in the table. Here's the necessary code:

```
1000      REM table
1010      DATA "1", "1E", "446", "4F4E", "5400", "0", "0"
```

We can't explain table creation in detail here, but briefly, the items in the data list represent:

1 : number of procedures

1E, 446, 4F4E, 5400: data on name and execution addresses for the procedure

0 : closing marker for procedure data

0 : number of functions.

Loader

The standard QDOS procedures include a subroutine which can be used to add new resident procedures and/or functions. Three steps are necessary:

(a) A pointer is set to the table we drew up above:
LEA TABLE(PC)

(b) A call is made to the subroutine, by putting its vector number ($110) into register A2.
MOVE.W $110.A2
JSR (A2)

(c) Control is returned to Basic:
MOVE.Q 0.d0
RTS

In machine code, this gives us the following data statement:

```
1020    REM loader
1030    DATA  "43FA",  "FFF0",  "3478",  "110",  "4E92",
"7000", "4E75"
```

Our 'table' code took up seven words (fourteen bytes) at the start of the reserved area, so this 'loader' code will start at address base + 14. To execute the subroutine and add the new procedure to Basic, we need to:

CALL base + 14

Error-Param

As we mentioned earlier in the chapter, any errors generated during a QDOS trap routine are reported in register D0. This brief routine simply enables the 'bad parameter' error to be returned when necessary. Here's the code:

```
1040    REM error-param
1050    DATA "70F1", "4E75"
```

Start Procedure

This routine checks to ensure that the correct parameters are provided for passing to the 'font' trap. Either two or three parameters will be needed:

(1) The channel number (i.e. of the channel for which the font will be used).

(2) The base address of the first font to be used.

(3)   (optional) the base address of the second font to be used.

We use a QDOS utility routine to enable us to pass these parameters. Because of the way in which the routine works (which we can't explain in detail here), it's necessary to do some careful checking and manipulating of the data. If the parameters are not provided correctly, this routine branches to the 'error-param' routine described above. Here's the code:

```
1060      REM start procedure
1070      DATA  "C36",  "92",  "B801",  "66FA",  "C36",  "2",
"809", "660A", "95CA", "6010"
```

3-params

This routine continues the error-checking in the 'start-procedure' routine, and is called by that routine when there is a third parameter provided:

```
1080      REM 3-params
1090      DATA  "C36",  "12",  "B809",  "66E0",  "C36",  "2",
"B811", "66D8"
```

Get Vars

Once the parameters have been checked, this routine uses a QDOS vector to help put the parameters into the appropriate registers.

```
1100      REM get-vars
1110      DATA  "3478",  "118",  "4E92",  "C43",  "2",  "6704",
"2471", "E808"
```

Get-id

Just to make life difficult, the channel numbers used by Basic do not correspond with the channel numbers used at a low level by QDOS! It's necessary to pass the QDOS channel number, not the Basic channel number, to the trap. This routine obtains the QDOS channel number from the table which the SuperBasic interpreter maintains for each open channel and puts it into the A0 register.

```
1140      REM get-id
1150      DATA  "COFC",  "28",  "D0AE",  "30",  "2040",  "2070",
"E800"
```

Change Font

At last we can call the font function! Four steps are necessary here:

(i)   First, the identity number of the initial parameter which selects the font function (25) must be put into register D0.

(ii)   Now, it's necessary to set a time-out.

(iii) Trap number 3 is called.

(iv)   The routine returns control to SuperBasic.

Here's the last section of code:

```
1160     REM change font
1170     DATA "7025", "7600", "4E43", "4E75"
```

Once you've run the initial program to write the data to memory and thensave it to microdrive, you can use a routine like this (either separately, or as part of your BOOT program) to active the new procedure.

```
10    a = RESPR(200)
20    LBYTES MDV1-FONT-MC, a
30    CALL a + 14
40    NEW
```

You will then have a new procedure called FONT (#n, x, [y]) which can be used like other SuperBasic procedures. Try it out on channel 2 (the listings channel) with a statement like:

```
FONT#2, 26,26
LIST
```

As there is not a valid font starting at memory location 26, the listing will be blank. Return quickly to the original font, with

```
FONT#2, 0, 0
```

Of course, though we've produced the FONT procedure, we haven't yet actually written a font! It's essential to do that in order to use the procedure properly. Here's a short program that will generate a single-character font; you can extend it, of course, to generate a full-length font:

```
10    a = RESPR(100)
20    FOR x = 0 TO 10
30    READ y: POKE x+a,y
40    END FOR x
50    DATA 65,0,24,24,24,24,120,120,120,120,0
```

This program starts its font at code 65 – i.e. the normal capital A. You can save it with a statement like:

```
SBYTES fontname, a, 100
```

and reload it with a short program like this:

```
10    b = RESPR(100)
20    LBYTES fontname, b
30    FONT#n, b
```

CHECK YOUR OPERATING SYSTEM VERSION

We checked the program above under version 1.02 and 1.03 of QDOS and it worked fine. However, it is possible that you may have to make some amendments if you use it under subsequent versions of the operating system.

It could be useful, for this as well as for other purposes, for you to find the number of the operating system version in your QL. You can't do this from SuperBasic, as you can find the Basic version number with 'PRINT ver$': instead you must use a QDOS trap. Figure 15.2 lists a short program, adapted

Figure 15.2 Find Operating System Number

```
100 REMark find operating system number
110 RESTORE
120 BASE=RESPR(200)
130 ADD = BASE
140 REPeat PUT_CODE
150 READ A$
160 POKE_W ADD, DEC(A$)
170 IF EOF THEN EXIT PUT_CODE
180 ADD = ADD + 2
190 END REPeat PUT_CODE
200 PRINT "OS version is ";
210 CALL BASE
220 FOR b = 0 TO 3
230 PRINT CHR$(PEEK(BASE + 14 + b));
240 END FOR b
250 DEFine FuNction DEC(Z$)
260 LOCal HEX$,T
270 HEX$="0123456789ABCDEF": VAL = 0
280 FOR T = 1 TO LEN(Z$)
290 VAL=16*VAL + (Z$(T) INSTR HEX$) - 1
300 NEXT T
310 RETurn VAL
320 END DEFine DEC
330 DATA "7000","4e41","43fa","8","2282","7000","4e75"
```

from the loader we gave above, which will do it for you.

There are only six machine code instructions in the routine, as follows:

7000	MOVE#0.d0	get system info.
4E41	TRAP#1	get system info.
43FA 0008	LEA 8(PC).A1	provide data space
2282	MOVE d2.L.(A1)	put QDOS vers. in d-space
7000	MOVE#0.d0	normal return to
4E75	RTS	SuperBasic

This time, as you see, we're using trap vector number 1, with the parameter 0 placed in d0 (first line). This routine is 'System Information', and it returns the operating system version (in four bytes: 'n.nn') in d2.L (i.e. register d2 used as a long word). This information is moved to the data space immediately following the machine code routine and we then read it using SuperBasic POKEs (to memory locations relative to the start of the space reserved for the routine) in the main program.

Note that in the listing we've used lower-case letters in our hex statements. These are often easier to type and the INSTR operator in the 'dec' function is case-independent, so it's quite practicable to do so.

16

The QLAN Local Area Network

The QLAN local area network is basically identical to the Sinclair Spectrum local area network and it is possible, by using the network, to link QLs not only to other QLs, but also to Spectrums and even to other computers. The QL User Guide gives only very brief details of the network and here we provide more details and suggestions on using these facilities.

Note that while QLs and Spectrums can communicate with each other, the QL cannot read Spectrum programs without special software. The Spectrum saves Basic keywords in a 'tokenized' form and the QL would need to be able to decode the tokens in order to make sense of a program. Though such software is not difficult to write in theory, it is not available (to our knowledge) as we write. It is certainly *not* provided with the basic networking system.

Note too that Spectrum computers only possess networking capabilities if they are fitted with the ZX Interface 1.

It is also possible to send communications from computer to computer using the RS232 serial link. However, in this chapter we concentrate on use of the QLAN/Spectrum network.

WHAT IS A NETWORK?

A network is simply an assemblage of two or more computers, linked together and able to share information and resources. For example, the second computer might wish to make use of a printer or microdrive attached to the first and *vice versa*. Sharing resources such as printers and microdrives is done simply by sending information, thus causing the computer with the resource to use it in the appropriate way.

Each computer linked into the network is called a *station*. In order to distinguish the different computers, each is given a 'station number': of course, all the station numbers used in the network should be unique. Valid network numbers are from one to sixty-three; zero is used for special purposes. As the numbers must be unique, this means that a maximum of sixty-three computers can be combined in this particular network.

Communication across the network is achieved by:

(a)   physically linking the computers, using the network lead provided with the QL (or a similar lead).

(b)   opening a software communications channel. The OPEN command used for all channel purposes is used here, though some other commands implicitly open channels.

(c)   one computer sending a message via the open channel.

(d)   one or more computers receiving the message.

Functions (b), (c) and (d) can all be achieved in SuperBasic: there is no need to program in machine code in order to use the network. Of course it is possible to handle network communications in machine code, but in this chapter we concentrate on SuperBasic operations.

The computer that sends messages is known as the *source* station. Computers that receive the message are called *destination* stations. Sometimes the sender will designate a particular station as the message destination. At other times, it will 'broadcast' a message which can be received by any station in the network. Here, station number '0' is used as a dummy destination number.

USES OF A NETWORK

You might wish to use a network for any of the following purposes:

– To send simple messages from one computer to another, providing a rudimentary electronic mail system.

– To transfer data files from one computer to another.

– To transfer programs from one computer to another. (Note the difficulty of swapping Spectrum and QL programs, noted above.)

– To enable one computer to access peripheral devices (e.g. disc drives, microdrives, printers, modems, plotters etc.) that are linked to a second.

You can perform all these different tasks using the same QLAN network.

THE PHYSICAL NETWORK

At the back of your QL, you will find two ports labelled 'net'. The two are functionally identical. You can plug your network lead into either port and the other end of the lead into either port on a second QL. The two ports are provided so that a chain of QLs can be linked together. Figure 16.1 shows how this works. As we mentioned above, up to 63 QLs can be linked in a ring or in any other arrangement which connects all the machines in some way. For example, the rather awkward arrangement shown in Fig. 16.1 would work perfectly well. It isn't necessary for two computers to be linked directly in order for them to communicate via the network. Indirect links (with other computers providing the junctions) work just as well.

Figure 16.1 Network Structure

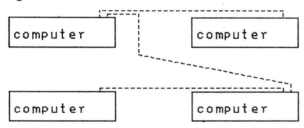

```
This is only one of many ways
in which four computers could be linked
```

   The network leads are just as simple as they appear. They contain just two wires. One wire acts as a ground reference point and nominally carries an OV. signal. The other wire is used to carry zero signals. When active (which in this case means carrying a zero signal, not a one as you might expect) the wire sends a positive pulse of current (nominally 5V); when inactive, it is nominally at OV. We say 'nominally', because actual voltages may fluctuate around the OV and 5V levels. However, the two states will usually be easy to distinguish.

SETTING UP THE SOFTWARE

This is what you must do in order to prepare your QL to participate in network communications.
   First, you must assign the computer its unique network number. The SuperBasic NET command does this. NET 5, for instance, assigns the station the network number 5. If no number is assigned then the system will assign

the default number 1, but as it is undesirable for two stations to have the same number, it is always best to assign a number.

Lower numbered stations have a slight advantage, because should two stations 'compete' to send signals at the same time, the lower-numbered one will gain priority.

Next, you must open a network channel for communications. Some network-oriented commands (e.g. COPY and LOAD) do this implicitly. In other cases, you will need to use the OPEN command, like this:

    OPEN#4, neti__2

or

    OPEN#3, neto__1

Though there is no specific assigning of input or output functions to the serial communications channels on the QL, and the same channel can perform both tasks, it *is* necessary to select and assign either input or output to a network channel that you open. It isn't possible to use the same channel, at the same time, for both purposes. 'neti' is of course an input channel; 'neto' an output one. The number following is *not* the network number of your own computer: it's the network number of the computer to which you wish to send a message. (More details on this below.)

The channel is used only by your own computer: its number does not affect the rest of the network and there is no need to consider other computers in the network when assigning a number to it. Sending and receiving computers can use the same channel numbers or quite different ones: it won't affect reception. However, you must ensure that you assign a number that doesn't clash with any other channel functions within your computer. For example, you can't use channel#6 both for networking and as a console channel!.

When outputting data, you will direct it via the channel number you assign, in order to send it across the network. When inputting data, it will come in via the assigned channel. However, you will have to do something with it – read it into variables, direct it to another channel (e.g. a microdrive file channel) – once it arrives. We explain below how to do this.

The CLOSE command is used to close communication channels when you have finished working with them. This is particularly important in networking: you may have to CLOSE your output channel immediately your message has been sent, in order to ensure its correct reception.

If your station is to act as a source (i.e, you have opened an output channel) you must select a destination for your message: either another specific station in the network or destination '0' if you wish to broadcast the message to all stations. If you want to send a message to two specific stations (for example) then you must do this serially: sending first to one, then to the other.

If your channel is to be a destination (i.e. you have opened an input channel), you might 'listen out' to station 0 in order to pick up broadcast messages or you might make specific arrangements with a source channel whose number you have given in the channel opening statement. The QL User Guide suggests that giving your own channel number as the source in an input station will enable you to listen freely to network communications. We did not succeed in making this (or, indeed, the 'broadcast' signals) work.

Now it is possible to send and receive messages, using the network compatible commands: PRINT, INPUT, LOAD, SAVE, LBYTES, SBYTES, EXEC, SEXEC, LRUN, MRUN, and MERGE. Before giving some specific examples, however, we'll explain a little more about how messages are sent and received, in order to help you in handling network timing and to understand what can go wrong.

CLAIMING THE NETWORK

QLAN is a very simple networking system, without all the elaborate protocols that enable more complex systems to handle multiple messages at once. Confusion can result in more than one station attempts to send messages across the network at the same time. The network has some inbuilt protocols and precautions that should help to minimize such confusion, but it *is* possible for two stations to 'broadcast' at the same time and any destination station should be alive to this danger.

In order to understand how network resources are allocated, we must look a little more deeply at how messages are sent.

The network as a whole can be in two basic states: *resting,* and *claimed.* When resting, the network isn't in action; no station is attempting to send messages (though some stations may be ready and willing to receive messages). There is (of course) no signal being sent along the signal wire, and this will be in its inactive (power level around 5V) state.

When a station wishes to send messages, it attempts to claim the network. It does this by performing a special sequence of operations. These operations are performed automatically when a station is programmed to send a message by a SAVE or similar command: there is no need to program them specifically.

First, the station proceeds to 'test' the network to see if it is indeed 'resting'. As the signal channel will in any case carry regular '1' signals while a message is being sent, it is necessary to make checks over a longish time interval, before deciding that the network really is in a resting state. The time interval consists of a basic time period plus a randomized additional time, a system that's designed to minimize the risk of network collisions. If any sign of activity is detected during this test period, the station fails in its attempt to claim the network and it starts the test again. There's no need to program the re-try: this happens automatically.

Though the 'test' period is long enough to enable the station to detect station-to-station broadcasts, it is not long enough to distinguish a genuine resting state from the much longer breaks that can occur between blocks of open broadcast messages (see below). It is because of this that two stations may end up alternately broadcasting blocks of data: and a receiving station must watch out for this eventuality.

Once the 'test' period has been passed, the station proceeds to send out a 'scout' signal, which consists of a 'leader' pulse (state 0) followed by eight bits of the station number. As station numbers vary from 0 to 64, the most significant bit will always be a zero. The bits are inverted, with the most significant bit being sent first and the least significant last.

After each bit of the scout signal is sent, the station checks the network to ensure that the signal wire is in the expected state. If it's not, this may signal a clash with another station's scout or broadcast signal. The attempt to claim the network is aborted and the station reverts to testing for a resting state.

Other stations in the network which are waiting to receive data will listen out for scout signals and use them for timing purposes. However, they don't actually make use of the data that are contained in the signal. The sender will repeat its station number in each message block that is sent.

Once the network has been successfully claimed, the source station can then proceed to send a block of data making up part or all of its message. The block (of up to 255 bytes) is preceded by a 'header' which contains, among other information, the source station's number and the destination station number. It also indicates the number of the block being sent (e.g. blocks making up a long message will be numbered 0, 1, 2, etc.) details on the contents of the block (e.g. full block or partial block making up the end of the message) and various check and control data.

After the header is sent, the source will proceed to wait for a single bit of acknowledgement from the destination, if the message is not to be a general broadcast one. Only after this acknowledgement is received will the rest of the block of data be sent.

RECEIVING SIGNALS

If your station is a receiving one, its task is a little easier. The receiving station simply waits until the network is 'claimed' by listening out for a 'scout' block. It doesn't make any attempt to identify the sender of the block: all subsequent headers will be read.

When the station subsequently reads a header to a block of data, it will then decode the header and check to see:

– If the source station is one from which it is willing to receive a message. For instance, if the destination is specifically waiting for a message from station 3, it will reject any messages from stations 1, 2, 4 etc.

— If the destination station is either 0 (i.e. open broadcast) or itself.
— If the block number is correct. The block might, for example, be a repeated broadcast of a block which was received correctly, but for which the source station failed to receive a correct acknowledgement.
— If all the check data indicates that the header has been sent correctly.

If the information received is satisfactory and the message is not a broadcast one, the destination station will then send a single bit of acknowledgement. The block of data is then sent. Once the block is complete, the destination checks again to see if the check data is correct. If so, an acknowledgement is sent to the source station. If not, no acknowledgement will be sent and this acts as a prompt to the source to repeat the block.

TIMING

As you may understand from the description above, it often doesn't matter in which order source and destination stations are programmed to send/receive a message. Using most network commands, the source station will continue to try again and again to send its data, until a suitable acknowledgement is received; and the destination station will continue to wait to receive the message, until it is received successfully. Of course, this is not true in the case of 'broadcast' messages, when the receiving station must be waiting to receive before the broadcast begins. It is also not true if the INKEY$ command is used as a timing device when waiting for input.

In practice, we found that it could take several seconds for a message to be sent and received, even using a simple two computer network. Don't be impatient and break into the communication too soon: allow some time before concluding that the system has 'stuck'. Note, too, that it seemed to us that CLOSEing the source channel was necessary before the message receipt was acknowledged by the destination station.

SENDING AND RECEIVING MESSAGES:
SOME SIMPLE EXAMPLES

We tested QLAN by setting up a simple two station network of QLs, labelling the two stations NET 1 and NET 2. Using this simple network, we succeeded in sending messages and transferring files from station to station with few problems. We were not successful in sending and receiving general 'broadcast' messages, in spite of repeated attempts. This may be due to our failure to use the correct statements or sequence of activity, rather than to any inherent fault in the QLAN system.

Here's a simple set of test programs, to check that your network works correctly. They include all the statements necessary for operating the network:

Station 1 (output)
```
10     NET 1 (optional)
20     OPEN#4, neto__2
30     FOR n = 1 TO 50
40     PRINT#4, "TESTING NUMBER"; n
50     END FOR n
60     CLOSE#4
```

Station 2 (input) d
```
10     NET 2
20     OPEN#3, neti__1
30     FOR n = 1 TO 50
40     INPUT#3, a$
50     PRINT a$
60     END FOR n
70     CLOSE#3
```

Here, as you see, we are simply using PRINT, directed to the network channel, to send our messages. At the receiving end the messages are INPUT to a temporary variable and then printed on screen.

This even shorter command sequence enables us to send a program held in the memory of station 1 to station 2. We use immediate commands in this case, so that the listing will not be affected:

Station 1	*Station 2*
NET 1	NET 2
OPEN#4, neto__2	LOAD neti__1
LIST#4	
CLOSE#4	

As the LOAD command automatically opens and closes a network channel, there's no need to give OPEN or CLOSE commands for station 2.

Finally, this last example takes a file on microdrive at station 1 and sends it to station 2. We simply read it into memory at station 2, but you could use a second COPY statement to save it directly on to station 2's microdrive – or (preferable, we think) save it subsequently.

Station 1	*Station 2*
NET 1	NET 2
N mdvl__f$ TO neto__2	LOAD neti__1

17

Expanding the QL

Though the QL offers an impressive amount of computing capability as it stands, it becomes an even more exciting machine when we look at its expansion possibility. In this chapter we look at why you may wish to add to your QL system; at what you *can* add to it; and at the advantages and disadvantages of various add-ons.

We wrote this book shortly after the QL was launched and before a wide range of QL add-ons had been launched. As a result, we are unable to discuss actual products in this chapter. Sinclair and other manufacturers have indicated their general plans for add-on production and it is not difficult to tell from the machine's design and architecture how it can be expanded. Therefore, we look at a range of possibilities for expansion, not all of which may have been realized in practice when you read this. We also look at some more speculative possibilities, which offer a possible pattern in which a family of QL machines might be developed.

WHY ADD ON?

First, why add to the QL at all? What capabilities does it lack in its present form?

In fact, the basic machine doesn't totally lack many capabilities at all — with the obvious exception of a parallel printer port. (Though you can connect a serial printer directly to the QL, this is a serious omission for those who already have, or prefer to obtain, parallel machines. We discussed printer interfacing in depth in Chapter 2.) But it does have some obvious shortcomings, which will be apparent to you if you have used it extensively.

It's slow in operation. There are two reasons for this. First, though the 68008 chip works at a spanking pace (7.5 MHz), the complex QDOS facilities and the SuperBasic interpreter slow down the pace of the machine severely. Though the QL has such a powerful main processor, in many applications its operation is no faster than that of typical eight-bit microcomputers. Secondly, though the microdrives compare well with cassette storage systems, they are not as fast in operation as disk drives.

Its internal memory is limited. Though 128K of memory seems a massive amount to those familiar with home computers that have typically offered from 1 to 64K, it still isn't a great deal when it comes to running highly complex application programs. The machine's memory map (discussed in Chapter 14) dedicates large chunks of memory to the bit-mapped display and for other purposes and this can leave application programs short of working memory. The Psion programs certainly are short of memory, as we saw earlier in the book: there isn't space to draw up a really large spreadsheet using Abacus, for example.

Its external memory (storage device capability) is also limited. The two internal microdrive cartridges hold only around 120K of data each. Though this is adequate for Basic programming, it isn't adequate when it comes to handling large databases or for a number of other purposes. (You can only store data on four bit-mapped screens on a single cartridge, for example.)

It doesn't run any industry-standard operating system. A large quantity of business and general software is written to run under popular eight- and sixteen-bit operating systems like CP/M (in its various manifestations), MSDOS and Unix. The QL as it stands does not support any of those operating systems and this cuts QL users off from this reservoir of software.

All of these shortcomings can be alleviated if you add on sufficient equipment to your computer – or, in some cases, simply replace the existing components by newer and more powerful ones. Of course, you may not find it practicable or desirable in every case to extend the QL in order to obtain the missing capabilities: the answer might simply be to buy a different computer. But if you want to do it, the chances are that someone will make it possible for you to do it.

WHAT TO ADD ON

The add-on devices that are likely to be made available for the QL come in three different broad classes. We'll outline these classes, explain the general purpose of each type of add-on and then go on to look at each in detail.

Additional Internal Memory

Perhaps the most simple and desirable add-on of all. Adding more memory, to bring the QL closer to the maximum 1Mb memory addressing capability of the 68008 chip, will make a very obvious difference to the operation of almost any large-scale program. With more memory, it's possible to fit larger files into RAM, to manipulate bigger spreadsheets and to word-process longer documents. It's possible (with suitable software) to fit multiple program and/or data files into memory, to support concurrent operations. With the less frequent microdrive accesses that more memory can mean, this add-on should make a massive difference to the overall working speed of your system.

Additional External Storage Devices

Additional plug-in microdrives will make it possible for you to hold more information on-line at the same time, simplifying complex application handling. Adding hard- or floppy disks as a replacement for the microdrives will not only increase your system's storage capacity: it will also enchance its operating speed and improve its reliability. While microdrive cartridges remain disproportionately expensive, using disks instead will reduce your bill for disposables! (Though of course, the capital cost of such an add-on will be quite high.)

Additional or Replacement Processors

A co-processor designed to work with the QL's existing 68008 and its support chips (including 8049 second processor) could much improve the machine's performance. It should speed overall operation, and add special capabilities: for example, enhancing the low precision maths capabilities of SuperBasic. A more drastic option is the supplementing or replacement of the 68008 with a quite different processor, designed not to work with it but to act as a main processor in its own right. You might opt to incorporate a popular chip like the Intel 8086/88 into the machine, in order to give yourself access to proprietary operating systems and software running on such a chip. Another option could be the replacement of the 68008 with another, more powerful, chip from the 68000 family.

Though these are the major types of device, you can of course expand your system in a variety of more general ways: by adding joystick controllers, new or enhanced input/output ports, or by connecting peripheral devices such as plotters and modems.

ADDITIONAL RAM

All of the QL's complement of RAM is volatile. Memory contents are lost as soon as the machine is switched off and there is no battery backup to enable part or all of the RAM contents to be retained permanently. It's particularly sad that a small CMOS battery backed RAM hasn't been included, because its absence largely negates the value of the QL's internal clock. Though the clock is real-time, it has to be set every time you turn on the computer!

There has been an increasing trend to the expensive but extremely useful non-volatile forms of RAM over the last few years. One likely enhancement of the QL is the provision of some non-volatile RAM: either a small quantity (under 1K, say) simply to act as a clock backup and for similar housekeeping purposes or a full complement, which could act as a form of 'silicon disk' and would make the machine more competitive with the latest generation of portable computers.

Most RAM expansions, however, are likely to be of the conventional, volatile kind. They will simply increase the amount of RAM available within the computer.

The 68008 has the capability to address directly up to 1 megabyte (1000K) of combined ROM and RAM, as we mentioned earlier. In fact some very sizeable ranges of addresses are reserved for input and output purposes and on the QL's memory map (see page 199), just 640K is allocated to RAM. This comprises the 128K of inbuilt RAM and a provision for an additional 512K (half megabyte) RAM. A practicable maximum for conventional RAM add-ons will be 640K, but if the demand appears for a still larger RAM, it's conceivable that enterprising add-on manufacturers will devise ways of freeing more memory for this purpose. Of course, with a second or replacement processor the QL's addressing capability could be much enhanced; and the use of 'paging' techniques to switch in and out blocks of RAM would enable much larger amounts of RAM to be handled. (Note that the 68008 does not directly support paging, as do many other processors.)

A 640K RAM would put the QL into the same class (in memory terms, at least) as typical configurations of popular business microcomputers like the ACT Sirius and the IBM PC. It would certainly provide the capability for fairly sophisticated multitasking, and we can look forward to the development of integrated program suites that make much fuller use than do the Psion programs of the 68008 chip's multitasking facilities.

The blank space inside the QL's case at the left-hand end (looking at the machine front-on) seems the obvious place for a RAM expansion board to sit. The board would be safe and unobtrusive inside the casing and it should be possible to duplicate the expansion port provided at the left-hand edge of the circuit board, so that the left side of the case will still provide a full expansion port for additional devices. It's possible, though that some add-on RAM boards won't fit this space and instead, will be fitted externally, rather like ZX81 and ZX Spectrum 'RAMpacks'. If you have a strong preference for an external or internal board, do check to see which type various manufacturers provide.

USING ADDITIONAL RAM

If you look back again at the memory map on page 199, you will see that the expansion RAM will join with the basic RAM to provide a solid block of RAM addresses within the QL, from &20000 to &40000. RAM will continue to be filled from both top and bottom, as with the basic arrangement, leaving a block of 'spare RAM' around the middle of this address range.

There are a variety of possible ways in which programs might make use of the additional RAM:

The provision of very complex suites of programs may itself take up a large chunk of RAM. Holding a large program entirely in memory, instead of relying upon microdrive overlays (as do most of the Psion programs in their basic versions) will much increase operating speed: but it will also eat up the available memory!

Handing very large files (e.g. database files, spreadsheet data or word processor documents) mainly or entirely in RAM will certainly improve the scope and versatility of the system. Many users would welcome the facility to work with larger spreadsheets than Abacus can cope with in its basic version. Many would also welcome the increased speed that Quill might operate at, if moderate length (say, up to twenty page) documents could be held entirely in RAM.

The provision of extra RAM makes it more feasible to consider the handling of additional screen display data in memory. Setting up an alternative screen memory would enable programs to swap instantly between two different displays: e.g. Easel might hold two different graphs in memory simultaneously or could switch to the second page to display 'help' messages without the need to re-draw the original graph when returning to it. Using additional memory to hold screen display data could also open up the possibility of genuine 'windowing', in which superimposed windows do not erase the material that they cover temporarily on display.

QDOS includes some very complex provisions for the use of 'spare' RAM as 'filing system slave blocks'. The operating system automatically handles the duplication of data that are written to microdrive, within this chunk of unused memory. Tables are maintained indicating the allocation of memory to the slave block system and the status of blocks within the memory used (for instance, empty, true representation of the microdrive file, questionable representation (for various reasons, e.g. unverified, not certain that the microdrive write was completed correctly and so on)). It's then possible for programs to use this section of RAM as a form of 'silicon disk'. Data can be retrieved from the slave block much faster than it could be retrieved from the microdrive itself, and this will considerably speed up overall program operation. As all data are written to the microdrive as well as to the slave block, this system doesn't increase the risk of data loss through power cuts or other unforeseen system failures.

The slave block system operates with the 128K RAM, as well as with the extension RAM. However, there inevitably will be far less free RAM when only 128K is available in total and the advantages of the system certainly are not visible in the early versions of the Psion programs for example.

ADDITIONAL MICRODRIVES

Though the QL has just two inbuilt microdrives, it also has a microdrive expansion port, which will permit up to six more microdrives to be 'daisy chained' on to the system. This would give a total of eight microdrives, which should be enough for the most enthusiastic microdrive user: though it would be possible to cope with far more drives on a QLAN network with multiple QLs.

It's easy to see the advantages in providing one or two additional microdrives. Often Drive 1 will be used to hold a program cartridge, leaving just one microdrive for data. It's necessary to do a cartridge swap in order (for instance) to merge a Quill document on one cartridge with a second document on another. Providing two or more drives for data cartridges will facilitate mail merging and other multi-file operations.

Further drives may seem an unnecessary luxury but they could be extremely handy, for instance, if more than one microdrive based program is to be run simultaneously using the multitasking facilities. They also increase the maximum amount of on-line storage capability and this could be particularly handy when trying to manipulate large and complex databases. On the whole, however, we feel that users intending to run applications large enough to demand more than two or three microdrives would be better advised to consider a disk expansion. Using more microdrives tends to make the disadvantages of this medium more, rather than less, apparent and a multi-microdrive application would almost certainly be painfully slow in operation.

FLOPPY DISKS

Though Sinclair microdrives are a welcome improvement on cassette storage systems, they are no substitute for floppy disks. They hold less data than a high-capacity floppy (around 120K, compared with up to 800K); in our experience, they are considerably less reliable than even conventional floppies, let alone the more robust mini-floppies and they have the disadvantages of being a non-standard storage medium. Sinclair are currently the only suppliers of cartridges. They are both overpriced in comparison with disks of comparable storage capacity and often difficult to obtain. As no non-Sinclair computers use microdrives, there is no question of swapping the cartridges between computers or reading another make of computer's files directly from the cartridge.

Microdrives are a serial access medium and this does mean that access can be slow when the data is a long distance from the read/write heads. Though Sinclair have quoted a typical access speed of 3.5 seconds, the actual time for the reading or writing and verifying of even a short file is considerably greater than this. In addition, serial access makes it very difficult for programs to set up complex file structures. QDOS does provide for a relocatable file pointer, which can be used to produce a very basic simulation of a random access file, but there is no proper provision for the setting-up of conventional random-access files on microdrives.

Sinclair themselves have announced no plans for the development of the QL so that it will support floppy disks. However, we think it extremely likely that other manufacturers will develop add-on hard- and software that will enable floppy disks to be interfaced with the system. As there is so little standardization among floppy disk operating systems in the sub-business market, these add-ons might either make it possible to interface existing models of disk (e.g. Commodore or BBC Micro compatible disks) to the computer, an option which would be extremely useful to those upgrading from a different model of computer, or they might develop compatible disks and suitable device drivers for QDOS from scratch.

Floppy disk drives are not cheap and a pair of drives (one drive can be even more awkward to use than are the microdrives) could cost considerably more than the QL itself. Interfacing floppies to the QL will be particularly appealing to those who already have disk drives or to those with a particular desire to use their QL in conjunction with a compatible disk-based computer. Other users may find that a hard disk (an option which Sinclair has indicated it will offer) proves a more worthwhile investment.

Finally, adding one or more disk drives would be a particularly appealing choice if you decide to expand your QL with a replacement or supplementary processor so that it can run a proprietory operating system, making a wide range of disk-based software available to you.

HARD DISKS

Hard disks are expensive. But a hard disk interface will be made available for the QL: almost certainly from Sinclair themselves and, almost as certainly from other manufacturers. A hard disk would so enhance the QL's capabilities that this could very rapidly become one of the most popular of add-ons – particularly, of course, if the disks on offer are competitively priced.

The great advantage of a hard disk is the massively increased amount of storage capacity that it opens up to users. 5, 10, 20 Mb or even more is directly on-line to the computer. Access to that data is slower than direct access to RAM, but it is very much faster than access to data on a floppy disk and very much faster than access to data on a microdrive. No practical limitations on file size; no need to change disks; great reliability; no more delays while the cartridge whirrs away. No wonder this is such an appealing option.

Ideally, a hard disk added to a QL ought to replace the microdrives as a regular storage medium almost entirely. The microdrives could then be used largely as a backup to the disk. (Hard disks are not normally replaceable within the drive: it's necessary to use an entirely separate medium as a backup of disk contents, so that you can recover in the unlikely event of a major disk breakdown.) However, it may not always be possible to transfer programs on microdrive cartridge (in which form they will still reach you) to the hard disk and some programs may not be able to take full advantage of the hard disk's capability to hold long, random access files. Certainly if you envisage using a hard disk system to handle long database files using Archive or some other database system, you should first check that the program you have in mind will in fact let you do so.

REPLACEMENT PROCESSORS, SUPPLEMENTARY PROCESSORS AND CO-PROCESSORS

The QL already has an impressive complement of processing power, with the combination of its 68008 main processor, the 8049 secondary processor and Sinclair's custom chips to handle screen display and peripheral functions. However, there's quite a lot of scope for the changing or supplementing of this processing power and we will look at this next.

Naturally the software and hardware aspects of making different processors work together are extremely complex and it is by no means certain that some of the suggestions we explore will be realized in practice.

Basically, the provision of new computing power might come in any of four directions. The 68008 processor (or, much less probably, the second processor) might simply be replaced by a chip that slots into the same socket on the main board. At the moment, this seems a fairly unlikely option. The specific support that the rest of the QL's circuitry provides to the 68008 means that only another chip from the 68000 family might reasonably replace it: and the different numbers of pins on the different chip models would make it impossible to replace the 68008 with either the popular 68000 or the fully thirty-two-bit 68020.

A very similar main board to that of the original QL might incorporate a more powerful chip like the 68020 instead of the 68008. Such a board would most probably be provided in later additions to the QL family; however, it is just conceivable that it might also be sold separately as a replacement for the QL board in the original model.

The original circuit board might be boosted by the addition of a support chip such as the 68010 maths co-processor, designed to supplement the 68008 and to enhance its performance. This seems the most likely option for users of the original QL at present.

Complex circuity might be devised to enable a completely different processor to run the QL. The new processor might take advantage of many of the control capabilities of the existing machine, but it would run different operating systems and software. You may be aware of this type of option in existing 'alternative processor' computers, including the BBC Model B and a variety of business micros. The QL's architecture is not designed specifically for expansion in this kind of way (as is the BBC's with its 'Tube' arrangement, for example) but it is quite probable that a 68000 processor could be added to the computer in this way. It's also just conceivable that enormous success for the QL might open a market for a device such as a replacement or supplementary 8086 board for the QL, allowing QL users to use their computer system resources for running sixteen-bit software under MSDOS or another popular proprietary operating system.

Adding a 68010 Co-Processor

The 68010 is among the most attractive of potential co-processors for the 68008. It is a mathematics oriented co-processor/support chip with a great deal of software applications programs written to take advantage of it. A solid repertoire of known ways of implementing powerful mathematical algorithms on this chip already exists. Speed enhancements of four- to five-fold could be expected on average, even within a Fortran environment where the efficiency of conversion via a well-established compiler of machine code is already high.

It is known that a Fortran compiler is under development for the current QL, but the frequently required ability to handle double precision, particularly for recursive algorithms, may well result in very slow processing unless a 68000 processor is provided, with or without the 68010.

Using the 68000 in QL-Type Systems

The provision of a 68000 processor, instead of or as well as the 68008, would completely change the application potential of the QL. Apart from opening up the vast and as yet unexploited repertoire of Unix linkable software to the micro market, the 68000 is even better established as the base processor for very powerful graphic design and graphic manipulation software.

The Unix operating system, which runs on 68000 based machines, has established itself as the premier operating system in the sixteen/thirty-two-bit section of the mini/micro market and can be expected to become still more popular over the next few years.

Although speed of execution is obviously important, the much longer time delays in developing and proving software as opposed to getting hold of existing software are incommensurably more important. In the graphic handling field, for example, much creative work could be carried out on a suitably supplemented QL, tested, and directly made available to a more powerful mini- or mainframe computer when fully developed. In this sense, the adoption of the 68008 as the first QL processor has provided a bridge (though not a simple one) into the world of powerful software, as distinct from the simpler software packages developed from the pure micro market.

VARIANTS ON THE QL

The use of co-processors or alternative processor leads directly to the possibility that much of the basic QL machine will find its way into the OEM (original equipment manufacturer) market, in which equipment from initial manufacturers is tailored to specific markets before being sold under a different brand name. We can expect the QL's base board to be extended to give a specific capability in a functional application such as mathematics or graphics or even to make it a very economic intelligent terminal to other hardware systems.

Sinclair have already announced their co-operation with ICL and the likely incorporation of a QL board into an ICL desktop computer is likely to lead to linkages between this machine and other ICL systems. Should (as we would expect) the QL achieve volumes of production approaching the order achieved by the ZX Spectrum, then the experience curve which dominates the economics of volume production of electronic goods must come into play and a virtuous circle of reducing costs and expanding markets of application be achieved.

SOFTWARE AND LANGUAGE ISSUES

Already Logo and Micro-Prolog developments for the QL have been announced. Sinclair's original product announcement mentioned a C compiler and 68000 assembler and other popular languages such as Fortran and micro-Cobol should also appear before too long. Though SuperBasic has many attractive features, it is highly desirable that a variety of languages should be made available for the machine and we expect this to be the case.

A particularly attractive speculation, once the RAM expansion and a better secondary storage medium becomes available, is the potential for implementing the Smalltalk language on the QL. Smalltalk is the education-oriented language developed by Xerox's research team. It has influenced the development of 68000 based computers like the Apple Lisa/Macintosh and though it is still not commercially available as a language environment, it may yet become available in this way.

All these language possibilities are inherent in the initial choice of the machine architecture and this is one major advantage of the selection of an advanced processor able to address a sizeable memory. In this sense, the QL can be seen as a machine which contains the potential for users to experience the kind of capability that would be provided on a mainframe or powerful minicomputer.

Perhaps QDOS and SuperBasic will have to be modified considerably in this process of extending the QL family, to take account of the various expansion possibilities. It is to be expected that a variety of operating systems will be developed, even for the current first QL version, let alone for extended versions of the machine. It is also to be expected that a variety of instruction sets will be made available on a proprietary basis within SuperBasic. (Of course, the language and operating system specifically support the development of new command procedures.) The current version panders, from a computer science viewpoint, towards a very simplistic view of data types.

These comments are not criticisms, but reflect the necessity which many other manufacturers of micros have relatively ignored – that of establishing a marketing niche with minimally adequate performance, but without restricting the potential for breaking out from that niche into other, more substantial markets where greater performance may be justified. Such things as the use of channels for input and output, internally or externally, may seem an irritating and tedious procedure to those used to more conventional micros, but the recognition of their necessity in order to provide greater transparency and user-friendliness in the much longer-established mini and mainframe developments in software was not without good cause.

In relation to this potential, the early hiccups and minor adjustments to design philosophy on the QL are trivial in relation to the teething problems usually associated with much more powerful machines. Within a relatively short time many of those problems have already been overcome and the obvious goal of accessing the well-developed power and capability of a whole cornucopia of applications software (but this time at a very low price of admission) will undoubtedly drive QL development in many, if not all, of these directions.

Index